About the Author

The author is one of a rare breed in that he is a first generation farmer. Armed with little more than self-confessed optimism, the company of angels, a stubborn determination not to fail and driven from an early age by family tragedy, he recounts in a sometimes poetic, generally amusing and always conversational style the characters, places, circumstances and struggles that have way marked his journey.

Principally this book has the late twentieth century U.K. farming scene as its canvas. On route to his present Dartmoor farm home and Pyrenean mountain retreat, he worked for eighteen months on a religious community and spent time in central and southern Africa. From here, he traded two plane tickets for a couple of written off Land Rovers and drove the resulting hybrid across newly independent Africa along with wife and six-month-old baby before converting the vehicle to collateral in the "no man's land" between international borders, this was to part finance the venture into farming.

Always preferring a "yes" to a "no", he has obviously enjoyed the not too occasional battles with self-important authority and pointless bureaucracy.

UNDER THE ROPE

Clive Venables

UNDER THE ROPE

Vanguard Press

VANGUARD PAPERBACK

A CIP catalogue record for this title is
available from the British Library.

ISBN 978 1 784655 9 90

Vanguard Press is an imprint of
Pegasus Elliot MacKenzie Publishers Ltd.
www.pegasuspublishers.com

First Published in 2019

Vanguard Press
Sheraton House Castle Park
Cambridge England

Printed & Bound in Great Britain

Dedication

During the past ten years or so two of our three sons have married so expanding our family by two daughters by choice and now five grandchildren. This book is not about them, it is largely for them. I see them in the sparkling dawn dew hanging in luminescent droplets from bursting hazel buds on a May morning. I see them in the leaping of the trout into the gnat filled summer dusk and in the first magical snowflakes falling hesitantly out of a heavy autumn sky.

If my life has been a metaphorical slow-moving train, then my brother, Neil, has been the engine stoker. Without him I'd have hit the buffers long ago.

Sometime into the journey I met an angel and married her. Without her saying yes rather than no there would have been no train.

This book is dedicated to my grandchildren Ella, Sam, Amelie, Joe and Isobelle, my brother Neil and my wife Gilly.

Acknowledgements

I am grateful to all who have helped me with the writing of this book but especially Jo Bee for typing up the original draft, various family and friends for reading though to check for accuracy and content and to Jo Teague and Pegasus Publishing for their invaluable help with the final draft.

Although I have tried to be accurate throughout, I have changed some names where I felt pedantic honesty was trumped by pragmatic sensitivity.

Preface

Eskimos may very well have fifty or more words for snow but for the purposes of this book I'll be more prosaic and settle for just two - bad and brilliant. Snow won't in any case get much of a mention so if it's snow that you are interested in take your time over the next few lines and skip the rest.

Firstly, there is the bad sort, the wet blocks of dirty, edge of the road, pushed over grey stuff with oily blue water leaking out from underneath as harassed commuters slip slide begrudgingly over it on route to their daily grind. And then there is the really good sort, the silky, silent, spindrift accumulations of fluffy powder gently laid down, softening the jagged peaks of mountain tops as if placed there by some benevolent creative spirit intent more on artistic effect than mortal aggravation. An all-enveloping, pristine winter duvet neatly arranged and tucked in at the edges to keep out winter's icy draughts.

The Pic du Midi just south of Bagneres de Bigorre in the French Pyrenees was just so coated last year, as my three sons and I followed others into the d'Oncet valley by getting off the cable car at the peak of this mountain pinnacle and turning left, ducking under the rope past the "Danger Don't Pass" sign and up the few paces to slide off point. Right led to the bar, comfort and rum-spiced hot chocolate and was the intended route. It is one of the highlights of my past year. We balanced together on a postage stamp of flat, well-trampled snow, some nine thousand feet above sea level, taking care to click down hard into skis on squeaky white powder, making sure that there was no accumulated snow between the boots and bindings. This was not a moment to lose a ski! After side-slipping down and round out of sight to the ridge above Lac d'Oncet, followed by a tight left turn, we momentarily took in the view, steadied the nerves and savoured the silence. Then there was just the beating of the heart and the quiet "issing" of skis mostly submerged in baseless icing sugar powder.

There was never a moment when we weren't going to do this but now it was a physical as well as a spiritual necessity. I'm not a good skier; ambition exceeds my competence, but I'll usually give most things a go. Age and circumstances were not on my side but other things were and as we slowly negotiated this steep mountain descent as a family group, each encouraging the other but with the lion's share of counsel coming in my direction, I thought fleetingly that to die there at that moment of time, thighs burning, heart pounding, surrounded by family and kissed by sunlight would be a good end.

The skiing in all fairness was not that difficult, just extremely steep. I know now that it has been the claimer of the lives of others. I don't know if they shared with me my brief unfulfilled premonition. I do know that without that left turn at the top of the cable car underneath the "Danger Don't Pass" sign we would have all been drinking rum-spiced hot chocolate and life would have been the lesser. Once down the main narrow gulley descent we were out of the main avalanche risk and we skirted right-handed around the temptingly untouched but flat snow-covered ice of Lac d'Oncet and carved elegant, or in my case staccato, curves in the caressingly soft and reassuring powder and onto the lower gentler sun-drenched slopes. Chattering like chaffinches on a spring morning, we paused and shared a knee-stiffening chocolate bar before heading off down the groomed piste to meet up with the rest of the family.

My life, and that is what the rest of this book is about, has had a fair few left turns below the warning signs on breachable barriers.

I would not have made the descent on my own; I was lucky to have company and encouragement. Throughout my journey I have had both assists from numerous friends and family; to them all I am indebted. Others have just been acquaintances; we passed each other without consequence, like silent ships on a dark still sea. They sadly didn't matter to me nor, I suspect, me to them.

I know very little about my own grandparents. If they left anything for me or other grandchildren to read, then they carelessly forgot to leave any clues about where to look. So, to my grandchildren, bad luck, no excuses, this is it.

What I do know about my grandparents is this; on my father's side my grandfather was a blacksmith living in a small village called Wall near Lichfield. He worked in a coal mine when there was work on and when there was no work there was no money and little else. His work included shoeing the pit ponies and the maintenance of the bogey tracks which were important in the extraction of coal. With my grandmother Annie he had eleven children, nine of which survived to be adults, my father was the youngest. As such he, my own father, was somewhat pampered, if you can call living in a small overcrowded cottage with intermittent income coming in and a rural culture more akin to middle ages feudalism than the present-day norm of democratic meritocracy "pampered". My father was helped by his older siblings to make the most of whatever was on offer. He had a fine singing voice and that got him into the Lichfield Cathedral choir with its associated improved schooling and a half step out of the grinding poverty that had defined his childhood. The Second World War came and along with its misery and wastage it brought about much-needed social readjustment and reform.

On my mother's side my grandfather Frank Gunning was a tenant farmer on Lord Bath's estate near Warminster. The farm was and is known as Cley Hill. He and my maternal grandmother

Hilda had four children, three girls of which my mother was the third, followed by a son Gerald who was no doubt expected to take on the farm. My mother, Patricia, remembered that my grandfather was innovative and successful in his day; one of the first to own a car, he quickly recognised its potential and hitched it up to the hay rake in lieu of the horse! His interest in horses eventually superseded his interest in farming. He had some success in racing ponies and was tempted to dabble in the horse racing game. His best horse was called Birmingham's Glory. He entered this horse in a novice jump race early one afternoon, expecting to win but it came in a dismal last. Convinced that the jockey had deliberately pulled the horse up, he then entered the same horse in the closing race at the same meeting and on the same day with the same jockey and a significant threat to the jockey's wellbeing if he didn't win! The jockey lived to see another day, so I guess he won!

Sometime later, after some sort of family crisis around the time of the Second World War and just before I was born, they moved away from the identity-defining life in rural Wiltshire to the colourless miasma of suburban Birmingham. Both my grandfather and his history died soon thereafter.

Beyond that I know nothing of my grandfathers or indeed my grandmothers. My grandparents lived through two world wars; I have no way of knowing what they thought about politics, poetry, work, sexuality or religion and yet these are issues that dominate our every hour. I hardly know what some of my friends and relatives thought or think about such things even today! So, for what it's worth, this is my story. Mostly I have tried to record both what has happened and more importantly my reactions to what has happened. It is unashamedly my story; the thoughts are my thoughts and as such may occasionally be dismissed as subjective egocentric irrelevancies which they may well be and sometimes just as ramblings without conclusion; again, I'm happy with that since I see life as a journey best taken free of the need for a definitive destination or an empirical arrival. Where I have struggled, I think I've honestly recorded it; where I have been lucky, I think I've acknowledged it and where I've made my own luck, I haven't disguised it with false modesty… Any two of us placed in the same room for five minutes would describe the experience differently; what we see depends as much on what's hidden in our memories as what bounces off our retinas. When I see dark brown, hooded, sad gypsy eyes I see my mother. Another would just see brown eyes.

As I write this, Britain has just withdrawn from, and in so doing undermined, the European Union, triggering what I fear may be great social and economic change and a return to dangerous nationalism in Europe which for all my lifetime has enjoyed unheard of economic prosperity and more importantly peaceful coexistence. In the endless and circular political debates on Brexit we seem as a nation to have lost sight of the fact that political union in Europe was the hopeful dream of two generations of our recent ancestors as they sought out an alternative to indiscriminate slaughter from the squalor of mud filled trenches. "If only we could get to the point of mutual dependency based on trade, we would be unlikely ever to go to war again!" Not a bad idea!

Throughout my childhood with different groups of friends, there always seems to have been the odd one or two who could be relied on to splutter out the phrase, "well it wasn't my idea in the first place," as soon as a window got broken, a car got scratched or our best made plans unravelled in any way. It's not really what we wanted to hear; they were no doubt wanting to separate themselves from the negative consequences of the activity of the group. Today I have the same reaction to the ever-growing list of politicians as they splutter out the phrase, "we're just delivering on the result of the referendum" and "following the will of the people." Listen carefully and you might imagine you hear the stealthy shuffling of slippered feet as they collect by the insufficient life boats of HMS United Kingdom ready to sing the "well, it wasn't my idea in the first place" chorus. They will remember it well from their childhood!

I'm scribbling most of this from a small house high in the Pyrenean Mountains of France which Gilly, my wife and I bought last year. It was what the French call "une affaire de cœur", an affair of the heart; as it has worked out it now feels like a poke in the eye for fortress Britain and the creeping and insidious rise of exclusive and nationalistic government policies. In England we have a farm in Devon which we moved to as tenants some thirty-two years ago with boundless youthful optimism and little more than loose change in our pockets. Before that I worked for four years in two very different parts of Africa and spent my childhood years in a largely featureless suburban Nottingham in the austere post-war years. We have three sons who may from time to time get a mention, but their story is for them to tell.

The social, political, economic and communication changes that have taken place in my lifetime have been unprecedented in the scope and speed of their arrival and it's largely these I want to chronicle as well as giving a word picture of how we got to where we got to, and in particular our journey into farming. Apart from a small family inheritance shared with my sister after my father's death when we sold his bungalow, we have not received any financial input other than normal interest-incurring commercial borrowing from different sources.

Our farming venture was started at a time in the 1980s when agriculture went into steep decline and virtually all the farming journals were bemoaning the lack of opportunities for new entrants and the virtual impossibility of establishing a new farming business without family or outside money —something they have kept doing for the last thirty-plus years. A farming friend of mine describes me not intentionally kindly as being an opportunist. He didn't mean it as a compliment, but he was dead right; farming for us has been all opportunism, the time to make hay is when the sun shines, sell when the price is high, buy when the rest of the market is eating lunch! Mistakes happened but we didn't allow ourselves the luxury of repeating the same experience twice; we left that for those with money and time to spare! Charles Dickens had it spot on with his Mr Micawber, just spend less than you earn…

I don't think that amongst all my faults that I'm guilty of taking myself too seriously; I have certainly aimed not to do so. I have tried to be honest but memory works in funny ways and if I have gilded the lily or tarnished the gloss occasionally you, dear reader, will have to see it as poetic prose rather than as an empirical account.

Chapter 1
Early Years

My childhood was spent in a suburb of Nottingham where we lived in a semi-detached house on a small, gently rising hill called Woodland Grove. The other side of the house was lived in by an elderly childless couple, Mr and Mrs Ward. They had an enormous cat with which Mrs Ward had a mutually beneficial relationship. For her part Mrs Ward seemed to enjoy chopping up then cooking the butchers rejects, liver and lungs etc. in her kitchen, twenty-four hours a day; the house stank of it. The cat for his part seemed to enjoy nothing more than eating the culinary results of his benefactress's efforts and sleeping off his indulgences in the middle of the garden. Very occasionally my elder brother and I would disturb his calm by launching a football over the hedge and into their garden. It was always my job to go around, chat up Mrs Ward and retrieve the ball. My brother Chris, who was five years older than me, would usually be the one that put the football there in the first place but at that stage he was twice my size, so fairness didn't come into the arrangement! On the uphill side of our home lived Ernest and Mrs Chamberlin. Ernest was some eighty years older than me; he smoked a pipe and grew magnificent hybrid "T" roses, which was a shame in the sense that they and our footballs were mutually destructive. However, he didn't let that get in the way of good neighbourliness and would have long one-sided conversations with me about his time working as a station master which would usually conclude with his panacea for long life: "Eat to live rather than live to eat". My experience proved less straightforward!

Chris was the first of us three children, followed by my sister Anne who was the darling of both of my parents and some three years senior to me. She was obedient, industrious, pigtailed and smiled a lot. She and I got on pretty well in contrast to Chris and me; we never really hit it off. Chris was good at football and since this was my father's consuming interest (he had played for West Bromwich Albion before the war), he got a lot of paternal attention. By the time that I arrived I slipped by much of the paternal scrutiny that was so heavy for my older siblings, almost unnoticed. My mother may have had some input into this, but I was too young to know what was happening at the time. Poor Chris used to have his every contribution to any football match analysed and dissected critically by my father. I guess this did not really help in building up his self-esteem. Looking back from where I am now, self-esteem was something Chris always seemed to be short of. Sadly, he died several years ago and in all our lives I never really got to know him.

My parents met when they were both in the Royal Air Force during the war years. My father first remembers mother as a squint-eyed pupil on the rifle range where he was an instructor. The story goes that he supplied her with a penny to put over her squint eye and this helped her considerably. He stuck with her in an attempt to retrieve his penny, though knowing my mother I doubt he ever did. The war and the breakdown in social barriers that accompanied it had thrown my parents together; unfortunately, they in turn replaced the external barriers with internal ones. Consequently, my childhood memories are dominated by my parents' constant squabbling and bickering at each other. I would have given anything or done anything in order to have some calmness between them. Retrospectively I think the problem was that my father always wanted to do the right thing and provide for his wife and family but never believed himself to have quite hit the mark. Perhaps my mother should take some of the blame for this; from my position I couldn't judge, but I think I always tended to side with my mother in the way that sons often do.

Over the years to come, the bickering gave way to a very destructive possessiveness on the part of my father, particularly with my mother but also with my sister. My father worked at the local Raleigh factory where he packed bicycles for export. In his own mind I think he felt this was beneath his potential, which in common with many of his associates, it undoubtedly was. But these were post-war years, beggars could not be choosers and the weekly wage earned just paid the bills when paying the bills was always a challenge. My mother had a little cash box which she divided into segments using cardboard; each segment would have a small amount of money put in to pay specific expenditures. I remember well the little "I owe you" notes that she would put into the compartment for holidays as she borrowed to pay the rates or the grocery bill etc. As summer time approached one year, I sneaked up into the wardrobe where she kept this private bank to check that there were still funds in the holiday compartment, only to find three "I owe you" notes! Somehow against all expectation we had a holiday that year as we did every year, either to Skegness which was the nearest seaside on the east coast of England or to Rhyl in the far-away wilds of North Wales and eventually to the exotic and hedonistic extremes of Torquay and then Newquay. Here palm trees grew, girls wore bikinis and tomato ketchup was served on top of spaghetti…

Chapter 2
School Times

My early memories of school are a bit of a blur but at six years old I do remember being asked to accompany a four-year-old neighbour called Jonathan to his first few days at school. I suppose it was an ill-judged joke to have told him to stay close to me since there were bears at the bottom of our road on the waste ground opposite the recreation field. The result was that his mother, for the next few months, had to walk him round the long way to school. I always felt uneasy going around for a tea of fresh white bread and milk and to watch "Popeye the Sailor" or "I Love Lucy" on their black and white television after that event. (We did not have a TV at that time.)

Infant school melded uneventfully into junior school during which the only event that stands out for me was the unexpected arrival of a younger brother, Neil, when I was eight years old. I say unexpected, but I fancy my parents weren't so surprised! Neil and I were to get on very well as the years passed, somewhat making up for the poor relationship I had with Chris, my older brother.

Somehow at the end of my junior school years, when I was eleven years old, I scored enough points in the "eleven-plus" to earn a place at a local grammar school. I must have only just scraped in, since I had no choice of which grammar school to go to but was given a place at Long Eaton where they still had spaces. Long Eaton Grammar School was an austere red brick Victorian edifice with wooden prefabricated additions to accommodate the baby boom which followed the war and of which I was part. The area behind these wooden "huts" was ideal for hiding the schoolboy disapproved-of activities such as smoking and cross-gender fraternisation. For me I think the worst of my sins was to swap picture cards which we used to collect, of football teams and individual players. Once a team had its full complement of eleven players then other children would stump up the money to purchase the accumulation of cards. In time we devised a game to spice up our petty forays into capitalism. We would flick the cards deftly from between our index and middle fingers against a wall until one of the cards got completely covered. Then the winner took all, but there was always some debate as to whether the card was completely covered or not. These debates may not have always been amicably settled! For some reason this activity was frowned upon by the school authorities; perhaps they imagined that the footballers were not in fact footballers at all but scantily-clad ladies. I saw some of these cards but somehow never found out where to access them; I think if I could have, I would have!

Another activity that we used to indulge in which was entirely innocent was known as conkers. It necessitated making a hole with a meat skewer through the middle of a conker seed from a horse chestnut tree, swinging it around and contacting your partner's conker; the first one to break was the loser. We found that it was advantageous to either bake the conker in the oven or soak it in vinegar. I did at one stage have a thirteen-stage winner - possibly my most notable school achievement at that stage.

I never thought at school that I would need to know French and so treated the French language lesson as an opportunity to fool about with others who were like-minded. It didn't help that I did not like the French teacher, poor man. His name was Williams. Mr Williams smoked heavily; consequently, his teeth were yellow, and nicotine stained, and his breath reflected his smoking which was not pleasant if you sat, as I had to, in the front seat in the middle of the class. Here I was inconveniently and routinely sprayed with saliva as he enthusiastically emphasised the vocal delivery of the French consonants. One day as he was in full flow, I thought it might be amusing to the rest of the class if I turned his book, which he had deposited on my desk whilst he adjusted his glasses, around. Something broke inside him. I watched his grey, blotchy face turn to uniform pink then deep puce as he grabbed his upside-down book and used it to attack me at the front of the class, my ears seeming to form the focus for his targeting. It was as close as I got to actually hitting a teacher, which would have been an excludable offence and my life would doubtless have moved in a different direction. My track record and reputation would have not served me well should I have used self-defence as a justification. Justice and fairness in that sort of situation seemed stacked heavily on the side of authority, guilty unless proved innocent was the name of the game here.

The man who oversaw discipline at this school was nicknamed Fraz. He had a fringe of ginger hair around what was an egg-shaped polished dome of a head, small beady blue eyes through which he squinted from over the top of his tiny round glasses, and no chin to speak of but a belly to match the dome. He was altogether a very round man, such that I always half-expected him to snort, roll onto his back and scratch his belly with his toe; sadly he never did but he did once ask me, as I dawdled in his office just to see if this time he would, "Well, boy, what are you waiting for?"

In my confusion I answered, "Nothing, sir," and beat a hasty retreat - An unusual triumph of pragmatism over honesty. Fraz was not blessed with a sense of humour and his educational philosophy was more sadistic than sympathetic. He was the deputy headmaster, and if you were sent to his office it was not a question of whether you would be caned or not, it was simply how many times you would be caned. It helped not a jot to put an extra layer of shorts on or to stuff anything else down the back of your trousers for protection; he enjoyed his work!

Chapter 3
First Jobs

There were, no doubt, opportunities for drama and other after-school activities, but for me the opportunities were restricted. My working life started at twelve years old and my first job was to deliver newspapers to about thirty houses close to home. This I did before catching the bus to go to school, it meant that I was frequently late. Throughout my school years and beyond, I seem to have always been a persistently late arriver. This is a skill which I have honed to perfection in later life, persuading myself that I was always much too busy with other things to waste time arriving early! That was and is at least a little disingenuous and I apologise to everyone and blame my mother for indulging me! If I missed the twenty past eight bus to Swadlincote then I caught the twenty-five to nine bus which dropped me on the wrong side of Long Eaton and necessitated a run across the town, past the snooker hall, whose dubious attractions I was later to appreciate in fine detail, and on to school usually arriving after class registration. Occasionally I would be helped by a very kindly, elderly history teacher called Miss Brooks who lived in the same village as I did and drove to the same school, thinking as I did of the four o'clock end of school bell. We had that in common.

My morning newspaper round eventually gave way to a Sunday delivery round which was much more interesting. For reasons I have never quite appreciated, the Sunday round used to occasionally get tipped; one particular customer used to wait at the end of his house driveway to collect the paper from me. I was fourteen years old and perhaps a little naïve – one day I checked the contents of his delivery and found, neatly tucked inside the Sunday Express, a copy of the aptly if unimaginatively titled "Tit Bits" and an impossibly colourful publication known as "Parade" which was full of very scantily-clad ladies with big yellow stars placed as a sop to modesty. Whatever the weather and however late I was, this particular punter on the edge of the golf course was always at the end of his driveway, always gave me a tip and was always smiling. Mostly the ones who had the Telegraph were miserable, complained that I cycled right up to their front doors and had pockets too deep to reach into. After a while I used to check the delivery bundle for my friend on the edge of the golf course in case there was any content that might offend him; there never was and he didn't seem to mind that he was not the first person to have turned the pages! I don't remember ever bothering to check the contents for the Telegraph brigade!

At fifteen I graduated to delivering groceries, for which I had a bicycle with a large metal basket on the front. Into this I could load about three boxes of groceries, which were delivered by me from Marsden's the local grocery shop, to the middle-class customers who could afford such a luxury. My bicycle had no gears, wide friction heavy tyres and a tiny front wheel but my responsibilities were on Tuesday and Thursday nights only, which did allow me to take part in after-school activities that were mostly sports orientated. My grocery round paid better than delivering newspapers, though there were no awards given at the end of school for efforts to serve the community by delivering groceries; consequently, it doesn't appear on my CV. Best in the year or best in the class was not usually in the same line as Venables in my schooling experience. The job did have its perks though. One of my favourite clients was Mrs Guinevere. She lived at the top of a hill unfortunately, but she always met my breathless arrival with a large slice of cake and an all-encompassing bosomy hug. Those were the days when such behaviour didn't have to have a hidden meaning. I liked her a lot and I'm sorry I can't tell her now how grateful I was for her kindness. She lived in a detached house with a jungle like garden, plants escaping across promising looking paths and smoke rising from the chimney. The warmth of her welcome was worth bottling and her weekly sixpenny tip gratefully pocketed.

The summit of my career in child labour was to succeed my sister at Frank Nudd's garage in Attenborough opposite the Royal Ordnance Depot (a hangover from the war years). By this time, I was a very reluctant sixth-former with other reasons to be at school apart from studying. I never got close to my sister's achievement in removing the wrong reflector on a Humber Super Snipe car and filling the boot with petrol rather than the tank which was behind the other reflector! Personally, I blame the car designer, but such generosity was not in the gift of the recipient - whatever, Anne moved on and I moved in.

I suspect that we all have crimes in our past; one of mine (I may not confess to all of them) involved the sale of salvaged oil to customers from pint bottles. If I sold the genuine article with panache and a good patter, it was perfectly possible to save about one tenth of a pint from every bottle. The eleventh was mine - only about one every two weeks, but it went towards running my Lambretta scooter with its ridiculous ten-foot-long aerial-cum-flagpole. If I felt any guilt in this it was somewhat mitigated by the fact that at half past eight most Friday nights, Frank (in whose garage I worked and whose flat was adjacent to the garage) had a visit from the same blonde bulging lady in a little red sports car. She left regularly at ten o'clock, as I was packing up the garage. For a long time, I thought she must've been doing the cleaning! Since she clearly got extremely well paid for her efforts, I suggested to my mother that my sister might like to apply for similar work, but my good intentions were not well received! I was getting educated in the school of life but at a gentle pace!

Chapter 4
The Kindness of Friends

At about this time in my reluctant schooling experience I had a friend who is now a member of the House of Lords. Sue Campbell was a friend for me and the girlfriend of one of my buddies. She was Head Girl at the school, and I was the only sixth-former not to be honoured by any sort of badge of office. Even today I don't understand quite why, but it may have been to do with the time it took to master snooker on the battleship table (a half sized, beer stained, cigarette burnt and pocket torn snooker table kept in the far corner of the smoke filled Long Eaton snooker hall on which we school boys could play cheaply and mostly unobserved).Or perhaps skipping school for a day in order to widen my experience of life, (going fox hunting, of all things) before returning to school at the end of the day for a football match. Sadly, this same match was refereed by my form tutor, but then how was I to know? Thanks to my friend - she had moved to the school from some exotic previous existence in the suburbs of some faraway city - Warwick it may have been, I somehow survived the two years of sixth form. She knew how to press the right buttons when I didn't even know where the button board was! Whatever, she was "cool" to use today's parlance. To me she represented the middle class - she had a car, a Triumph Vitesse, her mum was kindly and welcoming, and her dad owned a furniture shop locally. Crucially they lived close to where I did and her parents seemed genuinely interested in me, what I had to say, and what I wanted to do. The same was true of my then girlfriend Elaine and her parents. For girlfriend read "girl - friend" or better still "friend - girl." These were days of honeyed innocence when to hold hands in a double seat at the Essoldo Picture House whilst watching Ben Hur was to be poised on the edge of conventional respectability before hurtling off somewhere; I don't know where, we never got there! With both girls and their parents, I had begun to become aware of a political side to life, to recognise that boundaries were flexible and frequently self-imposed.

Other things had happened in my recent life to make me consider the philosophical questions concerning the meaning of life, religion and its implications etc. I was living in the metaphysical space of the hopeful rather than the expectant and there I have stayed pretty well for fifty years, fed by visionary poets and battered by the arrogance of zealots and contradictions of religious pomp. The boy then and the man now, both of us despise the mind-numbing conformity and blind obedience so treasured by the religious bureaucrats of the main faiths. Take a good man, a great idea, a brilliant vision, give it to the "pen men" and hey presto, you've got a religion and a whole lot of thou-shalt-nots!

Whether it was the disharmony between my parents, or the fact that my elder brother Chris seemed drawn like a moth to a candle flame to his own and my parents' disappointment, or perhaps it was the fact that my sister had moved to Sheffield Teachers Training College, Neil and I became very close and spent a lot of time with each other despite our age gap. With my mother working in the kitchen or wherever else in the house and my father and my elder brother dissecting the latest football game and the qualities or otherwise of the referee, Neil and I played draughts, assembled Air fix models and built dens and walls.

At around this time my sister was heavily involved with the local church, her friends were closely scrutinised by my father as to who was suitable or unsuitable for her. I should have hung a health and safety warning around her neck to warn off any potential suitors, of which she had a few. On the upside of this I could be sure that anyone who was brave enough to court my sister was certainly serious; my father would've been quite a deterrent to most! My good friend and now brother-in-law John Smalley was man enough to stay the course, happily.

We suburban boys in the post-war years enjoyed fairly innocuous and simple activities. Together with my friends Robin Mellor, Johnny Porter, Richard White and eventually Alan Andrews we became excellent den builders, we played endless football and no doubt dreamt of starring in that sport for the local Nottingham Forest F.C. who had reached dizzying heights winning the European Cup twice in succession under the unconventional coaching methods of Brian Clough. One of the things that we did regularly was to place halfpenny pieces onto the railway line; these would be squashed flat and expanded to roughly the size of a penny which could then be used to fool the chewing gum machines into allowing the delivery of a penny's worth of chewing gum for a flattened halfpenny. For the mathematically challenged, that is a hundred per cent mark-up. On rare occasions, the Flying Scotsman travelled on our local line, which was a source of great excitement. Pennies created in this way by this train were treasured beyond their pecuniary value. Despite our hiding in the bushes while the train went past, we were usually seen, and I suppose reported by the driver at the next station either at Beeston or Attenborough. However, the response was so predictable that we were never apprehended.

Our den-building mostly took place near the railway line on an old neglected siding with gravel extraction pits on the other side. During the winter these gravel pits would freeze sufficiently for us to run across them. We had what proved to be an effective, if primitive, way of measuring the ice depth, involving concrete blocks and a foot bridge. The sound of concrete block hitting ice would resonate across the gravel pits if the ice was thick enough or just make a splosh if it wasn't. The gravel beds are now a nature reserve with the inevitable prohibitive notices posted. Whilst making these dens we also made plans on how we were going to conquer the world and other things. Life got in the way of our plans and I don't know what the others ended up doing; we drifted off in separate directions.

Chapter 5
Losing Our Working-Class Credentials

In the late nineteen fifties, as boys' hair was getting longer and girls' skirts shorter, my father, having resisted my mother's attempts to get us all on the immigration boat to Australia (all you needed to do was tick the boxes and pay fifty quid and you were on your way down under), quit his factory job at Raleigh in order to take on a job selling petrol for a new cut-price company called Jet. In the petrol industry to that date there was a cartel operating between the four major petrol supply companies. Jet, under the guidance of the managing director, a canny Yorkshire man called Bill Roberts, disturbed the comfortable arrangement of the big four. This he did by purchasing odd tanker loads of unrefined fuel waiting in the North Sea to unload, then renting facilities to refine the fuel and hiring surplus tankers to deliver to garages all over the UK and eventually directly to haulage companies and other fuel hungry businesses. My father was lucky to get in right at the beginning and he was very effective at his job. I would occasionally accompany him and remember once going on board a German crude oil tanker, sitting in what I suppose was the captain's cabin and getting my first introduction to schnapps. It was breath-taking, sweet and tasted altogether of a world different to the one I had known hitherto.

Suddenly, we had a car, a telephone, a television, and within a couple of years my sister even had her own pony, though somehow it fell to me to look after it! We may have had a new settee (not sofa) for the front room, I can't remember – I was hardly ever allowed in! Was it really possible to be working class and own your own pony? On top of all the other issues my family had we now had an identity crisis as well! Dad worked hard, albeit in a suit rather than his blue factory overalls. We children were schooled in how to answer the phone as everybody was a potential customer. My father combined his natural talent for organisational neatness and snappy presentation with his genie-like ability to secure football tickets to big matches for his best customers. The results were financially dramatic though I think I was always inclined to anticipate the storybook wolf arriving one night and blowing it all away.

No more was it necessary for me to skip school for the day rather than ask my parents for money to go on an organised trip, which in my child's mind I thought they could not afford. No more trips down to the "beer off" with bottles in order to claim the deposit or otherwise (some bottles didn't carry a deposit but under instructions from my mother I would take them down in the hope the shopkeeper might be distracted and pay up by mistake). Lessons once learnt though are difficult to forget and I've always looked after the pennies and had an unspoken respect for the same quality in others.

It was socially necessary for my teenage credibility to "have a girlfriend" from about fourteen years old onwards and I was blessed with a succession of girls who fitted the bill nicely. Sex then was not what it appears to be now to succeeding generations. In my sphere at least, to hold hands in a public place was serious. To go out together was to be "going steady" with oblivion, pregnancy and a mortgage just around the corner. I decided early on that oblivion was overrated and not for me, so boundaries were not carelessly breached. I did however hold hands with some very good friends, some of whom I am still in touch with today.

My sister Anne's pony arrived soon after the television and the Morris Minor car. This badge of arrival in the land of the affluent soon tarnished for Anne, and Paddy the pony effectively became my privilege, responsibility and cost! Not to be guilty of looking this gift horse in the mouth, I cashed in on the positives. I soon found that the pony riding fraternity was mostly female and so introductions were easily gained and I never had a shortage of girls who were friends. Paddy moved on eventually to be replaced by Empire Knight, a fifteen-two hands high (small by thoroughbred standards) two-year-old bought out of racing because of his lack of size and potential. He was registered with Weatherby's and had two Derby winners in his ancestry, Hyperion and Nearco. He needed only a handful of oats to imagine himself steaming down the Epsom finishing straights. He was not broken in as a riding horse so I bought a couple of books and did the best I could, but he was never quiet. In this endeavour I was encouraged by a friend, Gill Foulger, who was doing a similar job with rather more compliant, kind of cobbish pony called Robin. Gill was to become a vital family friend to my mother and a confidant to my father at a very difficult family time. She was some three years older than me and attractive in every way, but I never saw her in any light other than as family porcelain. We are still good friends today. She is a great artist. Perhaps there were moments, as there so often are, when a look or a word might have been seen or heard differently and things might have taken a different route, and perhaps the porcelain might have been broken, who knows? These moments come and go – the "what if" or "if only" moments that punctuate all our lives all the time.

My survival at about that time was quite unnecessarily put at risk by my own stupidity. We used to hire a field some two miles from the family home. Having broken Knight in myself, I had a misplaced trust in his reliability and in my own abilities and would occasionally ride him bareback and with a rope halter – a bit like sitting on the roof of an E-type Jag holding onto the windscreen wiper with a demon at the pedals and no steering wheel. One mid-afternoon on a summer's day I was mounted just so, flies buzzing lazily above the acrid, accumulated, soiled dust of a summer stable, when something happened (perhaps a bucket falling) and this ebony, frustrated Derby runner took off like a cork from a bottle round the five-acre field which was interspersed with the odd spreading oak and sycamore tree. There was a brief moment when I could have and should have slipped off, but I missed it. During his self-indulgent race around the field I ducked twice beneath deadly solid outstretched sycamore boughs, themselves the size of small trees. Each time we missed the branch only by just enough that it grazed my back through my shirt but crucially, missed my head. If I hadn't flattened myself on the withers of the horse or if he had been an inch or two higher, the result would have been painful in the extreme, though the pain at least may have been short-lived! Eventually he slithered to a halt almost exactly where he had started from and I slipped off his back onto shaking legs. My religious friends would have, and probably did describe it as a miracle that I survived, without thinking about the awkward implications of why me, and not someone else.

Sadly Knight, as he had come to be called, died about one year later after being hit by a lorry whilst being ridden by my mother on the Bramcote bypass. The circumstances were such that I don't believe the driver was at fault. Knight had always been much too strong a horse for my mother to ride.

It has often struck me that when catastrophes occur, they do so in clusters; perhaps we just take our eye off the ball or perhaps they just crowd out other memories and retrospectively they seem to queue up one after the other. The next few years were to be dominated by events that neither I nor my family had any control over and would go on to colour my, and doubtless their reactions, hopes and aspirations for all the years to come. If I had a concept of a just and responsive God up to this time it would prove ill-fated in the light of events to follow.

Chapter 6
Neil, Family Turmoil, Religion and All That

The sudden and unexpected diagnosis of a rare type of cancer within the spinal cord of my younger brother Neil came out of a rare blue sky in my family's emotionally turbulent history. Thereafter the blues were crowded out with greys and the stars ceased to sparkle. My brother was eight years old when he was first diagnosed and died some three years later. There are some people in my experience who are just good, for whom there is no "but", no "however" and no "if only" in their character. Neil was one. Coming as he did some eight years after me, I guess he would have been an accident of poor contraception - perhaps we all were - who knows? Whatever, he was for me a very special person and it mattered not at all whether his arrival was intended or otherwise, he carried his suffering heroically, and to his last day he had a smile and a greeting for everyone. I would have changed places with him for a bag of bananas, but the banana man must have been busy elsewhere.

After the death of Neil both my parents were, in common with others in similar circumstances, totally devastated. They had exhausted all possible avenues of medical and other aid but at that time cancer within the spinal column didn't leave much room for hope. During the three years of steady decline, clerics, doctors, faith healers, football stars (the whole Leeds United football team) trod the concrete path at the front of our house to comfort my brother and offer what help they could. The suffering that he went through was physical agony for him and defeating mental torture for us all. My parents' desperation knew no bounds: if you have been there, as many have, you will know what I mean. With no discernible miracle coming from the Almighty there was no doubt we would have dealt with the devil himself in a pact to secure a cure for Neil. There was to be no cure - Neil died lying on the settee at our home with my mother in the kitchen and me kneeling beside him. Until the last day he was kind, humorous and calm amidst the cancerous chaos of his medical condition and the emotional turmoil without.

Death for Neil was a release. For my parents it was the beginning of a dark road of aching emptiness. Whatever they had done, no more could be done. My mother, at reflective moments, for the rest of her life took some solace in the hope of an eventual meeting up with Neil in some yellow-brick road afterlife existence. I believe she was ready to take that step every day until she died some sixteen years later in a hospital bed after a massive stroke in 1985.

My father struggled in the stagnant, cloying marshland of bereavement for two or three years and would at times have been happy to have no shadow on cloudless days. Eventually he emerged into the pale sunlight and immersed himself in "Riding for the Disabled" and other organisations caring for handicapped children. He doubtless caught glimpses of Neil in the children he worked with from time to time. He used his canny knack to secure tickets and invitations to visit football matches, the Houses of Parliament, the Royal Stables and the White City Stadium where he would take groups of children to whatever was on offer. On one occasion (with my sister Anne's help) he took a group of youngsters from Dame Hannah Rogers' school for handicapped children to 10 Downing Street to see the prime minister. John Major was of course the Conservative prime minister who succeeded Margaret Thatcher and for whom my father, with his heavily engrained socialist background, had a deep-seated loathing. Whatever, my poor Dad had to swallow his political prejudice in order to accompany these children into number ten. To his great credit he never forgot John Major's generous spirit with his time and interest shown to the youngsters and I think he was more open minded about his politics thereafter.

My father was an inspirationally generous and dedicated man who expressed his religious beliefs in good works and generosity. As I have already said, the gilt on the gingerbread got a bit sullied by other characteristics but he had been through a lot and somehow kept going. I for one can forgive him his lack of perfection. I never heard him refuse anyone help and for me and my young family he was always there when we needed support, which was often enough. We all remember him arriving with Liquorice Allsorts, a bottle of Blue Nun wine and a box of Milk Tray and then spending the whole day on the farm concrete mixing, worming cattle or dipping sheep etc. He was frustrating at times but then so are we all. My father was a perfectionist, but our life didn't allow us that luxury. We had made a fine art out of cutting corners and making do, as was necessary in order to squeeze twenty-five hours into a twenty-four-hour day and eight days into every week. I can remember his constant refrains of, 'If a job is worth doing it is worth doing properly,' and 'Come on, we mustn't cut corners.' Poor Dad.

At one stage, having borrowed money from helpful friends, secured a bank overdraft on massively over-valued assets and a bank loan on the collateral of my parents' house, with fourteen hundred breeding sheep, forty cows, three children at school on a rented farm and Gilly studying for an Open University degree, cutting corners became a dark and vital art. Whatever - critical, helpful and a constant encouragement at a time when such encouragement was desperately needed, my Dad was always there with his half-drunk cup of tea.

So, what of religion on the back of this? Along with folk singer Nick Cave, I do not believe in an interventionist God. I can't. Many do and I'm glad for them if it is a comfort in their lives. Within our own circle of family and friends there are those who will call on the Almighty to heal a headache and help with the homework as if God in his capacity as a heavenly father figure deals out such goodies in the way his earthly counterparts might, knocking off points for bad behaviour and giving out dolly mixtures for the opposite. Others have prayer lists in the same way as I have a "jobs to do" list. Got a problem? Then we'll pray about it – finished! I remember once, in a God hunting moment in my life, some senior clerical relatives "thanking the Lord" for protecting an aged and amiable friend of theirs who had inadvertently driven her car the wrong way down a short stretch of dual carriageway. I couldn't help wondering why an omnipotent, caring, interventionist God hadn't disabled her car on the feeder road and prevented malaria! And then there was my brother!

My mum found solace in walks through the countryside. Something about the undeniable order and the interdependency of the natural world spoke to her of a world apart from the corrupted version that she had come to know. Her aversion to the suburban life rubbed off on me: together we both came to abhor the ordinary. Why be grey when you might be white, or black? Why say no when yes might take you to places you've never dreamt of? She found in the organised church a fair dose of greyness, a lack of spontaneity and in her view, hypocrisy. The popular self-advertised description of our church (in which I had been a reluctant choirboy) being a school for sinners rather than a society for saints cut no ice with her. If the message wasn't clear enough to see the difference, then just sit down and shut up. Her childhood had been spent at a convent school and she had seen too much pomp, too much ritual and too much grey.

Mum's character was direct. She would face a problem full on. The electric lamp by my parents' bedside had too long a flex.

She cut it off with a pair of scissors. Flash occurs twice in the next sentence. Quick as one she cut the wire, and then again before she ended up on her back on the floor of the bedroom. The scissors, still in hand, were left with a smart blue-edged hole in the blade and fortunately a blown fuse in the main box. It got straight to the problem but created several more. My father would have considered it, planned it and before he got around to doing it, we would have all forgotten what the problem was. Genetics are useful in blame games; brown eyes are not the only thing I inherited from my mother's genes! Mouth, open and foot are words we might both have benefitted from having printed on our metaphorical retinas.

'Carefully chosen soft words turn away wrath.' My friend now and wife of more than forty years must have whispered it to me a hundred times or more to my benefit, but I suspect my mother never heard them or if she did, she never listened. My Dad would let the wrath element accumulate till the dam could no longer hold the pressure. It all made for an uncomfortable and tempestuous atmosphere in our home. As children we learnt to walk on egg-shells and savour the occasional calms between the storms.

Today as I am writing, looking south over the freshly snow-capped Pyrenees towards Spain, whisks of cloud tethered by gossamer threads to the luminescent beech and birch trees in their spring Sunday best, cherry blossom rampant, swallows pausing on their journey North and crickets calling the close of winter in this high hillside retreat, I see things as my mother would have liked. She would have been comfortable here. Here she could have found solace in the natural pattern of life. Prayer for her in this place would have been just to breathe deeply in rhythm with the natural pulse. Prayer is such a personal thing it deserves more than one word to describe it, like snow perhaps. The next time I meet an Eskimo…

My father, having been schooled at Lichfield cathedral, saw things differently. But to him also religion was more social than spiritual. Say what you like, pray what you like, and promise what you like, it all adds up to a bundle of nothing without action. He had seen in his lifetime a shift by the Christian church away from being a major force for social improvement towards being a self-interest organisation concerned more with personal spiritual salvation than social justice and reform.

Dad believed that anything was possible. People were not gifted, some just worked harder than others. He would say often, 'The funny thing is that more one practises, the more gifted one seems to become!'

For myself, and I have been close to people with a spiritual interest for most of my adult life, "Look To This Day" from Sanskrit and the popular "Desiderata" touch me deeply and to quote modern parlance it is where I am at most of the time. My brother Neil's illness and death affected me greatly and prompted me at an age when I suppose most of us confront the bigger philosophical questions of life to actively look for meaning and reason. His apparently pointless suffering and passing fuelled in me a desire to make a difference. To make some sort of sense to Neil's short life, I had to make something of mine.

The "Children of God," a religious sect popular some forty years ago might have got their wires crossed on certain issues but their mantra that "I'd rather see a sermon than hear one any day" is close to the mark for me. I've heard too many sermons, mindlessly chanted too many trite responses and seen too often the smothering of simple goodness by the clerical self-aggrandising cloak of religious bureaucrats.

What we are (my parents were right) is better defined by what we do than by what we profess to believe. Amongst my friends I count both religious and non-religious, but the ones I like the best are the doers, whatever their motivation. I like the sound of Pope Francis, Desmond Tutu, Nelson Mandela and Bill and Melinda Gates. There are many others, but the common thread is their humanity driving them to create hope in hopeless situations and build oases out of mirages.

My youngest son worked for a while as a carer helping people with severe learning difficulties in London. One day he took them into a café as part of their life experiences. They disturbed the peace in a significant way for the only other client who was enjoying his lonely coffee. He got up and left soon after the noise brigade arrived and before my son could apologise and explain the situation. When it came to pay the bill, the proprietor explained there was no need as it had already been settled by the elderly gentleman. Well I don't know if this guy had had any religion, but I like the result, whatever the reason for his compassion.

Chapter 7
Education and a Second Bite at the Cherry

My offer of a place at the Royal Agricultural College was generous and conditional on only five moderate GCE "O" level passes which I got on the principle of writing down practically everything I knew that was remotely relevant to the question and making up the rest. Five years earlier I had scraped into grammar school and now into the best agricultural college in the country with a worldwide reputation for excellence. I did however return to school to study the sciences to "A" level, but alas with no need for the end of study qualification I largely squandered my time there. It was during this period that Neil was first diagnosed with cancer. My rebellious teenage frustrations were unfettered; I had little respect for the school system and even less for some of the teaching staff. I was, to put it mildly, not a prize student and would have rebelled against the colour of the sky if all else was right! The two years passed in a blur - I couldn't wait for it to finish. One of the highlights of that time was my girlfriend Elaine Jones. We spent a lot of time together; my father adored her, and I guess her parents saw something in me that most of my teachers didn't. They took me on holiday with them to Scotland when the tensions in our home had been sharpened by the onset of Neil's illness. I guess I felt guilty in an obscure way at taking any enjoyment whilst impotent to change the situation at home. Elaine and the Jones family were stars in a rapidly darkening night, and I am not sure that I would have been wonderful company. Regrettably, I have lost touch with them. Life for me at that time was urgent; I was an angry young man and like angry young men the world over I kicked out at what I didn't understand. Our friendship stuttered to an untidy finish some two years later on the altar of my tempestuous youth. I could not risk the perceived oblivion of the ordinary that my contemporaries seemed to be drifting towards. If my brother Neil's suffering were to count for anything then ordinary and I would not walk the same path.

School finished and I needed a minimum of one year's practical farm work as a prerequisite before taking up my college place at Cirencester. I got a job through my father's contacts at the Nottingham Corporation farm that was used for sewage disposal, some seven miles from home. My parents set me up with a little car – a Hillman Husky that drank both oil and petrol like my father drank tea. This job was as a farm student on a staff of eighteen and I lasted six months. The foreman, Harry Andrews was a flat-capped, miserable, incompetent bully of a man with small steely blue eyes and the charisma of a damp sponge. For him, every day was a gloomy Monday and I had been foisted on him. He and I were not to get on well. If this was life for some, it certainly wasn't for me. I learned a lot about how not to do things and something about valuing time. The next time I got a chance to study would not be wasted. After six months of this purgatory, punctuated as it was by the occasional weekend at home to share in the family turmoil, I packed my one suitcase to head off south in my car, (which was soon to be christened Penny Conk), to work on a distant relative's farm near Malmesbury, Wiltshire. Here, fields had names and dogs had manners.

Sometime during this period, I returned home for a long weekend and took Neil up into the Derbyshire Peak District for two nights camping, sleeping in the back of my car. At that time, he was in remission and we planned our futures far away from suburbia. My memories are through a veil of tears but included Australia, dogs and horses. At that time hope had not been completely flattened, although pragmatism would have shown our plans to be pipe dreams. The remission was not to last long; I do not remember anything other than Neil's steady decline thereafter. However, it was a few days and memory of them has stayed with me – a patch of colour against a grey canvas. Neil was to write to me afterwards with his latest collection of jokes and recounting the memories of the trip. I have his letter still and his picture on the wall of this Pyrenean haven, looking west over snow-capped peaks. Such is life. With all that has happened since, things that I have done, mistakes that I have made, dreams that I have fulfilled and others that I have fallen short on, my brother has been close by, a comforting star on moonless nights. Neil's death in 1968 was, by the time it happened, expected and if I am honest, welcomed. He had no possibility of recovery and his pain and suffering was such that to have wished him to stay alive would have been perverse.

It marked for me the advent of a serious quest for meaning and justice in life which stays with me to this day, tempered by cynicism and reduced expectation as the years pass. Most things I have attempted since then I have achieved. I don't think I have ducked many challenges nor cheated any moral charter. In the eyes of some it may seem that I have been inordinately lucky or even privileged and perhaps I have been but then my nights are never totally dark...

Chapter 8
Royal Agricultural College

My two years at the RAC coincided with a growing in self-confidence, a calming down from my righteous youthful anger stage and a none-too-soon revolution in my attitude to study. I was unfazed and stimulated by the different people that I met, their different backgrounds (many had gone through private education) and their different interests. Academically, the course was not taxing for me; I loved the logic of applied scientific practice with measurable end results. This all seemed good common-sense stuff. I am indebted to the RAC and the friends I made there for more than my agricultural education.

The library was like walking into a comfortable lounge, soothing and other worldish with its oak panelling and small leaded windows. To begin the day walking around the outside of this Cotswold stone architectural masterpiece with its clock tower and artistically extravagant, features after eating whatever quantities we liked of bacon, egg, sausage, mushroom and tomato served up in polished tureens by smart Portuguese penguin suited waiters, was to be in a world totally different from eight years previously when I peddled my pack of thirty newspapers around the streets of Chilwell.

The local villages with their flower-adorned gardens, golden Cotswold stone walls and chipper stone roofs seemed unrelated to the brick-built, uniform, semi-detached, smoke-stained houses of the Midlands. If the quaint wooden front doors of these Cotswold houses had been opened by Peter Rabbit or Mr Toad of Toad Hall I would not have been surprised. Flopsy bunnies and primrose banks were not the stuff of imagination. Here they hopped around and grew in profusion.

One from my group of friends at college came from the Falkland Islands and another was from the Isle of Wight. My geography was such that they might have been neighbours! I was on a steep learning curve and my horizons were widening fast!

Though today it seems a little odd looking back, the college was all male; conveniently some twenty miles north, up and over Birdlip Hill was an all-female teacher training college at Gloucester. My ever-versatile and reliable but thirsty Penny Conk got used to the route and by cruising with the engine turned off (no steering locks in those days) down the hills, we could get there and back on a gallon of fuel. It wasn't always my car; we were a democratic group to begin with and shared transport. Inevitably some of my friends got "hitched" which threatened the survival of our fraternity. The college dances and end of year balls were held in the Boutflower Hall (named after Robert Boutflower, a former principal of the college who made his name pioneering the scientific feeding of dairy cows for maximum yield - he was probably not so popular among the bovine fraternity whose mammary areas had to accommodate the increased milk burden).

I remember Elaine coming down to one of these dances and it was as if we were strangers having just met with little in common. With marriage definitely not on my agenda, our friendship came to an unsatisfactory end which I was sorry about. I think I had taken both her and her family's friendship a little for granted and it seemed a shabby and unnecessary way to finish, like closing a book because the narrative in the middle pages had slowed down a pace.

Chapter 9
Holiday Work

During these two years at Cirencester, every holiday was spent working either at Christmas time as a student helper with the increased postal deliveries, at Easter as a lambing assistant or in the summer helping with the hay harvest soon to be followed by that of winter barley and then wheat. I must have been reasonably competent as I was never without a job and usually invited back for the next season.

On one particular farm, the farm manager and I were just getting going with the barley harvest in the Trent Valley. The combine harvester was a small Massy Harris unit that had no discharge tank, meaning that as the grain came off the field it had to be immediately bagged up in forty kilogramme hessian sacks. That was my job. The farm manager John Sutton was a big jovial character and we jollied along nicely together. The crop had been laid low by earlier thunderstorms which meant that the pick-up reel had to be dropped low to the ground. These old belt-driven machines were designed for perfect upstanding weed-free crops. We were in a different ball game here; every few minutes I'd hear a high whining noise followed by an unprintable expletive from the normally mild-mannered John and our walking paced progress would become standing pace. Off John would jump and thump the top of the pick-up drive belt with his fist, the high-pitched whine would stop followed by the comforting familiar clatter as the rubber V drive belt took hold and off, we would go again. No doubt the instruction book was specific about turning off the engine and disconnecting the drive, but the whole point of the exercise was to get the V belt to tighten into the drive wheel. Only an idiot would hit the inside of the drive belt which, when it suddenly took hold, might carry the offending hand up into the drive wheel, twist the arm off at the elbow if he was lucky or drag him into the main drive if he wasn't. John was no idiot but somehow that's what he did. His first expletive was followed by a prolonged scream. I part leapt and part fell off my bagging platform to reach his driving seat and the "off" device. My leg was caught up in the iron skeleton, but I managed to pull the button and the deadly monster coughed twice, shuddered to a halt, and then died. Not so John's scream. His elbow was still intact; he was a big, well-put-together man but the four fingers on his right hand were streaming blood and trapped between the pulley belt and the drive wheel. Using a fence post left behind from an earlier job, I was able to reverse the wheel enough for John to remove his hand.

My shirt came off pretty sharpish to transform into a rudimentary dressing and he held his arm out for me to bandage his hand. Each finger was stripped of flesh down to the bone, but he didn't want to know that, and he wouldn't look. His scream had subsided to a heavy intermittent sob through clenched teeth which I can hear now as I write this. We walked steadily back to the farmhouse where he insisted on feeding his dog and kennelling it before I drove him to the hospital in Nottingham. In an effort to comfort him in the black manner that we were both familiar with I suggested that he might as well give me his guitar and look out for a mouth organ. He managed a thin smile but goodness, he looked pale. I finished the harvest off with his friend and we were never to meet up again as my parents left Nottingham for good to live in Gloucestershire in an effort to help ease the pain that my brother's passing had left. John Sutton as a character has appeared many times to me in different guises throughout my time in farming. Steady as a rock, totally reliable when trouble threatens, tough as nails and mild mannered but only up to a point (then watch out). I don't know if John ever bought his mouth organ but he sure as hell didn't give me his guitar!

Shepherding during the Easter break was something else. I followed a friend into Sudeley Manor Farm near Cheltenham. As it happens, I actually spent three lambings there. Peter, who pronounced his name pepper with the two middle "p"s sounded as a "t" was the Welsh resident shepherd on this beautiful Cotswold mixed farm and for the first week would only regard me out of the corner of his eye. That's what "college boys" could expect. We had to earn respect. He had two little sons who never seemed to get any older over the three seasons I worked with him. Mine was the night shift, from ten p.m. to four a.m. Peter would come on at six a.m. and woe betide if I didn't leave things tidy when I left. Inevitably we sometimes overlapped when things were busy, which earned me the occasional full eye contact. I slept in the big house and ate supper and lunch with Peter and his wife Margaret, pronounced Mag-ret.

Peter's lambing philosophy was tough; castration and tailing (i.e. the removal of all non-essential body parts which might cause trouble later, ears survived due to their convenience for tag attachment) was done as soon as the lamb was born on the premise that the little blighters might think that it was all part of being born. He may have been right and certainly didn't want any soft advice from me concerning the probable survival advantage of letting the lamb dry off and fill its belly first! He probably had the toughest flock in England. Survival of the fittest and Charles Darwin would have had a field day here. Each night at Sudeley I would creep back in the early hours to the big house and claim my bed next to which would be a flask full of the best hot chocolate I've ever tasted. The owner's children had moved off to college, leaving the nanny to pick up odd jobs around the place. Bless her.

I was for three years one of her odd jobs. Breakfast at nine a.m. was laid out; one place at the head of an oak table looking out westwards and towards Sudeley Castle. Next to my place was a copy of The Times. Breakfast was several courses served up when I was ready! Somehow, I got myself onto the farm with Peter by ten o'clock. Over the years to follow we have had on our farm many veterinary lambing assistants and I hope that they have enjoyed themselves, but I know for sure that they were never as pampered as I was at Sudeley.

My final interaction with Peter would come on the last night of my stay when he and I were packed off by Margaret to Cheltenham Town Hall for the weekly "pick-up" dance. Each time he presented me with a tie to ensure that we were allowed in and that was the last I saw of him until eleven p.m. What he got up to I have no idea; I drank a lot of shandy. On the last occasion we took a taxi back to the farm and Peter presented me with a green-tinted glass as a going away present; it was suspiciously like the one I had been drinking shandy from, but I thanked him all the same. As is the way with these things it was as tough as Peter and lasted for years to remind me of those times spent sheep farming... Peter, you have a lot to answer for.

One of my other harvest jobs was at Belvoir Castle in Rutland on a farm whose speciality was to grow, dry and pellet grass. The job paid well but was otherwise unremarkable. My digs were at the Red House, Knipton. One day whilst eating my "snap" (lunch) in the eighty-acre field where I was ploughing stubbles, a field mouse ran across my outstretched legs as I sat in the sun against the tractor wheel. He was temptingly close. I swept him up with my hand in one deft movement and popped him into my now empty lunch box; don't ask me why, I just did. Back at the Red House I made him a cage and a bed but alas next morning there was no mouse! It was a daft idea at best; I had a cursory search for my new-found friend but to no avail. Harvest finished some four weeks later, and it was time to pack up and go back to college.

These jobs combined with a state grant meant that I finished college not only qualified but debtless and a lot wiser to boot.

Pulling the sheets off the bed for the first time since the beginning of harvest at Knipton (at that stage I didn't squander too much time washing unnecessarily), I discovered my little furry friend had settled in comfortably between the sheet folds at the bottom of the bed. I awarded him full marks for ingenuity and made myself late arriving at my next stop by walking across the newly ploughed field to return him as close as possible to where I had found him.

Some years later I found a swallow which had snagged its toe between barbed wire on the south coast whilst waiting for the big push to Africa. Releasing her was tricky but successful and I live in the hope that such simple acts of kindness might help tip the balance in my favour at some ultimate divine court hearing. "Against you, Venables, we have this endless list; however, in mitigation…" I might need a lot of swallows and mice to speak in my favour!

The swallows have just arrived in the Pyrenean foothills and I am looking to see if any of them have a missing fourth toe! The soothing vocal magic of Enya is percolating up from downstairs, just audible through the floorboards and food is being put together for supper after a day collecting firewood for next winter's warmth; the sun is pushing a golden evening glow up the valley and the clouds of earlier which gave rain have dusted the mountains to the west with fresh snow. The high stratus is blushing with the last of the sun's rays and wisps of mist are hanging on to the tree-clad hillsides. If the scene were painted that way, it would appear as a vulgar exaggeration, but it is the real thing and there is nothing vulgar about this scene.

There are diamond moments in life, and this is one of them; I feel a thank you is in order, but I am not quite sure who I am speaking to. Perhaps it's the field mouse or the swallow. Who knows? Thanks all the same.

Chapter 10
Extracurricular Activity

During my second year at college, I blew away any chances of getting the Queen's Prize for academic achievement (although the simple fact that it was a possibility testifies to the changes that I had undergone since my largely wasted school years) by getting immersed in extracurricular activities. With a friend, Ian Clark, I relaunched the then defunct Cattle Club; I captained one of the football teams and introduced "3W1" to the RAC. We had regular meetings in what I think was the "George Wing", as we sat folded comfortably into the leather upholstered chairs, looked down on by grandiose paintings of past principals sharing hanging space with extravagantly-muscled and exotically horned cattle on the oak-panelled walls. Our cattle club meetings centred on the finer points of the double-muscled Charolais or Belgium Blue cattle and the attendant calving difficulties. Would they, or would they not replace the reliable British stalwarts such as the white-faced Hereford, or the easy calving Aberdeen Angus which usually produced calves the size of a lightweight collie dog?

I remember getting quite excited at the idea of diluting bulls' semen with egg albumen, centrifuging the cocktail and then using only the top (or bottom) of the resultant mixture to artificially inseminate cows. This was to be an aid in determining the sex of the calf – very valuable in dairy farming, where by and large only female offspring were required – heady stuff in those days.

We had a particularly good turnout to a presentation on the effects of heat on the fertility of bulls and rams. Too hot, and the sperm lose their vitality (I have sympathy with the little blighters). It was notable that there was a queue for the bathroom and a particularly high demand for hot water preceding the following dance in the Boutflower Hall and the arrival of busloads of girls from Gloucester. "Are you prepared?" and "Yep, I've had a hot bath," must have raised a few eyebrows.

On another night, Oscar Colburn, a local farming trendsetter, spoke about his Colbred sheep capable of lambing four to five lambs at a time instead of the normal one or two. My guess is that Oscar hadn't got close enough to the working end of a sheep to see that she has only has two (if you're lucky) milk bars. If he had, then for sure he hadn't spent much time rearing orphan lambs or totting up the costs involved. It takes a very special lamb to grow big enough and fast enough to justify the cost of the milk powder, and those that do have an unfortunate knack of turning up their toes the day before going to market. We would always entertain our visiting speakers with a glass of sherry before the meetings and that is my excuse for introducing him as Oscar Colbred and his Colburn sheep! The sherry habit has stuck.

The football was, as a comment on social order, interesting. Though most of the RAC students came from public schools (remarkable really in a country where less than ten per cent of the population was privately educated), all the football team were state school in origin. Nearly all the rugby and hockey lot came from purchased education backgrounds. What it says for a meritocratic society I'm not sure, but I guess we would have stronger national sports teams and probably government etc. if we all went through the same melting pot. Rowing, which was not a sport that attracted a lot of interest at Cirencester due to its not having any large river close by, had an interesting history. Apparently, the boatmen and lesser mortals who worked around the Oxford and Cambridge boats were not allowed to partake in the sport lest their performance intimidated those of the privileged participants. Things have largely changed now but not a moment too soon. Similar could probably be said of other sports; boxing, tennis and athletics were not exactly overrun by black sportsmen seventy years ago!

At about this time in the late 1960s, the newly independent Nigeria was torn apart by the Biafran civil war. Oxfam and other international charities were highlighting the plight of the largely innocent civilians whilst the minority political class tried to position themselves favourably to exploit that country's extravagant raw material wealth. Food shortages and famine were the main resultant problem, and to me studying agriculture and wanting to make a difference, this seemed an obvious area in which to get involved.

Through a childhood acquaintance, Richard Lee, who was studying medicine at Oxford, I got involved with and introduced the "3W1" (Third World First) concept to the RAC. The idea was to publish a magazine (later to become The Internationalist) in order to inform the public and in particular the politically interested of the next generation about third world issues and so pressure government to dedicate a significant expenditure (from memory I think this was two per cent of the GDP) to development in poorer countries. It seemed obvious to us then, and is now of course happening, that if the rich world did not share the cake more fairly then the poorest of the poor world would march up from the equatorial regions and help themselves. After all, what would they have to lose? I don't suppose we envisaged the likes of Idi Amin in Uganda, the rise in Muslim extremism or the fanatical self-destruction presently happening in Syria, but it does seem astonishing to me now that these problems were not anticipated by those whose job it was to influence international security.

Whatever, along with others at the college, some of whom were involved with the Christian Union, we encouraged a thread of social awareness to take hold in what was a fairly privileged and parochial environment. To their great credit, many of the students and staff were very supportive and we were able to significantly contribute to the launch of 'The Internationalist'.

I was not "burdened" with a family farm to go back to, the repayment of any educational fees, or any longer any wide-eyed beauty bent on marriage, but I was driven by a desire to make some social impact to society somewhere. The idea of tying myself to a cow's tail or contributing to the welfare of some wealthy capitalist on his or her country estate did not appeal and so to my parents' consternation, I took the then, to me, obvious step of applying to work in agriculture in Africa. At twenty-one years old and with sixty or so other volunteers I went to Kenneth Kaunda's Zambia with Voluntary Service Overseas after completing my agricultural studies at Cirencester.

Chapter 11
Zambia

Landing at Cairo to refuel en route for Lusaka (Zambia's capital), we sixty or so volunteers, some only eighteen years old and only just out of school, must have seemed an unlikely prospect for benefit to this newly-independent continent. The air in Cairo was heavy, humid and aromatic as it came across the Nile laced with sugary, tropical, organic scents and was both intoxicating in its promise of things to come and slightly nauseating to the hitherto unassailed sensibilities of this suburban boy.

Barbara Lou was a vivacious eighteen-year-old school leaver from Essex who had the seat next to mine and talked all the way from London to Lusaka, occasionally putting her hand on my arm to check I hadn't gone to sleep or missed any important nuance. I have no idea what we talked about but whatever it was we continued the conversation a year later whilst we hitch-hiked across central Africa and back in order to climb Mount Kilimanjaro. It was to be the first of three similar journeys with three different girls, the last of whom was my wife and we had a six-month-old baby with us; but I am jumping ahead of myself.

In Lusaka we were met by the people from the British Council, who did their best to give us some idea of what to expect wherever we ended up. But with four main tribal groupings, seventy different languages, life pattern influences varying from the industrially corrupted copper belt around Kitwe and Ndola to the agriculturally wealthy Mazabuka in the south to the forested Mwinilunga and the desert-fringed flood plains of the Zambezi, this was not an easy task. Our jobs were varied. My Scottish friend Don from Arbroath worked as a veterinary research assistant, others were nurses, some worked in the civil service and another friend worked in the Luangwa game park. I guess most of us were teaching in the new secondary schools that President Kaunda had instigated across the country, on the back of a ballooning world market for copper, which Zambia had in such excess that its parliament building was roofed with greenish orange sheets of it.

My place was at Kalabo, a small desert town on the northern edge of what was really the Kalahari Desert, about as far as you can go west before reaching Angola. Geographically it is interesting as it was on the Luinginga River before it joined the mighty Zambezi on its turbulent journey eastwards, tumbling over Victoria Falls and across central southern Africa, from Zaire to the Indian Ocean in Mozambique. Each year the Zambezi would rise above its banks to transform the land to a forty-mile-wide inland sea; this would be the trigger for the paramount chief of the Barotse people known as the Litunga, to climb aboard his black and white barge, the Nalikwanda, and with pomp and impressive ceremony, move from his dry land capital of Lealui to his wet land base at Limulunga. On route the Litunga, "Mwanawina the Third," thoughtfully called in at Kalabo on his way to Limulunga. The ceremony itself was called the Kuomboka. He left his dry land base at Lealui in traditional dress but arrived at Kalabo in a copy of the full British Admiral's uniform which had been presented by King Edward VII in 1902 in recognition of a signed treaty between Queen Victoria and his ancestor Lewanika .

The Barotse people then and now had a fiercely guarded independent streak. Topographically this ancient part of Barotseland, now incorporated into Zambia's Western Province, would have been part of Angola if the cartographers of the colonial period could have seen beyond the edge of their wooden rulers to the borders of the Zambezi. However, my job was to teach agriculture for a couple of years and that's what I did.

Chapter 12
Kalabo

I was given a two-bedroomed house all to myself but gave it up within days to move in with a tall guy from London who had come from Salford University, qualified as a teacher in Lusaka and was teaching English at Kalabo. Dave Cooke was as lean as a streak of bacon and had one pair of shorts which might have been white at one stage, two blue shirts and an occasional pair of plastic flip-flops kept mostly for special days. He ran the Young Farmers' Club and his students obviously thought the world of him. At the time it seemed obvious good sense to share resources, though I soon found that my resources, which all fitted into an old leather and canvas rucksack, were more than double Dave's. We led a fairly basic and bohemian lifestyle. What Dave lacked in his wardrobe he made up for in books. If there was any Russian author that we didn't have on the shelf it was because they were out of print. Thanks to Dave's introduction I got to know Dostoyevsky through his character "The Idiot". Other luxuries included a pack of playing cards, which facilitated many nights of bridge with various other members of the teaching staff and a portable spool-to-spool tape recorder with only one tape, which was Simon and Garfunkel's greatest hits. "Bridge Over Troubled Water" and "The Boxer" might now be part of the Barotse local culture!

The bridge evenings were sweetened by Castle lager, Welsh cakes (thanks to Ros and Brian Nelson) and thinly sliced (unchewable otherwise) Barotse beef. We shared our house with Wallace Kapenda, whose role was unclear. There is a limit to how much time one can take preparing bahobi (boiled maize porridge), pummelling, boiling and then trying to reinject flavour into the occasional much prized joint of old Barotse cow beef. Washing the odd shirt and underwear was prolonged by ironing; we probably had the best pressed and creased underpants in Africa! Having a house manager (embarrassingly still referred to as a house-boy at that time; Wallace was about forty years old) may seem extravagant, as it did to me initially, but Dave's logic was impeccable. Jobs were in short supply and it was our responsibility to provide employment, help with education and redistribute the quite generous (even for me as a volunteer) teachers' remuneration. Wallace used to keep his eyes skinned for the occasional old cow being walked on its last journey to the butcher's hut and then join in the queue with a saucepan. That meant we would have our fix of protein and jaw exercise for the week ahead!

Word travels fast in rural areas and we were soon to have a full contingent of staff to look after the house and garden, build grass fences, fetch wood and keep cattle and goats away from any vegetables that were brave enough to swap seed status for potential food supply in this Kalahari sand environment. There was some organic enhanced soil closer to the banks of the Luinginga, but this had to be moved by wheelbarrow back to the school compound – a job that wasn't on anybody's wish list.

The household was complemented by Dave's black dog Gus, a short-coated Labrador-sized mongrel who was totally loyal to his tall, socialist, English benefactor. Apart from spending ninety-five per cent of his time either looking for Dave or sitting at his feet, Gus provided host status for generations of extremely prolific and shiny black ticks. The other five percent of his time was spent having these ticks removed. Fortunately, blackcurrants were not part of our gastronomy at that time so there was little chance of them getting into our food chain!

Mangoes however were available and delicious, if stringy. Unripe they could be chopped up to make a sort of crumble, and ripe they were best eaten whilst sitting in the river as the juice ran everywhere.

Eventually we were joined, much to Gus's discomfort, by Pwuss (Wallace couldn't pronounce Puss). Pwuss arrived by plane one day, smuggled inside my shirt on a short hop from Mongu on the other side of the Zambezi flood plain, as I returned from collecting a batch of day-old chicks for the Young Farmers' Club. Mostly Pwuss spent his juvenile period chasing geckos up the fly screens that fitted across the otherwise open windows. I like to think of him progressing sedately into old age, spreading his genetic paw print across the area, but given the local appetite for any small catchable wild animal, I wouldn't rate his chances too highly once our protection was removed.

Our house, for some reason known as a B32, was situated on the edge of the school compound; that, linked no doubt to my housemate's deserved reputation for being a benevolent soft touch meant that we were the first and sometimes also last port of call for anyone with anything to sell, and I do mean anything! Soon after I arrived, an extremely black, wizened, old man with one tooth called in with some goodies which he indicated were for eating. Nothing in my suburban background had prepared me for fresh red chilli peppers. Pepper to me belonged in small jars with multiple holes on the top. Responding to my visitor's invitation to try the taste, I bit into the pepper. He was ecstatic and soon we both ended up with tears rolling down our cheeks but for different reasons. Nkodo was to be a regular visitor for a long time and I was always careful to direct him to any newly-arrived staff houses in the hope that I could join him in whatever the Silozi equivalent of schadenfreude was.

Close to our house, beneath one of the only trees in this sandy compound, lived the oldest staff member, Alan Rhodes. Like his more famous South African namesake he was a hangover from the recently replaced colonial era. Alan was genial, courteous, absolutely correct and precise. Thirty minutes before school assembly and the inevitable singing of the national anthem, Alan could be relied upon to leave his house and walk over to the school buildings with his measured short pace, long socks, sandals, papers in a file tucked beneath his right arm and single shirt button very deliberately left undone, his whole appearance being "precise casual". (I never could enthusiastically embrace this singing of the national anthem as part of my anti-nationalistic sympathies; pride in something one has no input into always seems a bit illogical. We don't choose where we are born and since our nationality is outside our control, there seem to be no grounds to hold it against one, nor reason to be proud of it any more than to be proud of holding a winning lottery ticket. Glad perhaps but being glad is not a line one often sees in a national anthem!)

Soon after my arrival, Alan took it upon himself to direct me on several walks. One of these took me past a local village. Since the topography was fairly uniform, getting lost was not difficult and this I duly did. Getting back to the school was not a problem as the sun was dropping low into the western sky and so solar navigation was simple enough. During my walk I happened upon what I now realise was a circumcision ceremony - or more probably, judging from the bandaged appendages and very stiff walking style of some of the boys, the recovery compound. I was made to feel clearly unwelcome by a masked, rope-clad, garishly painted elder, so judged it best to beat a retreat, carefully avoiding any habitation. Now the state of Zambia, in common with many of the other newly independent countries, identified tribalism and the associated tribal customs with some suspicion and as a threat to national identity, and so circumcision was officially frowned upon as a tribal custom. I didn't then and don't now often sympathise with the establishment but on this issue, I was not so sure. Local traditions are all very well concerning things like morris dancing and Dorset feather stitchery, but circumcision?

School days were routine and organised well by a combination of the New Zealand headmaster Pete Speers and the

Zambian deputy headmaster Steve Manengu. Steve, in common with other Zambians in local government, was posted to Kalabo from eastern Zambia. He was a member of the Bemba tribe and his relocation was part of the government's effort to break down the tribal identity which can be so divisive in many African societies.

It may have been that those of us from the "developed world" were resented, but if so, I never felt it. However, there was clearly a prejudice against people from other areas of Zambia. The proactive government of Kenneth Kaunda did much to keep the lid on intertribal conflict. Many other countries such as Rwanda, Uganda, Nigeria and Sudan have not been so lucky.

Conflict was never far away though, since Kalabo was situated on the Angolan side of the Zambezi where the long, drawn-out struggle against the Portuguese colonial rule was followed by a protracted fight for political control and threatened the whole region.

Another local field of conflict involved several football teams: the police, the Boma (local government offices) the teachers, the army, the students and others played regularly on the edge of the town. These matches were robust to say the least and technically a little different from today's premiership. The pitch was predominantly sand with small islands of grass on which we players perched. If the ball came towards you, the idea was to push off from the grass in pursuit. Stopping or changing directions was not an easy option. The referee's job was more to keep score than to impose sanctions, particularly when the army fielded a team, as it was their supporters' habit to fire off a few rounds harmlessly into the sky when their team scored. I don't remember any of their goals ever being disallowed!

These football matches were primitive in the extreme but as an introduction to people whose lives and priorities were unlikely to overlap with my own, they were invaluable and eagerly contested. The league was organised by Brian Hart, another of the English teachers in Kalabo on a Ministry of Overseas

Development contract. Other teachers came from New Zealand, India, Canada, Wales, Scotland and Ireland. The split was about sixty/forty expatriate to Zambian.

Supplies came into Kalabo largely by barge from Mongu, which took about one and a half days. Sugar, flour, salt, cement and beer made up most of the pay load. We were short of most things most of the time, but somehow beer was the last thing to become unavailable.

There was a choice of Castle lager, warm or not so warm but the not so warm was invariably out of stock. The social centre of Kalabo was the Luanginga bar about fifty yards from the barge tie-up area. Music was heavily dominated by percussion and a sort of twangy, upbeat, steel-strung guitar. Dancing, which would not have been recognised as such in Cheltenham Town Hall was largely individual, bottle in hand, elbows high, head low, hips steady and feet shuffling from the knees down. Progress was round an imaginary point in the sand. Dave was a regular and could usually be seen gesticulating intensely, beer in hand whilst persuading his audience of the ills of capitalism. He was and is a well-informed and engaging political animal. We are still good friends and meet up most years. It was not unusual to arrive at the bar and within minutes of being there for a row of green bottles to arrive for consumption, sent over by casual and vague contacts. It's difficult for me not to compare the memories of Sunday mornings as a choir boy and the Anglican exhortations from tight-lipped, fancily frocked priests to give and not to count the cost etc. to memories of that row of green warm beer bottles!

Here the frogs competed frantically with the African beat on the banks of the Luanginga. Here was a real world in which I felt very comfortable. But for circumstances and perceived family responsibilities, it might have been a world I spent the rest of my life in. Whatever, I had found a pair of shoes that fitted, and my outlook and self-perception were changed forever.

After about six months, with Wallace's help, I found and bought a dugout canoe which broadened my physical horizons considerably. With my makolo I was able to paddle up the Luanginga with its crocodiles (there undoubtedly were some but apart from the skins, which were regularly for sale, I never saw them), and past hippopotamuses which at the time I and my occasional travelling guest thought of as sort of armour-clad cows with a predilection for water and mud. Ignorance is bliss until proved otherwise and it's awfully difficult to feel threatened by something that appears to be smiling at you! About a mile downstream from Kalabo with its simple tie-up pontoon and the ever-open bar was a sand dune, which although possible to reach on foot, was difficult in its approach so I was fairly sure to be on my own. The sand was large grained and squeaked beneath my feet; sometimes in mid-afternoon it would be too hot to walk slowly on without flip-flops or rubber-tyre sandals. This footwear, popular all over Africa, lasted for ever and comprised of a foot-shaped piece of car tyre and some straps of old seat belt or inner tube held in position with clout nails. Once the radial tyre was introduced, with its integral steel threads, the tyre shoe became more difficult to source.

I don't think that I felt particularly lonely at that time, but I did take a sort of contented melancholy pleasure in being on my own on the sand dune as the sun sank to the west over this northern Kalahari landscape to become a red ball over Angola. This very African experience was accompanied by the coordinated orchestral cacophony of amphibious croaks. It was not incessant and there would be occasional silences when it seemed to me that these clownish frogs politely waited for their neighbours to start, but once the silence was broken, any politeness was superseded by competition for the loudest croak. A bit like the House of Commons today!

Night comes quickly near the equator and my paddle back to Kalabo was usually accompanied by a small company of Barotse children calling out 'Makuha makolo,' which I think translated roughly to 'White man dug-out canoe.'

My response was to call back to them, 'Mutia munsa,' equally roughly translated to 'Black boy.' Our conversation was therefore neither intelligent nor politically correct, but since we smiled a lot, nobody got upset; it was after all nothing but a statement of fact.

Another teacher, Ron Keeble, who taught woodwork, spent his spare time building a small motor boat. Ron and Angela, his wife, were a great pair. Angela doubled up as the school nurse so there was always a steady stream of visitors to their house, of students and staff nursing sore knees, heads and other body parts! I was never part of the stream but that was down to my lack of ingenuity rather than anything else; having Angela gently massaging an aching head, especially if it wasn't actually aching, would have been worth the subterfuge! Ron, however, who could no doubt have enjoyed such ministrations at any time, chose to build his boat. Once finished and fitted up with a mysteriously acquired lightweight outboard motor, it proved powerful enough for some of us to water-ski on the river. Turning was a problem, due to the lack of width of the waterway and loss of momentum, so it was necessary to swing wide against the reeds on one side, keeping the rope lead tight, whilst balancing on the ski back across the river to graze the far bank and back to base behind Ron and the labouring outboard. Bilharzia, (a liver focussed parasitic disease associated with slow moving water) hippos and crocodiles were all no doubt real threats, but we were all gods with a small "g" and as such immune to such risks. To paraphrase a war correspondent of later years, all those who went out came back.

Teaching was interesting and I hope but doubt that I was able to impart some knowledge in the classroom. With little else to go on, I presented my subject of agricultural science pretty much in the way that I had been taught myself at the RAC some two years previously. I attempted to give it a Zambian slant, but there was a limit to the amount of localisation I could give to the design of a self-levelling combine harvester! Bless them all; the students aged between twelve and twenty were so hungry for knowledge in this newly independent world they soaked up whatever was served with smiling enthusiasm and impeccable manners. It was all very humbling.

Dave had started the Young Farmers' Club before I arrived, and we took it on together. With the group, we kept and slaughtered pigs (somehow my experience up to that time left me woefully short in the art of pig killing and none of my animal husbandry books went beyond how to keep them alive). The enthusiasm for the event amongst the students was awesome. Pig killing days saw numbers quadruple and they mostly arrived with assorted weapons, mostly fashioned on the "wooden club and six-inch nail" model. I tried to civilise the occasion by delivering a sharp hammer blow to the head and cutting the throat whilst four of the stronger boys held a leg each. I guess from the pig's point of view this didn't seem very civilised, but it did avoid my nightmare vision of forty club-wielding students chasing a bleeding, battered and squealing pig around the staff compound. The resultant pork was always much in demand and the experience was probably the pinnacle of what I was able to contribute. I became expert at hammer selection and knife sharpening!

I am reluctant to relate the chick-rearing venture, but in the interests of integrity I am bound to do so. Such was the demand for animal protein, we decided to rear some pullets for egg production. What could be easier? I arranged for and collected one hundred newly-hatched chicks from Mongu, which arrived on the same flight as our smuggled kitten over the flood-filled Zambezi. The chicks had started life at Mazabuka, where my Scottish friend was working, some four hundred miles away. Amazingly, one hundred surviving happy chicks hopped out of the box, all yellow and fluffy with beady black eyes and gaping beaks. How they knew how to drink water at that age I still wonder at, but they did, and then ate grain meal. Hey presto. This was a learning experience for all of us; a handful of the most reliable students were designated to chick-feeding duties. The chicks were housed in an unoccupied B32 bungalow. Feed was easily sourced, but water was slightly more complicated. We only had water on tap for two hours a day, when the pump was working, so if you turned on the tap for one of the other twenty-two hours then no water would flow. This is a small but important detail - the sort that potential empires fail on... Enter young farmer number thirty-one. No water. Never mind, he thinks. He will return later. Sadly, he left the tap turned on and the water started to flow whilst he was away. Slowly, the bath filled up to overflowing and the B32 gradually succumbed to a gentle flood. Not deep, but enough to prove that although ducklings and Jesus could walk on water, chicks couldn't. It didn't lead to a complete disaster. Some twenty of the chicks survived by climbing on top of the bodies of their less fortunate cousins. They went on to produce a handful of eggs a day. I should have learnt at that time that livestock and a peaceful life don't go hand in hand.

Chapter 13
Mount Kilimanjaro

During one of the school holidays, a group of us, mostly VSOs, met up at a café in Lusaka with the intention of going to Tanzania and climbing Mount Kilimanjaro. We had three weeks to spare and after all, Tanzania was just the next country!

Although we were paid rather generously as volunteers, much of my money had gone into my housemates socialist-inspired, estate-management, labour-provision initiative. Having already bought my boat and bus fares to cover the seven hundred kilometres between Kalabo and Lusaka, I was all but spent up, so for me hitch-hiking was the order of the day for the rest of the journey. Lusaka North to Kapiri Mposhi was not a problem. The secret lay in having a pretty hitch-hiking companion and a big tree for me to hide behind with the luggage. Once a driver had stopped, they usually found it difficult to drive on again. Kapiri Mposhi to Tunduma and thence on to Dar es Salaam was somewhat more difficult. My hitch-hiking buddy was Barbara Lou whom I had sat next to on the plane to Zambia. She had all the right credentials, being both pretty and interesting company. What's more, she still had half her life story to tell which I hadn't yet heard!

The yet unfinished "Great North Road" was being built by the Chinese at the beginning of their "colonisation by commerce" era. Most of the traffic seemed to be concerned with road building, and many of the vehicles were driven by Chinese men who were under instructions either from their employers or wives not to pick up western girls, however big their smiles or tight their T-shirts. After twenty-four hours waiting, we persuaded a Zambian lorry driver to allow us to ride on his truckload of drainage pipes as far as Mbeya in Tanzania. We were glad he agreed and left him with a share of our food and some kwacha currency but believe me, think hard before travelling hundreds of kilometres on the back of an open lorry in the African sun with three-foot drainage pipes for seating. On the positive side, we had horizontal shelter, and nine more years of my little buddy's East London life to hear about.

Close to Mbeya we found a guest house run by two elderly tartan-clad Scottish ladies who wanted to know what our relationship was before allowing us their cheapest room with one bed and a mattress on the floor. Supper was beyond our budget and anything other than sleep (in any case it wasn't that sort of relationship) was beyond our capability. The next day, accompanied by knowing winks and smiles and much 'Och ayeing' we set off for Dar es Salaam on the Indian Ocean. The journey was relatively easy and unremarkable, and astonishingly we met up with our spendthrift friends (they had travelled by bus) on the beach at Dar. There we swam, ate and camped for two nights before setting off for Moshi and Kilimanjaro. I have no idea how we travelled. Our sights were set on the snow-clad nineteen thousand, three-hundred-foot peak called Kibo. When we arrived at the first of three base camps just above Moshi, I had travelled some three and a half thousand kilometres by boat, bus, car, lorry and culvert pipe in seven days. Not the best preparation for an ascent to slightly more than nineteen thousand feet. None of us had any equipment (Kilimanjaro was in any case a walk, not a climb) apart from a few extra clothes and a sleeping bag. Walking boots would have been useful but I chose a bottle of wine and two cigars instead. I have no idea why, since I don't and didn't smoke and the wine, when we drank it at the crater's edge, tasted like vinegar.

If any of our group knew what mountain sickness was, we kept it to ourselves. The ascent took four of us three and a half days in soft shoes and anoraks. The remaining twelve, including Barbara Lou, stopped at fifteen thousand feet by which time oxygen was in noticeably short supply and altitude was taking its toll. Unfortunately for me, or as it worked out, fortunately, I developed a throbbing headache and a severe attack of what in India would be called "Delhi belly" as we moved out of the forest area into the giant plantains, thorn and lobelia. The border is abrupt; it is like walking out of one room into another, Narnian in its suddenness. My malady was probably well timed in that I drank gallons of water for obvious reasons. That fixed my headache and the other slowly succumbed to kaolin and morphia as we trudged across below Mawenzi peak to the third rest hut at the base of Kibo, we were met by a group of extravagantly well-prepared and fit-looking German climbers with ropes and boots (no less) walking down, having failed the ascent. Only then did we recognise the possibility of failure.

Whether it was the kaolin and morphia, exhilaration or just fortunate acclimatisation, I was feeling better as most of the group began to feel worse. I slept solidly for seven hours until three thirty a.m. when, under instructions from our guide, we got up to zigzag the course up to the snow on Kibo peak. Only four of us were able to make it, everyone else succumbing to mountain or some other sort of sickness. On the cusp of the volcanic ridge, we opened the wine and in dramatic fashion, lit the two cigars and snapped a photo or two. The wine wasn't worth the carrying of it; it tasted like vinegar and since we were struggling to get enough oxygen the cigars were not helpful either, though the image recorded was worth

the effort! By the time the sun had been rising for thirty minutes above the Indian Ocean, we were off the softening snow and onto the scree. The exhilarating feeling as the air got richer in oxygen was worth the step by step trudge of the ascent - four shuffled steps then pause for breath. To make it worse, I think the guide could have run up! My memory tells me that we ran all the way down to Moshi Base Camp, but I think it's lying!

As was traditional at that time, the four of us who made the summit were presented with a head band made of everlasting flowers and the rest got a posy. It was for all of us a memorable time, prior to Kilimanjaro becoming a backpacker's "must do" experience.

The journey back to Lusaka was largely uneventful except for the two-night stops. Having waved goodbye to our group as they gained the Lusaka-bound bus from Moshi, Barbara Lou and I walked off in the same direction thumbing for a lift. The area around Moshi was verdant by comparison with most of Tanzania, verdant in vegetation that is, and traffic-less alas. With not much left of the day and not much hope of a lift, we began to cast around for a safe place to sleep. As darkness threatened, a sparse smiling man came out of nowhere and offered us hospitality. It turned out he used to work for the hospital in Moshi and in his mobati (corrugated iron) roofed house he had a discarded dentist's chair which doubled up for him as a single bed. Our new friend not only gave up his bed for Barbara Lou but provided me with blankets and shared his supper of rice and beans. On our leaving the next day, he refused payment. This level of generosity was not uncommon; on the grand scale I hope we have been able to match it even in a small way. As a family today we try to do so but I am constantly uncomfortable with the knowledge that we have the equivalent of many dentist's chairs in a world rich in refugees.

The next night saw us again with the tartan-clad ladies at Mbeya. There was much sucking through teeth and knowing smiles, but they gave us the same room, this time including supper, and the same winks and nods when we left. Jokingly we said we'd be back; we never were. Some years later I went close to it but this time with my wife and my six-month-old son; it didn't seem appropriate to call in!

Barbara and I continued our journey back via Lusaka to Western Province. I left her in Mongu to travel down to Senanga where she was teaching and returned myself to Kalabo, to the students, to the sand bank, to the football, to the pigs, to the chickens, to Dave Cooke, Gus and Pwuss. Apart from an awkward half-term visit to Senanga, where Barbara and I tried to pick up where we left off as travelling companions, our friendship stuttered to a stop. For the second time in my life, a great friendship foundered on the reefs of different expectations. Since we could no longer be buddies travelling, it seemed we could not be buddies at all. In due course, we went to each other's weddings and the last I saw of Barbara was her back as she headed back towards London. Not, I hope, to a life in the suburbs; daisies (and she was one) don't flourish in the desert.

Back at Kalabo, things progressed on the socialist estate. The labour units totalled five, with various responsibilities, and Dave's steadfast determination to plough unconventional furrows seemed chinked by a single new female arrival on the scene. In due course, she would introduce curtains to the house and substitute our tin mugs, powdered milk and world food programme biscuit routine with a pot, tea cups and home baking...

In England, my father's health was to be balanced on a knife edge following my brother Neil's death. I made the beginning of one emergency return to the UK and got as far as Lusaka, only to be told that actually my father was OK, and I need not return. However, these experiences added up and I felt unable in the long term not to be close to my family and there to help if need be. By this time, I perceived myself to be the only son in terms of family expectation. Reluctantly I made preparations to return to the UK, leaving a place and a shoe size that I had felt totally comfortable in.

Dave and Merryn, (the force behind the curtains and the tea cups) were in due course to get married during the following year.

Chapter 14
The Journey Home via South Africa

I headed off down to Cape Town with Scottish Donald, Miracle Man Miles in his hand-built Volkswagen Beetle and a girl call Clare who had been working with VSO in Lusaka. We had not met before. We made up quite a load for Miles's Volkswagen Beetle, so its wishbone suspension was in a constantly flexed state whilst we were travelling with its rear located sump dangerously close to the ground. The journey south through Livingstone towards Bulawayo was hot and uncomfortable but compared to a concrete drainage pipe lorry it was first class; we took turns to sit in the front passenger seat and to drive. Donald, who at six feet five inches was some five inches taller than me and built like a good rugby second row, just folded up enough to fit into the back seat. It was a good job he had such a genial nature - his cup was usually half full rather than half empty. We knew that when he was getting impossibly uncomfortable, he would retell the same story of caber tossing at the Scottish Games in Braemar with engaging Celtic charm, always finishing with a long blue and white sigh, that was the time to change seats!

What it is that makes for good social cohesion rather than the other is not clear, but part of the recipe must be not to be precious and to enjoy a common new experience. Our journey through these Capricornian countries was certainly new, none of us were precious and Miles, who had glued together the Volkswagen Beetle, was a practical and unflappable mechanical genius. These qualities were to prove to be invaluable. Whilst driving through what was then the Wankie Game Park to look for elephants and ostriches etcetera, he did not bat an eyelid when, taking my turn to drive, I bounced his low-slung car over a middle of the road boulder with the front of the car just low enough to hit the sharper end of the boulder. This same rock then turned up, became a lot larger and as the back of the car went over, thumped the sump good and hard although we were not to discover the consequence immediately.

Some short time later, overladen as we were, I was too slow to change gear as we approached the dusty dirt rise out of a parched river valley along which we had been driving. It was Clare who noticed the thin black trail as we freewheeled backwards back into the valley to try the hill again in another gear. Linking the oil stream to the earlier incident with the boulder did not call for rocket scientists. As it turned out, we were down to one and a half pints of oil. At what point a Volkswagen oil pump stops circulating I don't know, but we must have been close to it. Under-vehicle repairs to cars are not normally done in African game parks, but we reckoned that it would take a particularly ambitious carnivore to take on Donald, so he was charged with security and armed himself with a tent pole. Repairs were simple enough for the resident on board genius - we drained the rest of the oil, flushed out the sump with a bit of petrol and glued up the crack (luckily not a hole) with epoxy resin glue which reaches its full working strength in forty-eight hours!

Clare hitched a ride in one of the few passing cars to the nearest game lodge and in the late afternoon returned with two white Rhodesian game wardens who were only too happy in their semi-inebriate state to tow us back to the game lodge. We must have mentioned elephants in our conversation because they went out of their way and off their route to take us across a dried-out lake and salt pan to get an up-close and personal view of these humble monster first cousins to the mouse. All this was at forty miles per hour on the end of a ten-foot rope in a cloud of dust with freshly emptied beer cans thrown at regular intervals through the windows of the rangers' towing Land Rover. Brakes were pressed and pulled but in retrospect, such caution was pointless. Luck or fate would smile on us or otherwise. It did and we survived to tell the tale. Two days later, with a glued-up sump, we were on the road again south towards the eastern Indian Ocean coast and the so-called garden route down to Cape Town. Details of this drive include blue skies, crashing surf, white sandy beaches, heat, whitewashed Dutch-style farmhouses and a profusion of red, purple, orange and green colour; this was indeed a rainbow country. Suburban UK seemed a long way away.

How it happened, I can't remember (the travelling arrangements were very cramped), but Clare and I got on rather better than fairly well by the time we reached Cape Town. It ought to have been uncomfortable given the gender and makeup of our group, but it wasn't. Clare had an engaging habit of giving full attention to anyone in conversation, partly I think since from her early childhood she had been seriously deaf and so eye contact became particularly important. She also laughed a lot, perhaps to cover the fact that she was not sure what had been said but it gave me the impression, falsely I suspect, that she appreciated my idea of funny. I learnt quickly that if I needed to tell her something to look out for or important to avoid, I should speak really clearly and with lots of lip movement. We were in a heaven partly of man's making, partly of our making and partly topographical.

For a few weeks, we were oblivious to all, floating on a cloud, immune from the cares of the world, a self-indulgent unit untroubled by family, politics, money, history or practicalities. The future was ours and we allowed ourselves to dream. This was new territory for me, perhaps for both of us. The next few weeks took me by plane to England where my father had been hospitalised yet again. Clare returned to the UK some weeks later with Miles, Donald and the patched-up car. We were ready to carry on where we left off, but the skies were no longer blue, the petals had faded and fallen and the worry-free visions of the future gave way to present and past intrusions of family, money, jobs etc. Our candle had burned bright, but our hopes and dreams had taken a nosedive – like the moth whose wings are singed by the heat of the flame, we were grounded in the miasma of suburban England, reluctant hostages to the stultifying mudflats of middle-class mediocrity. For a short time, what we had shared together was good but once the flame started to flutter, it floundered, and succumbed to the drear drizzle. The inevitability of its going out was unstoppable. On a dark November day in a featureless grey town in the south of England, we abandoned our dreams and went our separate ways. In due course, we were both to return to Africa in different circumstances, but we lost touch for ten years or so after this.

Clare was to complete yet another degree, treating her hearing disability as nothing, and then go on to work in Ethiopia. We renewed our contact some years later when, sitting in my then wife's parents' house, Clare appeared in the headlines of the Ten o'clock News. She had been abducted and held hostage and walked more than a hundred miles through the sparse and arid bush terrain of Ethiopia. Her release had become international news and it was just chance that I happened to see it. We picked up our friendship then and are still friends now, ironically both now living in South Devon although completely independently and our routes for getting there have been very different.

Chapter 15
Cinderella's Footman

My father's health problems, which centred on the death of Neil, gradually came under control and to his great credit he spent the best part of the rest of his life doing what he could to help children, suffering one way or another through medical problems, to enjoy an improved life experience. He was heavily involved with a new organisation called Riding for the Disabled, which brought some other form of mobility to otherwise physically handicapped children. Dad thought nothing of contacting the prime minister or secretary to the queen to arrange for groups of physically and mentally disabled children to visit Buckingham Palace, 10 Downing Street, the Royal International Horse Show or any other event or venue that he could get them into. He was in many ways an exceptional man, who struggled to overcome difficulties, both real and I think sometimes imagined, to do the best he could to better the lives of others. He was as hopeless at accepting presents or praise as he was generous in his efforts to give. His ideas on gender roles, politics and sport did often conspire to camouflage his generous nature, but in the long term, in the great heavenly scale, I do not doubt that the needle would drift emphatically in his favour. He was a good man who believed deeds to be more eloquent than words.

The winter of 1972 saw me back in the UK, with no money, no ties, no direction known. I was a Bob Dylan lyric in common with others for a revolution that to many of us was only retrospectively obvious. My parents were still in Nottingham, where I had grown up, but I was a different person from the insecure four-year-old who refused a car ride in his uncle's car because, well just because. The world was my oyster. It was post-Beatles, post-Rolling Stones and post-austerity but definitely pre-excesses of the cold war with the Soviet Union. We were to all live-in fear of the bomb for perhaps ten years or more.

On the "anything is possible" ticket I bought, with a borrowed twenty-five pounds, an old railway freight box and got it parked in the car park by the stage door of the Nottingham Theatre Royal. My previous project rearing turkeys for Christmas in my parents' greenhouse had only been partially successful in that expenditure had exceeded income. The theatre venture, however, was to be mildly successful both commercially and socially. I took the job as ostler to a Bristol hustler who hired out miniature ponies to theatrical companies. The Theatre Royal in Nottingham was putting on Cinderella, who needed ponies to take her to the ball. With my help and a contribution from Arthur Askey and Dicky Henderson, the beautiful Cinders got to the ball every night for eight weeks (I ended up on the stage with white britches, a pink waistcoat and a silver wig), as Cinderella's footman, quite considerably in pocket and with a new friend called, impossibly, Trixi van Bourne. Trixi was very definitely all girl; she had legs that would have graced a gazelle, the mischievous smile of a meerkat and a sleek cascade of hair which she tossed back at will like a well-trained Lipizzaner horse. She was cast as Dandini. Dandini was the love-struck sidekick of Cinderella's Prince Charming. This was some departure from the life I had experienced hitherto – colourful, glitzy and a bit on the racy side for this suburban ex-choirboy. But fascinating all the same. Now Dandini was supposed to be a man; how many children left the performance in a gender-confused state we will never know. Trixi liked the ponies (and me, a bit, I think) so after a few weeks, Arthur Askey and Dicky Henderson were a tad put out to have more kids waiting to have their autograph book signed by Trixi and me (on behalf of the ponies) than by these household comedy names of the day. I was accepted into this eclectic mix of chorus girls and boys as something of a novelty and occasionally included in their after-performance revelries. But for her father's intervention, Trixi and I were due to cycle down through Europe in the early summer of 1973. I never met her father, but his intervention saw Trixi go instead onto the "Benny Hill Show", "The Avengers" and the "Cats" musical in London rather than gallivanting on bikes with some total stranger! (The cycling trip had to wait some forty-five years, but did happen, over a thousand miles, sixteen days from Dartmoor to the Pyrenees, partly to "feel" the distance and partly as a pro-Europe anti-nationalist statement. We certainly felt the distance!)

Instead of this proposed biking adventure, I joined a religious community in North Devon, after several months milking thousands of cows as a relief herdsman in various parts of southern England. A sort of office temp in wellies who couldn't type, I found the job dirty, lonely and inconvenient but well paid. Sadly, after an unsatisfactory ride on the celebrity bus, Trixy was to meet an untimely and unexplained death some fourteen years later. It seemed that she walked deliberately out towards the sea on a cold January day in a nondescript town in southern England wearing not a lot and then lay down on the beach to meet death by hypothermia. What if we had instead gone cycling? I have an American friend today and we often swap notes on proactive parenting in this liberal post-authoritarian age - when to intervene, when to stand aside. We rarely reach a conclusion, but I often think of Trixi and her father, perhaps cycling would have proved to be the better option?

Chapter 16
Lee Abbey

The religious community I joined as a short-term member was Lee Abbey in North Devon. It's a film set awaiting its day, positioned as it is between the rugged bracken-clad, goat-occupied Valley of the Rocks and the cliffs, dominated by densely growing twisted oak and lichen, of Woody Bay.

My time spent milking cows as an itinerant was to be repeated at odd times in the next few years and meant that I was never to be dependent on the state for my welfare, although in recent years I have been glad to accept assistance with the health side of her provisions. We learn many things in the various schools of life, but I fancy that the most effective schools I ever attended were the ones that taught me what not to do. Subsequently, I decided in this bovine-dominated period of my life that whatever the future held for me, it was not to be in the cold, wet, concrete prison of the milking parlour. I sold my time and some of my integrity for money; it was a purely financial contract. I took some comfort in the fact that I might have been in banking...!

The same school taught me not to waste energy on taking myself too seriously, to treat the tinsel of urban life for what it is, urbane, not to follow any political or religious dogmas, and never to underrate the appeal of looking behind the closed door or passing the forbidding notice and squeezing "under the rope".

The best wave to catch would be when the beach was empty; the best time on the mountain was when the weather threatened, always against the flow.

Lee Abbey was largely Anglican but in theory was non-denominational. It provided, and still does provide, holidays and acts as a conference centre for largely Christian groups. It functions by charging slightly less than commercial rates and subsidises this by rewarding its working staff members sparingly and not seeking to take out a profit other than for reinvestment. It works as a community by having an ultimate non-challengeable authority and ambition - that being to represent the Christian message both within and without the formal church. As such, most of the community, if not all, within my time at least, were immersed in the religious (Christian) journey of the soul. Some felt themselves to have arrived but most of us I think were still travelling. I most certainly was. Some were professionals in the Church. There were some super-committed evangelists convinced beyond rationality of the rightness of their beliefs and a few other members who were recovering from trauma of one sort or another. My arrival there was, in my perception, random. As I have said, I couldn't believe in an interventionist God but most of my fellow community members did. Whatever, the result was a great living testimony to the Christian principles of care for the individual and respect for creation. It was for me a formative and overwhelmingly positive experience and I deeply value the many friends I made there.

Before my move to Lee Abbey, I had accumulated enough cash to own a car. However, six months tied to a cow's tail was not conducive to a good social life, the need for which the last few years had done much to awaken in my appetite. I arrived at Lee Abbey, where the estate was clearly desperate for someone to milk the cows, to be met by the effusive Caribbean estate manager, Amos Mcgann, and a diminutive, wiry, bow-legged elderly lady called Ursula Kay. Ursula was a long-time member of the community and had set up the farm. I was flatteringly hailed as an answer to prayer, a gift from God no less; my mumbled attempts to suggest that the welcome might have just been a fraction over the top were lost in a chorus of "Praise the Lord" etc. I was ushered into the parlour to look at these special cows and see if they were anything different to the ones I had been used to. They were unusually brown and white, suggesting that they were Ayrshires rather than their black and white cousins from Holland which I had been used to milking. (The Dutch Friesian had come to dominate the English countryside; their conformation spoke more of coat hangers than of sirloin steak, but they did produce a lot of milk.) For the Lee Abbey cows there was a mouth for goods in, whilst at the other end there was a tail and udder etc. for goods out, pretty standard; the difference I was told was in between the ears; they were indeed the most placid and patient cows I had ever come across. They had obviously been more influenced by the New Testament than the Old! It helped that we were milking about thirty cows rather than the more normal one hundred and thirty, but they were indeed docile and kind animals to work with. There was a lot to be said for rising at four thirty a.m. to open the gate for these buttered-up bovines to walk into the parlour, hang the clusters on the first four and then enjoy a cup of tea with cream from the top of the churn whilst looking down over the fields to Lee Bay and the Bristol Channel towards America. I never tired of this. I enjoyed it with many different people over the eighteen months I stayed there and carry with me to this day memories and friendships begun and nurtured as we watched the sea come to life, ignited by the rising sun from the East.

Hurrying along through the potholed Valley of the Rocks in the early morning, watched by the imperious wild goats with the churns of cream topped milk on the back of the wagon to meet the churn lorry before seven fifteen a.m., brewing beer in the dairy discreetly so as not to offend anyone's sensibilities, Hungarian circle dancing in the octagonal lounge with unsophisticated enthusiasm from all partakers and endless dramatic presentations ranging from the traditional Christmas story to the plight of the

Caribbean sugar plantation workers – these all became regular features in a weekly routine. The communal mid-morning "elevenses" frequently dragged on to become "twelveses" as we consumed whatever food was left over from the night before and agonised over the authority (or otherwise) of Saint Paul and the actual divinity (or otherwise) of Christ. These were jewel-filled days. I listened to and saw the lives of many totally committed and evangelically motivated Christian believers who embraced absolutely the message proclaimed in the four gospels. But for all that, I was never able to reconcile those beliefs with a troubled world and, to my mind at least, an apparently unresponsive God. I recognised absolutely that others could, and respected both their opinions and their sincerity but if there was such a God, then I could not excuse him or her or it for apparent inaction in the face of so much suffering through wars and disease etc.

Lee Abbey left me with an improved ability to live uncomfortably with what I perceived to be religious contradictions. I lost some of my youthful righteous anger, though still struggled, and do to this day struggle with the Christian perception of their God being the "only one true God." This to me seems provocative religious arrogance. I had little common ground with the occasional proselytising zealots. One in particular organised the summer camp. He was very large, very loud and had lots of teeth! Cold showers, camp fires and choruses accompanied hapless children being asked to accommodate Jesus in their hearts after confessing to total strangers how unworthy they were! These kids were ten-year-olds for goodness' sake; they hadn't had time to be unworthy! He seemed put out that I didn't want to join in his indoctrination process and then rather movingly upset when upon greeting me as his "fine, Christian friend" one day, I told him that he was wrong on all three counts! Fine according to my Oxford dictionary suggested elegant, extremely thin or showy (not something I'd been accused of before); Christian is and was a subjective description requiring exhaustive qualification, so it was unlikely that I would tick any of his boxes; and friend I thought didn't fit on any level! We seemed to get on better after that as long as we didn't meet up.

Unlike my toothy and zealous acquaintance at the summer camp, I had the philosophical problem of distinguishing between faith and belief. Do you need faith in something that you know to be true? Then surely, it's a fact and faith is unnecessary. If you have a belief, then that is just what it is, a belief, and it is sustained by a faith. There is room here for hope but not for certainty. Within the Church there always seems to be this push to assert that one believes something or other as if, if you believe it hard enough, then it becomes a fact. To say that one believes in "the one true God", "the divinity of Christ," "the existence of the Holy Spirit" or "the authority of Saint Paul" is not the same as saying it is fact. I have heard many of my Christian friends talk of knowing God or knowing Jesus. The leap in faith that they often explain is necessary for this grand statement is to me a departure from logical reason. It seems to me to be a substitution of reasonable faith necessary to sustain a belief, with simplistic, non-evidence based, comfortable assertion. It may well be better to know than to hope, but not if knowing means getting off the train. The comfortable state that they then inhabit seems to me the comfort of the arrived. Questioning is tiring but it keeps you on your feet. It is unlikely that wars would have been fought on different beliefs but misinterpret belief as fact and you have a whole new can of worms.

One of my regular early morning tea tasters looking out over the Bristol Channel towards America was David Gray who had escaped the confines of a nine-to-five job at Rolls Royce and the promise of a clock upon retirement so that he could count away his remaining hours. David gave up his job at Rolls Royce and moved to Japan where he became a church worker, after a period at Lee Abbey. He was the most precise person I have ever known, never without a tie or an ear-to-ear smile; his tie I think he put on each morning, his smile I think he slept with. It was always a challenge to know if he was serious or not – usually not, and always loyal. David eventually married his beautiful Japanese wife and produced two lovely kids, one of whom was to work with us for a short while on the farm some twenty years later, and the other, Elizabeth, is now a classical dancer in Okinawa. Sadly, David was to lose his life drowning at a supervised swimming pool, leaving Keiko to carry on the church work and bring up the two children.

My days certainly started even better in my second spring at Lee Abbey, when tea was expanded to include Weetabix, brown sugar and cream scooped off the top of the churns before any disturbance. Not a recipe for a healthy heart and perhaps and I paid for it later… My indulgence was assisted by another community member who had been parked at Lee Abbey by her parents, newly returned from Kenya where they had been working as missionaries with the Church Missionary Society. Gilly would put a plate of Weetabix and brown sugar, smuggled out of the kitchen where she worked, on top of the churns after the afternoon milking for my consumption in the early morning. These dawns were to become even better when she joined me on her days off from work in the kitchen.

I first saw Gilly the day she arrived with her parents, sister and brother, all sitting very upright and not comfortably on hard backed chairs in the octagonal lounge as if awaiting a dental check. They all had a slightly lean and weathered look, but Gilly was the one I went back to take another peek at through the glass of the closed lounge doors. Her sun-bleached hair, tumbled over her right shoulder and down to her waist, held in place by a magic tuck behind the ear, pale Caribbean Sea-blue eyes, high sun-blessed cheeks and turned up nose above a wide engaging smile made her look pretty good head to toe. There was no shortage of pretty girls with interesting stories at Lee Abbey, but Gilly was definitely a notch up, in a class all her own. We are still of course in the realms of perception and belief… !

Parked there for her safety until she could take up her university place, I did not see the parents again for six months. I don't believe that they were ecstatic in the way that events developed, but I may be being over sensitive. If they were enthusiastically supportive, then they disguised it very cleverly.

Gilly and I became good friends in the most innocent of ways. For six months we saw each other every day - worked together, danced together, walked together and dreamed together. Here was someone who seemed happy with not knowing what tomorrow held. We got up early to walk the cliff paths to Jenny's Leap, shared sherry at Ursula's cottage and beer at Woody Bay, fished for crabs with bacon rind and string out of rock pools, foolishly canoed out into the Bristol Channel in my double canoe as the tide ebbed and tried earnestly to find common spiritual ground. This last endeavour eventually presented difficulties.

It was the sort of romance that gave comfort through a brushing touch with the back of our hands and an unobserved approach viewed through a car mirror, a smile across a crowded room and it's lasted forty-five years, mostly without a break. If we've had differences, and we have, they have been dwarfed by positives. Our journey together started in September 1972 and the rest of this book is about that journey and a farm that we built together along the way.

Chapter 17
Gilly

One difference that Gilly and I struggled with and proved more difficult than we might have expected was Gilly's belief at that time (to quote from Nick Cave's 1997 song "Into My Arms ") in an "interventionist god". This was fundamental because, as I have made clear, I didn't, and I still don't. Doors for me were a challenge and the tighter they were closed, the harder I kicked. If it was God who opened them, then why did my toe hurt so much? To replay the surf metaphor, we were not some bit of marine flotsam washed willy-nilly on the whim of a divine will, we chose which wave to join, and when to push off for it, and when to roll off. For me, the interventionist God idea was too comfortable, too much like fatalism, too easy to blame when things go wrong. I don't see any reason or rhyme for cancer; like war, it's there because we haven't yet worked out how to crack it. In our lives, much later, Gilly was to become very ill; things were looking pretty dire and the response from a close contact of ours was, 'why?' I could have screamed at the naive simplicity that suggested the existence of a divine chess player pushing us around, doling out cancer here and good exam results there. I didn't scream and Gilly got better thanks entirely to the excellence of her care and modern technology. My brother had died thirty years before due to the lack of exactly the same things and I don't believe for one moment he died as a result of some divine plan.

Gilly was to take up a place at what became Oxford Brookes University to study large scale catering - we had talked around the subject of marriage and family etc. in the way that young people everywhere do, without considering the logistics of how we might get there, but nowhere had we considered the need for "large scale catering". True, I had a good appetite but the tureens that Gilly was looking at were something else. For one year after Lee Abbey, she fought her way through the economics of hospital catering and the right way to make a three-gallon pie. She was not where she ought to have been. The course she had embarked on was the result of a "stick the tail on the donkey" approach, some six thousand miles away in Kenya where Gilly had done all her schooling. She was no more suited to work in a large-scale municipal kitchen than a hamster was to live in Harley Street.

I had enrolled at a technical teacher's course in Wolverhampton which I duly commenced in September 1973. The idea was to convert my National Diploma in Agriculture, via a teaching qualification, into a degree which I could then use to work in the third world with the Ministry of Overseas Development, for whom a degree was a prerequisite. Like Gilly, I was in the wrong place at the wrong time. The Students' Union idea of an entertaining evening was a bar striptease in a seedy pub. This was a far departure from Lee Abbey and in any case, the packaged item was usually well past its "best before" date!

The older guy in charge of my teaching practice couldn't remember anyone's name and insisted we teach using his "failsafe" question and answer routine, i.e. ask the questions and don't continue until you get the required answers. This was about as inspirational as a trip to the dentist on a wet Monday in November! The course was only three terms and I completed two, but in all conscience, I couldn't bring myself down to the level that we were asked to teach at. Not lacking in self-belief, I considered finishing the course and refusing the qualification, but I was also short of cash, so I left with only the 't's to cross and the 'i's to dot. It was a grand gesture but left me high and dry financially and practically rudderless.

With limited options, I went back to my itinerant cowman job to scrape a few pennies together. I ended up conveniently close to Oxford and Gilly, at Lambourn, the home of so many great race horses and stables. Park Farm was owned by a guy called Neddy

Ayre. His assistant cowman had left suddenly and after two weeks the head cowman left too, then the tractor driver was taken off stock duties to get on with the spring cultivations. Bingo, I had three people's jobs to do and a boss that didn't mind paying overtime. For the first time in my life I was paying tax and still needing a second piggy bank to store the excess.

Neddy Ayre, my boss, knew little about farming but in five minutes one morning taught me a lot about man management. If anyone ever tells you that a herdsman's job is easy, be sure of one thing - they've never done it. With some six hundred gallons of white stuff in the bulk tank, I finished the second milking by switching the system over from milk collection to acid cleanout. Normally, I watched the clean acid water mix chase the last of the milk through the transparent pipes and then removed the pipe from the bulk tank just as the last of the milk entered the tank and before the acid-contaminated cleaning mix entered the tank. On this occasion, the Hereford bull that we had running with the herd to mop up (impregnate if you will) any cows that had not succumbed to the tender ministrations of the artificial insemination man, forced an entry back into the parlour looking for extra food. His timing was inconvenient and as a result, whilst dealing with the bull I allowed the acid to follow the milk into the tank. Not a lot, but enough to give a watery green tint to the milk. Whether or not the average Oxford punter would have noticed this on his cereal I don't know, but I tipped the whole lot away down the drain and went up to see Neddy in his grand south facing house to break the news. He smiled sympathetically, put his hand on my shoulder and said he thought I probably hadn't done it deliberately and hoped the rest of my day would be kinder to me. I learnt a good lesson that day.

On the strength of my now bulging piggy bank, Gilly at twenty and I at twenty-five gave substance to our dreams with an inexpensive ring. I proposed to her formally at Westonbirt Arboretum under a spreading chestnut tree surrounded by extravagant autumn colours on a stunning September Sunday. She said 'Yes...' I had hoped she would...

Doubtless Gilly's father would have preferred the formality of my asking for his permission etc. (in fact I think he would have preferred the whole event to have been a dream) but since we had no plan B, it seemed to me in my youthful arrogance better to honestly inform him of our intentions that to disingenuously lead him on in thinking he had any say in the matter. He was the dutiful child of a different age, formal and traditional and if I am to be honest, at least from where I stood, I found him not a little self-opinionated. Doubtless he thought I shared that same characteristic! It wasn't a good start. Skipping gently over the significant and none-too sensitively put father-in-law to son-in-law exchanges, it was accepted that we would marry in the following July - one year into Gilly's degree course, on the understanding that I would ensure Gilly would finish her degree course... Oh dear, the girl I knew was different from her father's daughter. About the first independent action Gilly took upon getting married was to walk away from the course at Oxford in favour of an academic English-based course sometime in the future. For the present, we were both to leave within twelve months for southern Africa to take up a two-year job in Lesotho with Christian Aid, but I am jumping the gun.

We were married on July the twenty-seventh 1974 at Bedford where Gilly's parents lived. Doug Constable, our corduroy-clad chaplain friend from Lee Abbey, hitch-hiked over to play Teddy Bears Picnic instead of Mendelssohn's Wedding March. Yoshtoka from Japan elegantly sang the "Come I'll Let You Have a Rose" ballad which was the Yugoslavian entry for the Eurovision Song Contest at which Doug had been a judge. He had transcribed the music to the translated lyrics. If we had used the British entry, then we would have been skipping down the aisle to Mary Hopkin and "Knock, Knock Who's There?". Gilly's godfather, in a grey suit and dog collar, wobbled on a rickety chair and said whatever it was that godfathers say and my brother-in-law, John, like the good man that he has always been, stood in for my best man whose wife inconveniently produced their first baby on the same day by caesarean section. We danced Hungarian circle dances with friends from many places and drank the least alcoholic punch I have ever tasted, until Gilly and I departed on a bicycle made for one – she on the crossbar – and swapped it a little way down the road for my Volkswagen Beetle in pastel green with black wings to hide the rust and Disney cartoon characters on the doors. Like weddings everywhere, it was a meeting of the generations, although in the '70s with the aftermath of the war, the Beatles, birth control, the atomic bomb and rock 'n' roll, the generation gap was perhaps exaggerated. Photographic evidence suggests it was a happy event and I think it was, and for the record, I am sorry that I didn't at least pretend to ask for parental permission, but it would have been a pretence so perhaps it is better I didn't.

We honeymooned in Scotland and it rained twenty-five hours of every day. We ran out of petrol on the motorway, the mosquitoes were the size of small birds and on the one night we didn't camp, the landlady of the cheapest bed and breakfast we could find chided us for trying to dry our wet clothes on the radiators. I smoked a pipe of clan tobacco for the first and last time in my life to discourage the aerial assault of the killer insects and we returned home early eager to begin the rest of our lives but apparently to the much-unspoken family concern. It went over our heads!

Chapter 18
Wytham

If evidence were needed of our good intentions for Gilly to continue at Oxford, we had rented a house from a Scottish farmer on the outskirts of Oxford. The village was Wytham – all thatched roofs, stone-built picture-book houses and a red telephone box. We called the house Shamba, Swahili for garden, as an ironic reference to the nettles that covered everything that wasn't concrete. Our arrangement with Bob Bilsland the farmer was that I would work in lieu of rent. We had advertised in the Oxford Post for just such a deal. Bob had been the only one to respond. A Sunday afternoon meeting was arranged, which proved to be a long, drawn-out occasion where politics, hunting, private education and Scottish independence were talked about. I needed to get back to Neddy's cows and Bob to his. I was to learn later with this Scotsman that life and comfort were definitely a first over his cows' milking routine. If he felt like missing a milking to suit his mood, well that's just what he did. Oh, the glories of being self-employed! We secured the cottage on the grounds that my hands were hard, calloused and rough with deep black grained streaks running down the insides of my fingers – the result of a farm cocktail of silage, cow poo, milk and iodine with which we cleaned the cows' udders. I was, in Bob's opinion, clearly a worker.

During the following six months at Wytham, and with Gilly free of the demands of the institutional management world, we made the first of many homes and were content in our uncertainty of what the future held. Gilly would take our pet sheep, Smudge, to graze on one of the many places in the village that were available and suitable for a very overweight first-year, Suffolk-cross, grey-faced ewe. There had been two lambs early on, a gift from the shepherd at Park Farm, Lambourn, who "couldn't be bothered with the little buggers." In the way that bottle-fed orphan lambs often do, the one called Freckles had keeled over, having drunk too much milk in one sitting – a lesson there to tell your greedy children! That left us with Smudge who was to be the first of many thousands of sheep we were eventually to keep and she herself survived eight years and multiplied her value many times over. This was a lesson to us for years to come. We then spent the balance of the days painting walls, digging up nettles and bottling (we had no freezer, an unheard-of extravagance) wild fruit. We had row upon row of bottled, burgundy berries gleaned from the perimeters of the fields. During the winter we intended to convert these to all sorts of delectable short-day culinary treats. The first jar we opened had a not unattractive white top to it, which we took to be sugar, as you sometimes get on homemade jams. Our enthusiasm was undiminished and complimented the apples wonderfully as an out of season apple and bramble crumble. There was, however, a difficult-to-pin-down, slightly musty flavour. The next jar to be opened was examined more closely. The white sugar layer on top of Gilly's preciously bottled blackberries had more to do with protein than carbohydrate. I don't suppose the small fly larvae (it sounds better than maggots) would have actually done us much harm. Many Africans treated their larger cousins as a delicacy, but apple, bramble and maggot crumble did have a slightly less appetising ring to it. Next time I looked, all the shelves were empty, and I thought it better not to notice!

We experimented with nettle soup, nettle and mint soup and nettle, mint and mushroom soup before accepting the conventional horticultural wisdom that nettles were a weed and best kept that way. There must be a parable in this somewhere. Brawn was one of the better experiments, which tasted delicious but unfortunately required half a pig's head, a very large pan and a steely disposition in the cook.

My arrangement with Bob was unspecific and soon I was working for him in a very informal way. One fine late summer's day, we were walking across the farm (probably looking for blackberries) and could not fail to notice that the combine harvester was static in the middle of the winter wheat field. The headlands had been cut, if cut was the right word - anyway the combine had driven over them, leaving six-inch wheel ruts in the soggy ground. 1974 was one of those rather damp summers and the crop in question would gain brownie points now as a contribution to conservation and birdfeed but was never going to enter the grain mountain debate. We followed the wheel ruts towards the combine, and I translated, paraphrased and sifted the dialogue that a slightly over-excited Bob was engaged in with his tool set and his combine, but I think Gilly, even with her genteel and protected upbringing was beginning to get the feel for the situation. Bob, by now aware of our presence, launched a heavy, open-ended, one-inch spanner into the inanimate and defenceless pickup vehicle, perhaps a little unfairly I felt, and said, since his argument as I understood it was either with the combine or the weather but definitely not the pickup. I thought then that the joke was OK, but I do accept the timing wasn't too hot!

He switched his attention from the combine to me, suggesting none-too sensitively that if I thought I could do any bloody better than I had better 'effing' well get on with it and 'effing' good luck to me. It wasn't really a conversation; I suppose it was a kind of friendly gesture to wish me good luck. Hitherto, my only combine experience was to bag off grain some five years earlier, but what I lacked in experience, I did make up for with a large amount of trial and error. I worked out eventually which lever lifted the pickup reel, which drove the beast forwards and how to discharge the grain and most importantly how to stop the lot when the tone of the clattering took on a slightly different note. It was like tuning a guitar, you just knew what it should sound like and anything different usually meant something was about to break or jam. Harvest progressed at a snail's pace and in a minor key more like a funeral dirge than a triumphant march.

I was still combining in November on the principle of cut what I could, fill the tank and then walk back to the farm to fetch the trailer, discharge the combine, do a bit more, discharge again then stop the whole process and drive the blue Ford County tractor, all wheels and exhaust pipe, back to the farm to empty the grain, by this time a sort of grey porridge, onto the barn floor. Gilly took turns to drive the monster but as it took a bit of driving expertise that Gilly was yet to acquire to reverse into the barn and tip the trailer with its faulty hydraulic connections, I had to be there in any case and it saved no time. She did however attract more glances than I, stuck in behind the steering wheel between the tractor's eight-foot wheels, her long, fair hair flowing out in the autumn wind.

For all that, I liked Bob. He was not well but when calm, he was good company and amusing. In common with others I have known, he took great comfort in putting a spanner into what he called the bureaucratic stew. Bob's particular forte was to deliberately let his sixty cows walk one after the other across the new Oxford bypass, which he hadn't supported the building of in the first place and so certainly wasn't going to make it easy for its users now; it had been built across his fields. His favoured time was eight fifteen in the morning and five o'clock in the

evening rush hour. Although his temper could be something special, on these occasions he maintained an irritating calm as he greeted the hooting and the road rage with gentle Gaelic platitudes, carefully composed for maximum effect. His curly grey hair tried with some success to escape from underneath his battered bowler hat, tied on to his head by red baler twine.

Being short of cash helped incentivise us but I don't think we counted ourselves poor - we just didn't have any money. Gilly taught herself to spin whilst I taught myself to shear. Thanks to Smudge's first fleece, I still have a pair of mittens, fingerless ones, and a scarf kept for skiing. We taught ourselves to do everything and bought nothing except that which came from the local auction house. Gilly was playfully referred to as "the scrapper" by the auctioneer because she would only bid five shillings for a bundle of six fire grates of which we only needed one. The other five did go for scrap on the same day and left us in pocket. We always tried to do it that way.

Some friends who visited for supper kindly brought us a bag of minced beef rather than a bottle of wine. We were part of the good life revolution without knowing that there was a revolution going on. No TV, no "what shall we do now" evenings - just work, sit down occasionally after one job and before another and sleep. At around that time, one of the tabloid papers ran a news story on the cost of setting up home for young marrieds; it came to just short of fifteen hundred pounds. Working on that basis, we had made a profit of around one thousand, four hundred and fifty so we felt rather smug. We were to later set up the farm on much the same principle.

With Gilly no longer tied to Oxford with her course, we explored other possibilities. This farm was not going to benefit from my prolonged presence. Our bank situation was not healthy, and we had set our sights on Africa. By February 1975, we had packed up the house, waved goodbye to our new-found neighbours and found temporary lodgings for Smudge the sheep. We were on our way to Uganda for me to work as an agricultural teacher at a Catholic mission school on the White Nile as it left Lake Victoria on its three-thousand-mile trip through Sudan and Egypt out into the Mediterranean. We were booked on a Sunday afternoon flight to Entebbe via Cairo. On the preceding Friday, British diplomatic representation was withdrawn from Uganda as a protest against the horrific excesses of Idi Amin, the politically self-appointed tyrant leader of Uganda. I think we would have continued with the plan, thanks to fatalistic naivety rather than calculated courage, but for the timely intervention of my father.

Pragmatism prevailed and we swallowed our pride and went back milking for six months on a sprawling commercially run farm in the Warwickshire countryside. Another farm, another house but we knew from day one that we would be here for a short time. Profits were squeezed out of the pips here, hedges shaved within an inch of their existence, machinery kept going with curses and baler twine and most of the farm staff stultifyingly non-cooperative. I met with the owner in his office every morning. He had inherited the farm and clearly knew the cost of everything to the last penny. His values however were foreign to me.

If the sun shone during our short time here, I think it was on the day he decided to sell the farm and buy a villa in Greece.

One gently amusing anecdote concerned a cow, actually a first lactation heifer which we called ironically, Teats, on the grounds that she didn't have any worthy of the name. In bovine terms, she was a skittish teenager whom I spent three months trying to teach to do what cows normally do in the milking parlour – that is, walk in gently, eat a measured ration of pumped up cereal, let down her milk quietly into the cluster of suction tubes supposed to imitate her long since removed calf and then depart in a controlled and sensible manner. This teenage cow had obviously stolen the bull, that is become pregnant too early and if cows can be said to have charms, well then, she was sadly lacking. She jumped, panicked, and trampled over everything in sight, including my hands, the cluster, buckets and the next-door cow. At my wit's end, I took to tying her back legs up individually to the tail rail. After two semi-successful milking's, she learnt that if she kicked with both of her legs together, she would end up in the pit of the parlour along with me. Once was enough. She was dried off hurriedly, that is not milked again. Since by this time it had been decided that the farm was to be given up for a Grecian villa, she wasn't moved on immediately but kept on for the farm's sale. When her turn came for auction, she snorted and pawed her way into the ring, looked for the smallest farmer at the ringside, took two strides, cleared the rails and said farmer, flat hat and all, and was knocked down by the unperturbed auctioneer for dog meat price as she hightailed up the lane for her temporary freedom.

Whilst at Kineton we got to know Mike. He had come straight out of school to work on the farm and had been there about two years and thought he had arrived in heaven ahead of time. Mike would fix most things and what he couldn't, he knew someone who could. He just had "it", whatever "it" was. For me he had an old tandem bicycle frame. Gilly had hit twenty-one in April and I needed to mark the event with an original present. Jewellery was considered between breaths, as were dresses (advice here is don't try it anyone – I did once and believe me, there's a lot more in shopping for a dress than I was ready for. You need to know things like bust size, length, material, pattern, sleeve design, neckline etc. I thought colour was enough!) I settled on Mike's steel, rusty tandem frame; we rubbed it down, painted it metallic gold, bought new bike parts for it, a set of derailleur gears and hey presto, an original twenty-first birthday present.

After the farm at Kineton was sold, we cycled the sparkling new machine down the north coast of Devon and Cornwall to Land's End and back again, camping where we stopped and getting to know each other on another level. If you want to rearrange your bottom-to-seat contact on a tandem, don't forget to warn your partner first! We found that people would come up and talk to us at stops along the way in the same way that strangers will strike up a conversation in a park on the grounds that their dog has funny ears. At one stage we were grinding our way uphill and therefore, down through the gears. Remember this all you cyclists, after one, go no further unless you fit a disc spoke protector. We hadn't and spent most of one day refitting sheared spokes and pulling the wheel back into some sort of shape on the side of a road somewhere in Cornwall. We never quite got the wheel true and could only stop the brake from catching by slackening off the brake tension to give space between the brake block and the wheel. The story could have had a sorry ending, but we in fact got back safely. We put the bike plus other bits and pieces into an old caravan in a friend's stable and headed off to Lesotho with Christian Aid. This is a job we had set up before our cycle ride and in the closing weeks of my last intimate experience with dairy cows!

Chapter 19
Lesotho

Lesotho is an African anomaly; it is a small country completely surrounded by one other single country, that being South Africa. It became a British protectorate in 1868. As the subject of a pub quiz question, it's great but its position relative to South Africa is and was the political equivalent of a rucksack full of rocks. Historically, Lesotho is a small twenty-mile wide strip of lowland bordered on one side by the Mohokare, Tele and Senqu rivers and on the other side by the Drakensberg Mountains (known in Sesotho as the Maluti Mountains). It owes its origins to Moshweshwe (later to be crowned King of the Basuto people). He made a stand against both the Zulus and the Boers at Thaba Bosiu, a high, natural fortress, easy to defend, with a conglomeration of small local tribes. First to be resisted was Shaka Zulu pushing down from the north, and later the Boer settlers pushing up from the south, harassed as they were by the British coming from the Cape.

In 1975, many of the young men and some of the women of Lesotho would work in South Africa, mostly in the gold and diamond mines around Johannesburg. The social squalor of living and working conditions for black migrant workers was renowned and in stark contrast to the glitzy prize to be found so abundantly in the asteroid- disturbed land around Johannesburg.

Lesotho was ripe for western involvement. It had the distinction of being the only country in the world that was surrounded by one other single country, South Africa. Undoubtedly, it was a poor country and at that time, the eighth poorest in the world according to some statistical analysis. It had little indigenous industry or production other than its labour force for the black holes around Johannesburg. Working in the mines had become a sort of rite of passage for young Basuto males; racism, tribal conflict, prostitution and physically strenuous work all combined to justify its reputation.

Lesotho at first glance might seem to be somewhat less of a country than its giant cousin further north, Zambia, with its vast inland waterway the Zambezi, its world-famous copper deposits and varied topography. Yet the borders of Lesotho had been fought for and defended by the feisty population; oblivion was the alternative. Old Moshweshwe knew what he was doing and what he was about. No colonialist cartographer's lying ruler was going to save the Basotho nor were any hopes of exploitable raw materials to fund the west's industrially exploding economies. Lesotho only mattered because it mattered to Moshweshwe and to his peers at the time. Later in life, he swapped his spear for a pen and played the proud Victorian British with perfectly timed political pragmatism to gain nation status and maintain it against all probability. Ironically, the development of a racially divisive and ultimately insupportable apartheid political system in South Africa is what put Lesotho on the aid map in terms of third world countries deserving of help. By the 1960s and '70s it was seen as a very vulnerable David relative to the Goliath that was South Africa, and for a while Southern Rhodesia. The rich west was falling over itself to be seen to help Lesotho as a cover for their inaction against South Africa which, despite its repugnant political philosophy, was too valuable as an industrial partner for the west to want to really hurt. Lesotho was in the 1970s a proud country whose people didn't know the level of their poverty.

In my time working there, I was to see immaculately built and maintained thatched rondavel houses with neatly plastered and painted walls and floors. The plaster was actually cow dung mixed with mud and had the feeling of cork to touch and walk on. These villages were largely built and maintained by women, the menfolk being occupied away in South African mines. They were surrounded in early summer by waving seas of blue and pink cosmos and were in stark contrast to the corrugated iron-clad shanties mushrooming around most African cities. It didn't deserve to become the AIDS capital of the world by the 1990s, with over forty per cent of the female population affected.

This was the country that Gilly and I flew to in August 1975; it was to be our home for two years. It is the only country in the world where its lowest point is above a thousand metres and this it exceeds by four hundred metres. It occupies some thirty thousand square kilometres of ground equidistant between Bloemfontein and Durban. It has a population today of about two million and is ostensibly a subsistence agricultural economy with some exploitation of diamond reserves high in the Maluti Mountains. Recently, it has developed a clothing textile business sector selling largely to America. It also supplies water to much of the Orange Free State of South Africa. However, by far the most important export is that of its manpower into South Africa. Remittances sent home from these workers has underpinned the struggling economy for years.

The small church-inspired college of Thaba Khupa would provide an alternative, though in truth, any industry or farming enterprise could only exist as long as the punters had funds to buy what was being produced - and we all know where the funds came from. However, oak trees grow from small acorns and snowballs must start somewhere.

My role was grandly titled "agricultural extension officer and teacher of animal husbandry". There were other white British people working at the college and a similar number of black Basotho; mostly at this time we were all living on site. Our first three months in Lesotho were to prove to be an emotionally testing period. We arrived bright eyed and bushy-tailed, ready to play our part in whatever way we could, but we were not prepared for what lay ahead.

Firstly, there were no work permits prepared for us; we were not aware that we needed them, so for six or so weeks we were on tenterhooks, thinking at one stage it was very likely that we may be declared persona non grata and returned to the UK. This was eventually resolved. Secondly there was an issue regarding housing; mine was certainly not a senior role at the college, and in no way justified the provision of a house far more comfortable, large and well positioned than the black lady deputy principal's house some two hundred yards away where she lived with her four children and husband. Despite my objections, this was allocated for us to use but not until the carpet had been replaced, as it was marked by a previous family's use! To make matters worse, the old carpet was then given to the deputy principal, presumably on the premise that she was black and wouldn't notice the shortcomings! The charity that we were working for was Christian Aid, the same one that my mother would go on house to house collections for in the UK as did many others. If she collected twelve pounds for her two hours' work, she would be cock-a-hoop. I was one thousand per cent sure that neither my mother nor the donors would approve of this plan. I objected to the proposed housing arrangement but was nowhere near forceful enough.

Thirdly, whilst waiting for this privileged house to be made "habitable", I was foolish enough to mislay some money, about one hundred rand. It was a large amount for us, but it was a lottery win for one of the students. However, it was my carelessness rather than anything else that meant that this money had gone missing and instead of seeking some quiet resolution for this situation, it was taken out of my hands and blown up to biblical proportions to involve the whole college, presumably on the assumption (possibly correct) that it had been stolen. Fortunately, whoever the beneficiary was kept quiet; I hope it went to pay his or her sibling's school fees. Whatever, it wasn't a good start for us. Lastly, we somehow got sucked up into a Mennonite Church in Maseru which might have been lifted lock, stock and barrel from the American Bible belt into Lesotho. There were lots of tea parties, Jesus jingles and "praise the Lord" choruses (yet again) along with fundamentalist bible study. The nod here was to treat everything as a gift from God and say yes please - a bit like Monopoly, advance past GO and collect two hundred pounds. No questions asked... Gilly was swept along on its comfortable tide whilst I floundered around in the dilemmatous surf.

I was beginning to feel that the comfortable shoes I had regretfully slipped out of in Zambia had been replaced by toe-pinching wooden clogs.

For the first time, Gilly and I found we had a disagreement so fundamental that we could not resolve it. With bad grace I put aside my qualms and we moved into the newly-carpeted house. It was a mistake and I should have stuck to my guns; without doubt this house should have gone to the deputy principal. Gilly saw it as a gift from a providing God, the existence of which I didn't recognise; we were fundamentally in different camps and spiritually oceans apart. The muddied pool that we eventually climbed out of left us both bruised and diminished. It may not seem a big deal now but at the time it was, and formed a dead, cold weight between us.

My shoes remained tight and only began to soften up as I gradually took control of our destiny. On a practical level, this meant that I separated myself more and more from the college campus, working predominantly with the students in their home situations, helping to establish some sort of farm business. Typically, this was rearing chicken for meat or eggs, and vegetable growing with the occasional rabbit-breeding enterprise. My attendance and later Gilly's at the chorus-chanting Mennonite

Church became very occasional. Religion for me had become a difficult struggle when held up against the coal face of life. With the poets and the psalmists, I celebrated the splendours of life and creation, but I couldn't get off the train; the stations looked too comfortable, the ambiance complacent.

We put our different perspectives on the top shelf, out of daily viewing and focussed on the things we agreed on, leaving the rest to the passage of time. It worked but slowly.

Soon the Basotho Hat Hotel in Maseru was to have its feathers ruffled by the building of the Holiday Inn as a venue for international aid seminars, of which there were many, and the provision of luxury accommodation for the very generously paid international aid brigade and not so publicly advertised casino activities. These were banned in South Africa by the high-minded nationalist politicians, presumably to earn them brownie points at Saint Peter's gate, whilst they hurriedly gabbled over the fundamental abuses of apartheid. We used to deliver chicken and vegetables to both hotels to supplement the college's income. There was always a distractingly bright if not generously clad group of girls drinking at the bar of both these hotels. We usually exchanged pleasantries; why not? After all, they were not selling chickens and vegetables! We were not in competition! They were the human urban equivalent of some bizarre, gaudy subtropical chattering birds pecking around at a watering hole, resplendent in gleaming plumage and looking for a mate with dollar bills under his wings.

At about this time our first son Daniel was conceived and when the "brethren" of the Church learnt the news, God was duly thanked and praised. I suggested that the explanation might actually be slightly more biological and more to do with hormones than the Holy Spirit but by this time I think I was seen as a lost cause and beyond redemption.

Gilly came out with me on some trips to the villages until the discomfort of dirt-graded, potholed and corrugated roads made such journeys too difficult. Daniel was to be born eighteen months into our time in Lesotho and at the Catholic Mission hospital in Roma. The Swiss doctor in charge, a Doctor Beeler, was a formidable lady who sent me packing the day before Daniel's birth on the grounds that the birth was not imminent. As with most things, I thought I knew better so although I did leave the hospital via the door observed by the said doctor, I re-entered by the window into Gilly's room some five minutes later and slept on the floor with the connivance of a friendly nurse. My excuse was that we lived a little way away, had no phone contact and I might be needed. After all, I had delivered multiple calves and lambs! Inevitably, the doctor was right - there was no action by early the next morning, so I quietly exited by the window and came in by the front door, making sure that I was noticed. Danny was born later that day and I was required, albeit only to point out that the hormone drip used to stimulate birth had been upset with movement and was delivering at six times the required rate. His fast and speedy arrival is a characteristic in his make up even today.

We returned to our house which now boasted solar heated, hot water as well as a new carpet! The solar heating system was primitive, relying as it did on cold water circulating through the black alkathene pipes looped around on the roof of our house. It was effective as long as you only needed hot water at the end of the day, the day had been sunny, and you only needed the equivalent of two buckets full! We had an alternative though, an outside boiler, which provided about one bucket full of warm water for the burning of ten fir cones (of which there was a plentiful supply). The fir cones fitted neatly inside a steel jacket of water. Later, a Swiss friend gave us his prototype parabolic reflector, covered in tin foil which, if we focused it correctly with the sun's rays concentrated on a strategically placed saucepan of water, would boil a litre pan of water in ten minutes. It was useful around midday and had the appeal of taking me back to childhood experiments with magnifying glasses, paper and ants.

Chapter 20
Agricultural Extension Work

One of my students, called Maryhale Tabola, lived at a fabulous village high in the Maluti Mountains. To get to the village of Mamahao required a drive-up country to Leribe on reasonable roads, followed by a six-hour drive on a very questionably negotiable mountain roadway hacked out of the hillside, more like a stairway crossing several culverted streams and eventually fording the Little Orange River.

Gilly had travelled up with me in the early stages of pregnancy. On this occasion, we were driving a Daihatsu double cab vehicle which foundered on the second stairway, not being four-wheel drive. With only one driving wheel in contact with the ground, there were always likely to be problems. After several hours walking, being encouraged at every corner and hill that the village was just a stone's throw ahead (Maryhale had a wonderful disposition and pointed, after a graceful sweep of her head, with her chin, in the required direction), thankfully we were picked up by a South African fisherman in his Toyota Land Cruiser. Being white we were given seats in the front; Maryhale sat in the in the open back with the luggage. He talked incessantly about what was going to happen when South Africa moved to a more representative political system (perhaps we would all sit inside, heaven forbid!). Whatever, we were glad of the ride and nodded a lot. He dropped us off at the supply station on the wrong side of the river, so we completed the last section on foot.

Eventually we arrived at the village and were met by Maryhale's family and a good number of their village members. Our arrival had been expected – the village was extraordinary – about as far as one could get from the capital. The rondavels were immaculate, the courtesies generous but not elaborate and the mountain scenery spectacular. Once it was appreciated that we would need to stay overnight and that Gilly was pregnant, Maryhale's younger sister was sent careering around the gardens to catch the biggest chicken, which had good reason to run and half-fly in its squawking bid for freedom. Happily, for dinner but not for our feathered friend, it did not escape and was converted into a very tasty, if tough stew in a decisive manner. Its decisiveness is both its best commendation and its reason for compulsive viewing. The sight of a headless chicken running its last journey is a disturbingly compulsive spectacle right up there with bull fighting. The feathers were not eaten but only just survived the pot. There is something very wholesome about the lack of waste in much of Africa's village life and the opposite is true about the waste in western living. (A friend of mine now, who used to be a ranger with the local national park tells me that his least favourite job was emptying the public waste bins of dead pheasants the day after a shoot.) By the time supper arrived, we were both starving. The meal started with a bowl each of matoho, (fermented sorghum porridge.) We received this in a rondavel set aside for us. Gilly, who was not usually at all squeamish, just couldn't swallow after one mouthful. A combination of being pregnant and the unfamiliar sour taste was blamed; not wanting to appear ungrateful and without Gilly's excuse I drank both portions. I should have just not finished the second. The message got back to the cook and more was sent in. On the grounds that chicken was to follow, we declined, much to the relief of the kids waiting outside for the leftovers. Chicken followed with bahobi, the ubiquitous maize porridge staple found in most of Africa. There were greens too as a vegetable relish and bottled apricots for pudding. (Pudding, notice, not dessert, I haven't lost all my working-class credentials!).

The leading light of the village was a tall, lean, immaculate and articulate guy called Joseph. Joseph had worked in South Africa and brought back all the best of what he had seen there.

When we left, he presented us with another jar of apricots. I hope we were able to be of some benefit to that wonderful place but anything that I could have done would have come a very poor second to Joseph's contributions. To me, that seemed proper development; copy the best, leave the rest.

We returned to base later that day thanks to the Irish brothers at the Catholic mission sharing their vehicle with one more person than the vehicle could possibly carry. That was the way of things – nothing wasted, not even a free ride perched on the tow bar of the vehicle. These Irish brothers who ran the mission at Mamahao really did have their hearts in the right place, usually establishing schools, hospitals and health clinics and doing what they could to improve the lot of the community of which they were part. They were robust, straightforward, good, selfless people and I don't remember hearing any of them preach. The spirit they were full of got things done. I had seen the same in Zambia. These folk were in it for the long haul, there was little evidence of any brand-new four-wheel drive, white Land Rovers with fancy motifs on the side of their bodywork. Already too many of these aid projects were staffed by career workers with their good eye fixed on home comforts and index-linked pensions. The mission vehicles were used for work, not advertising.

I had one more trip to Mamahao. This time Gilly was too heavily pregnant to come, and I carried one hundred one-day-old chicks, starter meal and vegetable seeds. The weather had been wet and by this time the college had taken delivery of a four-wheel drive Land Rover (so qualifying us for what Paul Theroux would later call in his book, "Dark Star Safari", the "aid brigade" – perhaps a little unkindly and I think in our case perhaps a little undeserved). We still made slow progress. At one stage, fearful that the one-day-old chicks would suffocate with all the lurching about, I stopped by a puddle and released the chicks for a drink. Within two minutes, all of them had learnt to put their heads down, take a peck of water and then heads up again to swallow it. Catching them up again, considering these little lemon-yellow fluff bundles were only a day out of the shell, was not the easiest job. In a few more days it would be quite impossible.

The rest of the journey was difficult but not eventful – I noticed whilst fording the Orange River close to Mamahao that the water seemed deeper than last time, but it presented no insuperable problems. On this occasion, I stayed a couple of days to help build a hessian and wire netting and willow-framed chicken pen. The theory was that a rudimentary frame was constructed out of the willow branches, and chicken mesh stretched across it, half covered with hessian and painted with cement. You could shoot holes through this idea from whichever angle you chose but it was quick and cheap and effective and lasted for a couple of years. I knew that my main priority was to get a turnover going quickly before the small amount of capital that the students returned home with was earmarked for someone's hospital fees or school bills.

I wonder now if what we did forty years ago was of any long-term value relative to the devastation that AIDS has brought to this mountain kingdom. For sure, Joseph would have scrutinised my efforts to see if there was anything worth learning.

What has become of my good friend and co-worker Morai Molemohi who taught animal science at the college in my stead and took over the village visiting when I left, I don't know. In an unintentional way, he was to have a very significant effect on our lives in the very near future.

Back to Mamahao, two days' work later, and a significant rainfall had swollen the Little Orange River to make it unfordable. I went down to look and there was no possibility; I did what Africans do all the time; I waited. There was no way of contacting Gilly; the age of the mobile phone had not yet arrived. After two further days and a drop in the level of water, I somewhat tentatively took leave of Mamahao and Joseph for what turned out to be the last time and eased my way with much furrowing of brows into the aptly named Orange River, now not so little. The far bank was about one hundred yards away and beyond the exit point was a supply store; it was that which I was aiming for and as the water was soil laden and opaque, I kept my eyes focused on. Whether we floated momentarily or not, I don't know, but though the route was in theory straight, the steering wheel had a lot of use. I had never been a great fan of Land Rovers, but on that day, it was a good friend; we got out, passengers and all. By the end of the day my friendship with the vehicle had intensified - I was deeply indebted to it!

About two hours along the rough stone track, we came to another crossing, much shorter and normally dry, on a concrete platform built above culverts. This time the culverts were overflowing with the mud-laden result of yesterday's storm and the concrete platform was invisible. My passenger at the time was a Basotho guy who spoke a lot but not coherently - not at least for me. Together after much arm pointing and tentative stick prodding, we decided on an entry point. I was not convinced but took comfort in the fact that even if we had got it wrong, we would be upstream of the culvert not downstream, so rather than being lost without trace, we would be washed up against the edge of the culvert, probably drowned but not at least lost! Inch by inch we moved forward; the rain had started again so things would only get worse. My voluble friend went very quiet until we suddenly dropped down off the edge of the bank, momentarily grounded, then when the bank gave way we levelled with the water over the bonnet for a moment and then as we established a more horizontal position, the bonnet re-emerged, and water filled the foot well up to just below my knees. At this time, the exhaust must have been submerged by two feet and the air intake just clear of the water. Whatever, the quiet of my passenger gave way to an exited nervous chatter, and short of any other ideas, I put the vehicle into reverse and kept my foot on the accelerator. In retrospect it was a good thing to do but there was no rationality at the time. We were there for enough time for me to compose, recite and amen a prayer if I had thought it was worth it, but I hadn't, and I didn't. Suddenly the churning wheels must have hit rock and we moved not too slowly in reverse up the bank we had just entered the river on. My friend became quiet again and smiled an apology as we emerged safely on the other side of the culvert, having re-entered some five yards downstream. Once off the mountains, I couldn't help feeling that there should have been crowds of cheering people on the other side of the road, but life was progressing as normal. If we had been washed away to oblivion, it would have been just the same; a salutary experience. Gilly had not been especially worried; she knew it had rained and guessed that I had been held up. I went into our bedroom, banged my head on the door and slept for twelve hours, the sleep of the grateful living.

The Land Rover washed up well and so did I, though the smell of mud lingered on, especially in the vehicle. It didn't much matter. Some few months later Morai, whilst driving into the Malutis to see another student, moved over to the edge of the road (that is the outer edge) to accommodate some driven cattle. The road gave way and the vehicle, driver, passengers and all slipped over the edge of this precipitous road and rolled side-over-side sixty feet down into a ravine (known as a donga in Lesotho). The cab had a fibreglass roof which went on the first roll and was followed by the two passengers and eventually Morai, one person per roll. Astonishingly, no one was seriously hurt. Morai's pride was dented and one of the passengers, the college's secretary, chipped a very large white front tooth which she displayed gladly to all and sundry with the slightest excuse. The Land Rover suffered no mechanical damage; even the windscreen wipers worked but alas there was no windscreen to wipe. The rest of the bodywork met a similar fate and there was a slight twist in the main chassis. Even in Lesotho, the insurance company reckoned it was beyond repair. Not one to look a gift horse in the mouth, I offered, after about twenty seconds of careful discussion with Gilly, to buy the wreck from the insurance company and finance the venture by selling our return plane tickets. Thereafter, it would just be a simple matter of driving home. However, I am getting ahead of myself.

We had slowly extracted ourselves from the bubble gum comfort of the transplanted church but remained on good terms with most of the people that we had met there. One couple working for the government in a legal capacity and from Tasmania came out in their Mercedes car to play bridge one evening. They were of our parents' generation and very correct, and a bit on the proper side of practical. I say played bridge, but it turned out that although David was keen, Melba, his new wife, was merely compliant. Bridge is a difficult game to follow at the best of times especially if snap is your only previous experience of cards. The evening was spent sweeping insects off the specially conveyed card table with its billiard like cloth-green surface. The flies and moths expired on collision with our paraffin-powered hurricane lamp without which Melba couldn't identify the cards. It pretty soon became apparent that whether she could see them or not made little difference. The end of the evening was a relief. I can still hear David sighing ruefully that no, the ace wasn't worth only one point and hadn't they gone over this five minutes previously? I don't think that Melba actually cried but she did whimper.

We eventually waved them goodbye as they slowly negotiated the potholed road driving into a full African moon, green table and all. The evening was not repeated. Rumour has it that David became an expert at patience - it only needed one player.

Our water supply depended on a two-mile stretch of one-inch bore, alkathene pipe delivering from an electric-pumped well and reservoir reserve. The system was simple and not unlike that which we now rely on at our farm in Devon. However, it worked better when the pipe was not punctured! The area between the college and the well was scrubland but did provide a sort of grazing resource for the local village. Since there were no field boundaries (or for that matter fields), the cattle and goats would be tended by young boys usually before they started school or older ones if no other work was on offer. Put yourself in their shoes; it's hot, you're bored and beneath the six inches of earth covering the pipe is cool fresh water! Puncturing the pipe was not a problem, drinking was not a problem, but resealing the pipe was. A woody stem sufficed for a short while and tomorrow it would be someone else's problem. When you're eight years old and thirsty, tomorrow is another world and so is someone else. We never did resolve the problem, and therefore frequently ran short of water. There were now goodness knows how many patches of car inner tube and jubilee clip repairs. After a while we used the real McCoy alkathene pipe joiners, but they were more expensive and required a lot of spade work.

Having got into the habit of use, break and repair as cheaply as possible, it is difficult to lose; consequently, now we live in a house and on a farm that is a cornucopia of imaginative repairs – some would say bodges. It is character building for anyone who stands in for us, farm sitting when we are away and satisfying not to have to call in a technician every time a repair is needed.

Leading up towards the birth of our first son and with an eye on the future return journey to the UK (he would only be six months old), I got hold of a supply of rattan from Bloemfontein and using a plywood base and an image of what I wanted to end up with, I fashioned a good-sized Moses basket which would support a mosquito net and mattress. The result wasn't at all bad and has stood the test of time in usefulness. Not only did it protect Danny on the prolonged journey back to the UK, but it was the first home for our other two sons born later and all five grandchildren born until today. It has, to its credit, proved to be resilient, insect proof, spacious and in a home spun do-it-yourself way quite stylish. As a business, I wouldn't rate it alongside merchant banking, but we do still use it forty or so years on and that's something your average banker can't boast. We live in the age of the 'Oh, I've just fitted a new kitchen' brigade; what they actually mean is 'I've just paid someone to fit a factory-made work surface with an imported German-made, pre-shaped sink, Chinese labour-saving gadgets, Swedish mass-produced light units (on a pound sterling to gram weight scale up there with the precious metals), all neatly set up with a Spanish slate floor, fitted by a Polish artisan and the end result is just like that at number 24A but the fridge is soft closing and holds one extra pint of guacamole!'

Anyway, returning to the Moses basket – it is still going strong and I am content to look at it today and know that all our children and now in turn their children called it home for their first six months. I get a similar buzz out of the wooden trike and trailer set that never had much shine but outlives even today all its plastic competitors. The wheels are from an old shopping trolley, the main body some reused polished plywood and the front stem assembly odd bits of recut roofing battens. It is now in its fortieth year and is still, even in this plastic computer age, the most used toy.

On another occasion whilst supplying chickens, food and cement etc. to a remote village near Teyateyaneng, Gilly was still in an expectant state so I dropped her off at the imaginatively named Blue Mountain Inn to where I hoped to return in an hour or so, have lunch and then we would go home. I hadn't driven ten minutes after dropping Gilly off before I managed to find a bottomless puddle to sit the vehicle in on route for the village. No amount of pushing, shoving or swearing could make it move, so all the bags, the chickens, the food and fencing had to be removed (at that time, food bags had forty kilos in them, not the delicate twenty-five kilos of today), and carried through the mud to dry ground – this time the pushing, shoving and the swearing worked and the car edged forwards. Now in South Africa I would be classed as white in skin colour and all my students and passengers, black. At the end of the day we were all a uniform muddy brown and happy to have shared the experience. The division of society based on skin colour and known in South

Africa as apartheid was clearly very flawed and must have been difficult for many white (do I mean pink?) South Africans, as it obviously was for the blacks (do l mean browns?).

I got back to the Blue Mountain Inn in time for supper with a very long-suffering Gilly. Unusually, I showered first. The food was fabulous in the way that food always is fabulous when you are hungry. The lady who served us had a relation at Thaba Khupa and she generously responded to my quip that the only thing I could imagine better would be the same again by bringing just that; oh, what it is to have an appetite.

There were frequently political squabbles going on between the respective governments of Lesotho and South Africa. When things got too bad, big brother Pretoria would crack the whip and Lesotho had no alternative but to dance compliantly. On one occasion, all animal food exports were stopped from South Africa to Lesotho. Unaware of this, my work partner Morai drove over the river with the Lesotho border post to the east and the South African border post to the west. He stood his place in the "nee blanks" queue on the South African side and then drove up to fetch the ten bags of starter mash, rather crucial to us and to all our students, to get the chickens going once they arrived, and they were due very soon. The trouble started when he attempted to return with the food. 'No go,' the customs man said, so back to Ladybrand for Morai and eventually back to Thaba Khupa with no food.

Now I have inherited, I think from my father, an invisible demon perched on my shoulder and when he hears 'No you can't' he says very audibly to me, 'Yes, actually I think you probably can.' He gets most excited when the target is in a uniform, not operating on my particular plane of logic and exhibits the slightest suggestion of pomposity or doesn't look me straight in the eye. I knew these jokers from old; my old scout master might have been one of them! The fact that they were only doing what they had been told was not going to be a meaningful defence.

I repeated Morai's journey without having to queue in the "nee blanks" section. Collecting the same ten bags of food, I stopped at the border on the South African side. 'Ach now, my friend, that's not possible.' I was expecting just that but hoped my being the favoured colour might have cut some slack - well it sometimes did but not on that day. My little demon on my shoulder was screaming at me to thump the little bugger on the nose and do a runner, but he only half got his way. Like a scene from the film 'The Great Escape', I turned the truck around and headed back towards Ladybrand as if I was going to return the food yet again. The Caledon River that separated South Africa from Lesotho was spanned by a narrow bridge with a road on one side and a railway track on the other. Respective border posts were about two hundred yards apart on their own sides of the water. Whether or not the South African border guards raised their heads from their desks, and if they did whether they felt for their hand guns which were prominently visible on their hips, I don't know because as I shot past the border post on the railway line, the suspension soaking up exposed sleepers and the four hundred kilograms of food on board, my eyes were set straight ahead. By the time I reached the Lesotho border post, we were slowing down whilst my heartbeat was speeding up. Feeling super pleased with this stupidly idiotic action, I drove home, and nothing was ever said. The next time I went to the border post, it was as if nothing had happened; the passport irregularity was not noticed, the chicks didn't go hungry and my demonic companion grew in confidence. In the farming years ahead, he was to prove a useful friend, without whom we might have foundered several times over.

One of my students had been given some land belonging to a local Catholic mission on the understanding that he would grow vegetables and allow the mission to use the venture as a demonstration garden. This seemed a great idea, especially as they had access to a small tractor and plough which one of the brothers was competent to use. I went to visit on the Saturday morning that ploughing was planned for. The scene was jamboree-like with everyone and their several dogs watching the tractor slide into action. The soil was sandy and dry and looked the same six inches down as it did one inch down, so they set it for deep ploughing in the hope of burying the weed seeds.

Now Lesotho is heavily populated with people and the winters are cold, so forget any visions you might have of herds of antelope, ear-flapping elephants and flamingos strutting their stuff – that all happens further north or west. The wild animals of Lesotho live close to the ground and of necessity are difficult to catch and secretive in their habits. The gerbils of Matsieng Mission, however, were in for a shock. Six-inch ploughing meant that their home burrows were disturbed and like seagulls behind the plough in the UK, the young boys and some of the girls too were dancing behind the plough, scooping up the saucer-eyed rodents and stuffing them into whatever containers they had – often just their shorts pockets. It may be that these cute looking creatures, often known as desert rats, were destined for cages in the pet shops of Europe but I think it rather more likely that their cookie looks wouldn't save them from the cooking pot. At least they had the dignity of knowing that they were not unappreciated! The vegetable garden got going with much love and a lot of work, with water carried to every plant to ease its first few weeks and always someone to look out for marauding goats or cows hungry for the colour green.

This student was lucky to have the land provided by the mission as the land tenure system in Lesotho was such that most of the land was owned by the king and administered by the head man or more likely the head women of the village. This meant that success or failure of the small-scale farming ventures depended heavily on the goodwill of the village elders. The prospect of a readily available supply of chicken meant that we usually won the day with respect to land allocation.

During the rainy season, usually October through to April, the rains are generally heavy and short lived. Lesotho is not the place to go for cloudy overcast skies (Devon fits that bill very nicely).

In October it is normal for the weather to break in late afternoon with spectacular lightning storms. Since we lived close to the mountains in the confluence of two valleys, lightning storms were particularly dramatic. Gilly was on the wrong side of fascinated by these natural electrical concerts and would take refuge in the middle of the sitting room until one day the light bulb joined in and flashed blue! I don't remember whether it was the same storm or not, but a family group arrived on our doorstep some few hours after a storm – their grass-thatched rondavel had been struck by lightning and the father had climbed on top to pull out the burning section and save the rest of the roof. Insurance wasn't an option for these folk. Catastrophically, the roof had collapsed – it was beyond saving and the father was momentarily in a walled cage full of burning grass. He got out but was badly burnt in the process. He was one of the group on the doorstep. They needed him to be taken to the hospital, and of course we were happy to help, having the only vehicle in the area. He talked and thanked us all the way to Roma, the nearest hospital town and then walked into its patient area. With nothing more to offer and nothing else we could do, we drove back home to discover three days later that he had suffered eighty per cent burns and had died in the hospital. I had had no idea that he had been so badly affected. This family would have doubtless had his hospital bill to pay afterwards which would have been an added pressure on the relatives. In the UK, hardly a day goes past without someone complaining on the radio or television about our National Health Service. What this family would have given for such a lifeline!

Not all mercy missions ended badly. On another occasion, a similar group arrived, this time with a lady who had been several days in labour – I say lady but in truth she was more a girl – in sheep terms she would have been too small to go to the ram... She was conveyed in a wheelbarrow until they got to us, where the

Land Rover was able to double up as an ambulance. Somehow, she was bundled into the back seat with several of her family. This time it ended well, I am glad to say and so the population balance was restored.

Chapter 21
Return to Kalabo, Flood and Mud!

Dave and Merryn Cooke, from Kalabo days in Zambia, had relocated to a school in Mahalapye in Botswana, which was the other side of southern Africa, wedged between what was then South West Africa and South Africa. They were planning a trip up through the north of Botswana and the Caprivi Strip, past the Victoria Falls at Livingstone and north to Mongu on the east of the Zambezi to spend Christmas in Kalabo on the other side of the river. We joined them and two of their Tswana friends after a pampered and luxurious train journey via Johannesburg. The train was still coal powered, the dining car had wooden panelling and lace tablecloths and tea was served by a white-gloved African waiter out of a china teapot! Astonishingly, it is still possible to travel in such style today in South Africa on the Blue Train from Johannesburg to Cape Town or Durban without having to take a mortgage out first. It might, however, be necessary to suspend any moral scruples when passing through the tin shanties of South Africa.

It was the school Christmas holidays, so there was not a lot of time to fit it all in, especially as some of us wanted to divert into the Chobe Game Park, which was still open, although under-utilised due to the hostilities around what was then still Southern Rhodesia after its unilateral declaration of independence under its white leader, Ian Smith.

We touched the hot sand of Botswana briefly before loading up into the old Land Rover that Dave and Merryn had bought and headed up northwards. The journey was hot but interesting, with its single-track tarmac and graded earth passing lanes. The idea was that you drove using all ten feet of the tarmac, as did the oncoming traffic and then peeled off to the side to pass the oncoming vehicle just before collision point and then back on again afterwards. It is obviously important to peel off on the correct side, as getting it wrong would change the shape of the vehicle somewhat!

Driving along at forty to fifty miles per hour with one side on corrugated dirt and the other on new smooth tarmac takes some getting used to, but we were young and invincible. The invincible bit was stretched the next day, when against Merryn's forcefully delivered advice I got out of the vehicle to get a better photo of some buffalo which were partly obscured by trees. Good thinking Merryn, but with all my experience of African bush life gained in suburban Nottingham and a vague idea that although aggressive, buffalo have poor eyesight, I stubbornly approached the group of buffalo on foot. They were contentedly chewing the cud, a bit like the cows I was used to milking in England. Merryn was getting a little excited and uttering rather unladylike oaths and one of the closer animals was doing the bovine equivalent of adjusting his glasses, so I retreated to the vehicle and we drove off. Merryn was not one to miss an opportunity to point out any weaknesses in my judgement and was in full flow for quite a while, such that I did feel for a moment that I would have been better to have taken my luck with the buffalo. She has forgiven me now but only just, and no longer are there buffalo in the equation.

We arrived in Kalabo for Christmas Eve to discover that food of any sort was in short supply – worse still, the Luanginga Bar had no beers and the police based at the BOMA (local government buildings) were not comfortable with, nor convinced by our little group wanting to spend Christmas in Kalabo! We had to check in each day that we were there, which took time but that was one thing we had plenty of. Our allocated days were tripping by and we were soon on route driving across the Zambezi flood plain with the water noticeably raised from the week before and black rain-laden clouds threatening from the south. My turn to drive once again led to problems. We were travelling in convoy with a police Land Rover and one other; I think it may have been army. We were third in our group of three and I somehow allowed the vehicle to get into the wrong wheel ruts. If I put it that way, it sounds partly the fault of the vehicle, but it wasn't – it was all mine. In my defence, I could say that because we were third in the little convoy, the track had already got significantly chewed up. Whatever, we ground to a halt when the sump was pushing up too much mud. Surprisingly, the other two vehicles could not pull us out and since the black clouds were now above us and emptying, they were concerned for their own safety. The police pointed in the direction of the nearest village and disappeared along with the army, no longer bothered about why we wanted to be in Ķalabo! (The same thought had crossed my mind, but I thought it better to not voice it, Merryn having already mentioned buffalo in her last conversation, slightly unkindly I thought). It was close to dark so we had no choice but to erect our tents on the driest ground we could find and attempt to sleep.

The rain crashed down most of the night and the driest ground of the previous night was decidedly soggy by morning. Dave was not downhearted – somehow, he had made contact with the village and they were going to come back later with oxen and plough ropes. As we waited, we identified two skeleton carcasses of drowned cars within the vicinity of where we were currently parked; the omens were not good. However, what was good was the promise of the villagers and they came out in force with oxen and ropes and small boys and noise. The relevant rope connections were made, and the noise levels built up. There was a great deal of hooting, whipping and arm waving but apart from churning up the ground to a sort of thick gravy consistency, the vehicle didn't move an inch. We spent one more night under canvas after having decided what things we might carry the next day on foot. Even Dave had given up the ghost.

At dawn, we had had little, if any sleep and about the same amount of food – we were wet, and I was wondering how many cows I was going to have to milk to buy Dave and Merryn a replacement vehicle. Into this desolate scene entered about six small boys, none of them older than ten. Their smiles were welcome and their enthusiasm infectious. 'Yesham, sir,' they knew what to do. 'Yesham,' they had done it before many times. 'Yesham,' we would be on our way by the end of the day. We watched as they fetched stones from goodness knows where and then started to jack up the vehicle diagonally, wheel by wheel from the hub caps. This meant that the springs were kept compressed and the stones could be forced under the wheels; simple, but ingenious. It took most of the day to raise the vehicle just clear of the ground, each wheel on a tower of precious stones. The tents and whatever else were laid out before the wheels and Merryn, being the lightest person, sat gingerly in the driving seat. Freewheeling hubs were checked to ensure we were in four-wheel drive, the engine was started, and second gear engaged, much discussion on not too many revs but whatever you do, don't stall, otherwise no pressure... On the count of three, the clutch was released, everyone pushed including our infant helpers, the vehicle toppled forwards off its tower of stones, the revs went dangerously low, but we were moving, wheels spinning, bits of tent wrapped around the axles, but we were moving forwards onto slightly drier ground. After two or so minutes, the Land Rover was clear of the bog and we could see daylight beneath the chassis.

We pooled all our cash resources after having already paid the villagers for their oxen-related efforts and thanked the boys in every way for their help. Impressively, the villagers with the oxen had at first refused to accept payments since they said they had not been successful. Dave was made of good stuff and he insisted, and I was glad he did. The chance of paid work for these people must have been pretty rare yet their sense of what was right and just overrode even their need for money. It is at least interesting to consider the origin of such a moral code. Religion of course would be one explanation but in the absence of religion, moral codes still exist and persist.

The journey across the rest of the flood plain to Senanga and down to Livingstone and the Victoria Falls was joyously straightforward. Buffalo rarely got a mention – the atmosphere was electric and buoyant and helped by the knowledge that at Livingstone there was a hotel which ran an "eat all you like" barbecue. We were all ready for it and happily they seemed ready for us. The problem with not eating for a week is that when you have got food on offer, the stomach capacity has shrunk somewhat, and your eyes are definitely bigger than your stomach. We all took more than we could eat and then had to decide what to do with the results of our gluttony. Gilly was the only person with a bag and as it was not acceptable to waste this food, we loaded all the meat into napkins and into the shoulder bag. Two hours later, we walked over the delicately lit footbridge spanning part of Victoria Falls on the Zambezi as it spiralled its way downwards and eastwards towards Mozambique. The sky was clear and the stars bright. Romance was in the air, but not for us alas – the smell of warm mutton wafting up from Gilly's shoulder bag might be just the thing for desert nomads, but it did absolutely nothing for me! Back to Mahalapye on the ten feet of tarmac – the exception was a four hundred-yard strip of motorway-type road which doubled up as an aeroplane landing strip – now there's an idea for Heathrow's extra runway!

We returned to Lesotho and to the college. From somewhere I had acquired some Californian rabbits. Like all rabbits, they breed prolifically and eat whatever greens are on offer. They seemed just the trick to provide a protein-rich alternative to the fattening chickens and would be more sustainable. With the students, we had constructed cages and to keep up with the numbers of residents, the cages had to multiply fast. They were positioned close to our house for security (as were the turkey chicks on the veranda - more later). I had not reckoned on the difficulties that would be associated with slaughter. Quite a lot must happen between the fluffy, docile, white, nose twitching rabbits, some of which had names, and a steaming protein-rich delicacy on a plate. The other thing about rabbits is that whatever you do with the meat, it always smells of rabbit. Having introduced the idea, I felt duty bound to see it through, but I have never eaten rabbit since - imagine you had twenty happy pet cats and... no, don't even go down that one! This was definitely an animal husbandry project; I passed it happily onto Morai as soon as I could with a muttered, totally fabricated and lame excuse.

My parents came out to visit us whilst we were in Lesotho; it was the first time either of them had been out of Britain, so we went up to meet them at Johannesburg Airport with an old Volkswagen Beetle that we had acquired. These cars last forever - well at least the mechanical bits do. The doors wouldn't lock so for security we tied them together across the seats with ropes whilst we were in Johannesburg. Of course, to do this meant opening the windows, it being a two-door car! The only reason it wasn't taken or worse, must have been that the possible beneficiaries felt moved by my simplicity. Somehow, I had thought that to tie the doors together and leave the windows open would be a deterrent. I had had a senior moment without actually having the excuse of being senior...

Some good friends of ours, an American family working for an international aid charity, came to visit one day and we took them down to the dam that was used for irrigation. I had made a sort of boat of plastic stretched over a simple wooden frame. Boat, in fairness, was a little bit of a grand title but it did float, for a while, and the water in any case was warm – we kept the lake stocked with carp which were easy to catch, ugly, tasted of mud and had bones seemingly unattached to any skeletal system. It was as if the only purpose of these fish was to choke anyone brave or desperate enough to eat them. It was a good deterrent. Darwin would no doubt have had an explanation for their bones, but I am afraid I haven't managed to find it. On this particular day a snake was seen swimming across the reservoir. My all-American action man friend was on the bank in a flash with the axe brought down with the wood for the barbecue. Snake and head were separated before I could plead its innocence and a case for its defence. The colourful serpent was placed in a carrier bag for the second of the four children to take to school as a trophy. Bag and snake were hung on the back of the pram brought along to house American infant number four. About half an hour later, American mother Kaye screamed as she saw the snake, with its head barely attached, climbing out of the bag some twelve inches from her sleeping baby!

On another trip with the same family, this time to Coffee Bay on the Indian Ocean, we all ate shellfish. They were a novel taste but not a good idea. It was to be, in our last few months there, a chance for Gilly to have a look at the top of what is known as the Garden Coast. The stucco-plastered white Dutch buildings, multi-coloured and manicured gardens (labour was not a problem unless you happened to be it; wages were meagre) all would have added up to a great place to live, setting aside the political system, the social divide and inequalities based on colour. It would certainly be a lot to give up in the years to come.

Back to the crustacean diet; I had had a bad one. Within twenty-four hours I was uncomfortable in every way one could be – a raging headache and all that is associated with severe internal chaos. If I could have been isolated or left behind, I would have been. Instead, there were nine of us in a car heading back for Lesotho and one of those was our new two-month-old baby,

Daniel. Somehow, Gilly's careful protection of him proved enough; in fact, no one else was affected. By the time I got to see a medic, the worst of the symptoms had subsided. Eventually, blood tests suggested that this had been typhoid fever, although a second lot of blood tests didn't reveal any typhoid antibodies. Whatever, it was a long time before seafood re-entered my top choice food list. I can, however, recommend it as a sure-fire way to lose weight.

Two other livestock experiences centred on the poultry. Poultry for meat had the advantage in Lesotho, as in many other areas, that the birds convert vegetable protein more efficiently than larger animals which need more energy to maintain their body temperature etc. Also, the food package at the end of the day is more family sized and affordable. We might have taken things a step too far in raising turkeys for Christmas but with such a large transient European and American population based in Lesotho, we felt it was worth a try.

We set up a paraffin lamp-heated reception area on our balcony for the arrival of the chicks. Turkeys are not normally known for their good looks or endearing characters. They start off OK and rapidly go downhill – I know people that have displayed the same characteristics! The turkey chicks were very soon looking scrawny and developed decidedly unchristian-like personalities. At two weeks old, they would identify the weakest of their group and conduct merciless hunting parties that only stopped with the demise of the quarry. I don't think they considered the fourth dimension very much or that they might themselves be the smallest tomorrow. The hunt usually started with the feathers being pecked from the tail end. This quickly revealed a bare rump, by which time the writing was on the wall. In an effort to educate them in a "don't do this, it is not nice" manner, I took to using an accumulated supply of Christmas and birthday present shaving foams to replace the removed feathers. Whether it did any good, I can't tell, but it was satisfying to watch the ringleaders trying to get rid of the shaving foam from around their beaks. In addition, it got rid of my unwanted presents. Why shaving foam even got into the possibilities list I don't know, since for most of my years I have had a beard. A bit like socks – it shows that the giver remembered the occasion but little about their creative imagination. When we moved the surviving turkeys to a larger home, we found a small cobra curled up beneath the false floor, which just goes to prove that if you provide suitable accommodation and food, friends and relatives will soon fill the space. That has continued to be the way!

The last of our Lesotho livestock tales involves the purpose-built broiler chicken rearing houses built neatly of dried mud bricks and wooden three by two-inch roofing supports with corrugated iron over the top. These had been built before I arrived and were used to teach the students whilst they were at the college. My input here was minimal, but a new batch of day-old chicks had arrived, and I would usually do an evening check on the heat lamps etc. It was normal to see the occasional rat, par for the course with poultry. I had heard said that if you see one rat you can be sure that there are another dozen or so just around the corner. Well, I hadn't paid such talk much attention, so I was not prepared for what was to follow. Delayed one night beyond dusk and into darkness, I arrived at the chicken houses, torch in hand on a dark night with only the reddish glow of the heat lamps. As I opened the door to check the new arrivals, I swung my torch up to the rafters, which were alive with white teeth and beady eyes. One of them must have squeaked, 'Panic!' and they all did just that, bumping over themselves in motorway-like collisions, off the rafters and onto the floor and, more pertinently to this story, onto me. I felt them hit my head and shoulders and scrabble for a foothold as they slid down my T-shirt, shorts and bare legs. Thankfully, no foothold presented itself, especially on my legs! The possible consequences make me shudder even now. My exit was on the sharpish side of fast. I was shaking uncontrollably and in a cold sweat. Give me a short-sighted buffalo any day!

Our time in Lesotho was coming to an end – Morai and I had been working together more closely and part of my job had been to hand over to a Basotho replacement. Morai couldn't have been a better person for me; we got on well and he was later to visit us in England. We had been privileged to meet a wide range of people in very different circumstances – we had travelled a lot, both for work and pleasure and we had started our own family. We had gone some way towards accommodating some fairly different perspectives in our own lives by concentrating on what we shared rather than what we didn't, and it is just possible, but only just, that we might have contributed something to our host community.

Now, having swapped our return flights home for two wrecked Land Rovers, we had to travel some six thousand miles with a six-month-old baby back to England.

Chapter 22
North Through Newly Independent Africa

The Land Rover we had purchased from the insurance company had not one body panel worth saving, so it was clear we needed to scratch together whatever money we could and go and buy a shell. One of the NGOs (Non-Government Organisations) in Lesotho had just the thing, an old, long wheel base, windowed safari vehicle whose engine and gear box had reached retirement age. It was to be sold via closed tender bid so (not for the last time) we counted out what we had and put in our bid (it was all that we had, and it proved to be enough). Removing the body from the new acquisition was simple mechanics and muscle power, and with a few new drill holes to compensate for the slightly bent chassis of the younger vehicle, we lifted and persuaded the replacement body into position. I had guessed the slight bend in the chassis was not going to be significant and so it proved. The resultant vehicle had an extra fuel tank, spare springs, starter motor, alternator and battery, seats right through and windows. We couldn't have asked for a better vehicle. Our learning curve had been pretty steep together but perhaps the one most important thing that I learnt was that Gilly was up for the adventure. I think I took it for granted then but looking back, so much of what we have done together couldn't have been done if either of us had been too concerned about the "What's going to happen if…?" Neither of us has ever been too concerned about tomorrow; today is the day etc. and tomorrow will look after itself, it's another world.

One thing we needed was a carnet. If things were to go wrong in mid-journey and we had to sell the vehicle, then the carnet would provide a cash guarantee to the importing government, which would be the equivalent value of the import duty that would be paid to the relevant state exchequer. In order to cover all eventualities, this was about three times the value of the vehicle, at that time, about twelve thousand pounds. My parents offered their house as surety (which represented all that they had worked for since the war). I pointed out to my dad that it was not beyond the bounds of possibility that it might be called on, but he just said, 'Well, make sure it isn't,' and that was it. My parents were to help us in a similar way some years later when we started farming, without which that similarly would not have happened. Given what they had been through, they could have been forgiven for pressuring us to settle down in a secure nine-to-five, gold watch on retirement type of job with gnomes in the garden etc. but I think they knew that it would be like a prison for me and they never mentioned it. It was important for them that I was "making a mark – colouring the canvas and all that." I am deeply grateful to them for that support. In response, neither Gilly nor I have ever been guilty of worrying whether we spilt a bit of paint in filling the canvas or not. Our lives have not been meticulously planned – we have been responsive to opportunities – more "Why not?" than "Why?"

We drove away from Thaba Khupa with Daniel, our first son, in the middle front seat between us, two hitch-hiking friends plus rucksacks in the back and a row of yellow plastic water carrying bottles hanging above the windows on the gutter line of our rebuilt vehicle. The home-made woven Moses basket was neatly wedged between the spare fuel tank and the always present nappy bucket; I think we knew that whatever was in front of us in the long term would be different from that which we were leaving. A child in tow certainly changes the equations, as do ageing parents, partner commitments and the need for housing and income enough to keep the rain out and the food on the table. But for now, our priority was our return journey. The intention was to drive up through Central Africa, across to the east coast, through the sisal growing lands of Malawi and Julius Nyerere's socialist Tanzania, then up to Kenya where we hoped to spend three to four weeks in the country of Gilly's childhood. From there we intended to either drive north through Sudan, then Egypt and across the Mediterranean and home via Turkey and Istanbul, or to take one of the fortnightly sailings on the Union Castle Line bound from Mombasa's Kilindini Harbour across the northern part of the Indian Ocean to Karachi and Pakistan. This trip was regular, reliable and relatively cheap, dependent largely on the demands of a very significant Indian population which had settled around Eastern Central Africa, making up the bulk of the trading community. At that time, it was unusual to find a hardware store or a clothes shop in the countries that we went through that wasn't owned by someone from the Indian subcontinent. As such and as a community, they were largely resented by the African population, perhaps in the way that the Jewish community was resented in areas of Europe in the nineteenth century and earlier. Uganda was in the grip of a madman, Idi Amin, who was the president and had all the qualities necessary for a career as a sadistic, demented clown but without being the slightest bit funny. As such Uganda was out of bounds for us with a small infant.

But Kenya was a long way off. The beginnings of our journey were similar to the earlier trips we had made by rail, except that we were driving. First to cross were the dusty, parched farming lands of the Boer-dominated and aptly named Orange Free State. We were very short of disposable cash, so stocked up with milk powder, maize porridge and fruit whenever we could. One of these places was a farm supply and hardware shop within South

Africa before going on into Botswana. Our Land Rover was obviously from Lesotho due to its number plates and obviously going north because of its paraphernalia and luggage. Within the shop was an elderly white South African man who may have overheard our conversation; he bought a torch, gave it to us, wished us good luck and left. It didn't cost him a lot and we might not have needed it but as a kind gesture, I remember it still, along with others. Kindness has its own luminescence. The entire white South African population was limited in its travel options due to the racist nature of its minority government and international sanctions. Many did not support the political system that entrapped them and the black majority population. As with too many political systems, they served the interest primarily of the politically powerful and not the majority population.

On we went into northern Botswana, past the Okavango swamps and back to the Chobe Game Reserve to take another look at those buffalo! Chobe had got onto the front pages of most of the broadsheet newspapers a year or two previously, thanks to the shenanigans of the self-indulgent rat pack members Elizabeth Taylor and Richard Burton. They had chosen Chobe's main game lodge as the site for their second marriage to each other. Whatever, when we got to the main entrance, we were met by a slightly incredulous guard. Yes, it was open, but we were the first people to visit for several days due to the political situation. This was a euphemism for the political anarchy and gun law that dominated affairs in the Caprivi Strip to the south and east of the Chobe Game Lodge, bordering as it did on Botswana, Zambia, Southern Rhodesia and Angola.

We took this as a good omen in that the animals that we hoped to see would not have been frightened away from the access routes, but were soon remembering, "Be careful of what you wish for." Within twenty minutes, we were slowly approaching a large group of amiable-looking grazing elephants, one eye on us and the other on the next mouthful of leaves, great grey ears gently twitching in an effort to move the insect nuisance. There was not an obvious route around them, so we stopped to allow them time to move on. The road was dusty and dry with occasional deep sand areas where recent rains had washed mini sand dunes into the road in the same way that wind blows snow in the northern climates. It was on top of one of these mini sand dunes that we had stopped, with the engine turned off so as not to disturb these gentle giants. As a precaution, I slipped out of my driving seat to turn the freewheeling hubs on the front wheels to "drive" so engaging four-wheel drive should we need it. Most things I had checked and double checked for efficacy, but freewheeling hubs were always going to be difficult to check and I hadn't. It soon became apparent that we had inadvertently positioned ourselves between a large female elephant and her baby, hidden in the bushes behind us. Now, forget the image of a smiling "Dumbo" with pink frills attached. This mother wasn't smiling and had no frills as she lumbered menacingly to Gilly's side of the Land Rover, ears flapping, trunk skywards and trumpeting in defiance. Her intentions were obvious, and she gained pace as she approached the vehicle. I hurriedly turned on the engine and engaged the gears for a quick exit. Hearing the elephants trumpeting, Danny decided it was a good time to cry, which Gilly countered with a deftly delivered milk bottle; the sound of splintering ball bearings, as the freewheeling hubs metamorphosed from ingenious technology to useless scrap, was a worrying addition to what was already a tricky situation. Someone shot a prayer up to the Almighty. The armour-clad, clearly irritated matriarch, ears still flapping madly, slithered to a halt, took several steps back to paw the ground and prepared for the real assault. On her second approach, she must have been very close, since looking across Danny past Gilly, I couldn't see the top of the approaching animal. Unable to move the vehicle with back wheels grinding into soft sand, I started to open the door on my driving side, intending to run at the elephant, arms waving and shouting, 'Shoo!' hoping that surprise would be on my side and she might spare the Land Rover and its contents. Beyond that, I didn't think, nor did I need to as she backed off with a last trumpeted utterance, an angry shake of her head and headed into the bush, baby and the rest of the herd in tow – perhaps there was a God after all! Apparently, elephants don't flap their ears when they really mean business!

Our two hitch-hikers and I earned our keep by pushing the stranded vehicle off the sand dune whilst Gilly kept the wheels turning. We stayed by the river, kept moving and approached Elizabeth Taylor and Richard Burton's patronised grand African lodge unconventionally across the lawns, past an unsurprised African groundsman, across the raised flower beds and down the small stone retaining wall. The rest of the day seemed a bit tame by comparison but did include a large amount of animal photography from afar, no other visitors and a magnificent African sunset. For once, we slept in accommodation rather than our tent. It was a sensible choice as the next day we were to meet up with the most dangerous of all African horrors in the form of a tanked up, angry, red eyed, AK-47-toting, hatless soldier who none too politely enquired of us whether we had realised that we had just run over his beret.

It all happened as we drove away from Chobe on the northern border of what was then Southern Rhodesia, eastwards on the way up to the Victoria Falls and the Zambezi. The Caprivi Strip is an unlikely panhandle protrusion of land belonging to Namibia and inherited during colonial times from the German colony of South West Africa. It borders Zambia and Angola to the north, Zimbabwe to the east, Botswana to the south and Namibia to the west. It was "given" to the Germans along with a small island in the North Sea in the nineteenth century by the colonising and imperialist British in exchange for the Germans giving up a claim to Zanzibar. The German Chancellor, Leo von Caprivi, after whom the strip is named, thought that access to the Zambezi, which the strip had provided, would give the Germans a water route linkup between its colonial territory of South West Africa (now Namibia) and its territories in East Africa. Sadly, for Herr

Leo von Caprivi, he forgot the slight problem of the world's biggest waterfall only some fifty or so miles downstream! This is a bit like somebody buying a house in Nottingham with sea views, if only Lincolnshire wasn't in the way! Incompetence or straightforward stupidity clearly isn't the prerogative only of some present-day politicians; it's always been there. Perhaps that gives us grounds for optimism?

Well, in front of us, perhaps one mile away, we could see a dust cloud which meant that there was another vehicle. After a while the dust seemed to have settled and a vehicle materialised. As we drew level with this vehicle, it was clear that it was full of soldiers, though whether they were involved with the Angolan Civil War, the fight against white minority rule in Rhodesia as it then was, or the lesser-known struggle for independence for Caprivi itself was not clear. All that really mattered was that our red-eyed, slurring interrogator had a gun and we were conspicuously white and had apparently run over his beret. This was a touchy situation and I thought it better not to offer him my dirty white tennis hat in compensation. Trying very hard to ditch any of the South African burr that my accent had picked up in the last two years, I apologised as profusely as I could for inadvertently running over his beret. In time he began to calm down and became slightly less threatening. Gilly was able to point out that our car had Lesotho number plates and yes, we had been working in Lesotho to help gain greater independence from the apartheid nationalist South Africans and that we were unlikely to be imperialists white spies with a six-month-old baby in tow. We were eventually allowed to continue and drove extremely carefully, lest we squash any other berets, up to the Zambian border post at Victoria Falls and comparative safety.

From Zambia, which proved comfortably boring by comparison, we headed up towards Malawi with its vast inland sea. Border posts always seem to present a problem, possibly because the opportunity for golden handshakes was so difficult to resist when the border guards were poor and many of the travellers massively wealthy by comparison. We were allowed in fairly quickly once the guards had checked through our luggage as far as the nappy bucket (disposable nappies were a luxury beyond our budget). There is something fundamentally final and convincing about a bucket full of soiled nappies! Gilly had anticipated the need for a long dress, and I was encouraged to swap my shorts for trousers. It was the first and last time my knees have been seen as a potentially corrupting influence! By this time, we had said goodbye to our hitch-hiking friends in Zambia so were careful not to park on any sand dunes. They had decided that they had had enough excitement and would continue the journey by train! What they missed, however, was Lake Malawi.

We drove up through Malawi uneventfully, past the comical baobab trees rising awkwardly above the wafting elephant grass, stretched out villages with old men sat in whatever shade they could find, watching whatever moved in their patch of this world. Women everywhere carried water pots or sacks of vegetables on their heads, moving slowly with duck-footed dignity and resignation written on their faces. For them, tomorrow was not another world; it would be much the same as today. Chickens pecked in the dust and played their name game with the passing vehicles. We joined Lake Malawi at Chiweta, a small market town two thirds of the way up the western side of this southernmost African rift valley lake. The ninth largest lake in the world, it has the most species of fish of any lake anywhere and from where we were, it might have been the Indian Ocean in that we could not see land on the other side. Livingstone named this lake "The Lake of the Stars" in recognition of the twinkling lanterns of the night-time fishermen in their boats.

Whilst at a market, we bought kapenta, a sort of dried sardine, from a pile standing three feet high and conical with a base ten feet across. There must have been a million and more of the dried, crispy, pungent smelling, shiny, tiny, grey fish in this pile alone. There were several others. Kapenta is an iron-rich source of protein purported to help prevent prostate cancer. Like its distant cousin the snail in France, you must know how to serve it. We didn't and it tasted like most other iron-rich medicines with a salty exterior, but this one was still in its tinfoil wrapping. We struggled through a plateful and had to admit defeat and gave the rest away to an enigmatic gentleman called Ali.

We met Ali whilst camping by Lake Malawi. Danny's wicker basket was suspended from a thorn tree above white sand surrounded by squares of white cotton drying nappies, like some war time aerial navigation aid. After the dust, the border post, the bantering, the flattened beret discussions and the elephant experience, this seemed several rungs up the ladder to heaven. At this stage we were happy to surrender some excitement for a bit of tranquillity. Ali had materialised as if he were a ghost and was sitting patiently some twenty yards away by the lake on a tree stump. His legs were crossed; he had a white skull cap, large white teeth with prominent gaps, and his face was dark, tanned leather creased by blackened scars of years past. His robe of faded blue and white was well worn and lent an air of mysticism to him. We hadn't seen him arrive and he made no noise, but he did respond to a wave. He spoke English well but in an almost over-correct way; his enunciation was slow and elaborate. There was something about this man that keeps his image crisp in my album of memories, whilst others fade and blend under the ruthless passage of time. It turned out that he just wanted to hold our six-month-old, blonde, blue-eyed son, which he did gently and caringly for ten or so minutes. It transpired that he was a conscientious Muslim who lived locally. Yes, he would be grateful to accept as a gift our surplus to requirement kapenta (although I would have preferred to have given him something that we attached more value too, as such, the gift seemed somehow diminished from my view point). In time, he moved off towards the shimmering, inland sea that was Lake Malawi. In my mind's eye, he has never been far away, yet we were together for a very short time some forty years ago. What his story was, I shall never know, but there was a haunting melancholy behind his smile as he held our son, and it etches its way into my dreamworld.

The Tunduma border post is on the way into Tanzania and it had an interesting slant to the usual in that one of the border guards was medically trained as part of Julius Nyerere's revolutionary socialist barefoot doctor initiative. He was quite insistent that Danny should have had a particular vaccination before entering Tanzania. Gilly had checked what was necessary and had been told in Lesotho that no, such a vaccine was not for babies. Like arguing theology with a fundamentalist, the discussion aspect pretty soon gave way to a pantomime "Oh, yes he does", and "Oh, no he doesn't" routine. Sensing my frustration, Gilly packed me off to the car and smooth-talked her way to reason.

About an hour later, we entered Tanzania, leaving behind a very buttered up border guard. In front of me, although I didn't know it then, would be forty years of, 'Go and sit down over there whilst I talk reason.' I felt then and still feel now that it has much more to do with my being six feet tall, male and not lightly built and Gilly being a slimline, smiling female who listens well and nods at the right times!

Whilst in Tanzania, we heard that this country had closed her borders with neighbouring Kenya, on account of a different stand taken against the other member of the East African Alliance, Uganda. We spent a long time in various offices in Dar es Salaam before securing a piece of paper with impressive looking stamps on it which should see us into Kenya. As a precaution, we drove up to the little used border post at Namanga. If there was a closed border initiative, then the man on the front line didn't know about it and we felt it expedient not to inform him. Gilly soon established common ground with him, having lived for some years with her missionary parents close to where he was born. The piece of heavily stamped paper stayed in our bag and it turned out to be the easiest border post to negotiate, despite our earlier concerns. We had been cautioned by many on the risks of travelling with a six-month-old baby and in retrospect, I guess it may have been a bit reckless if things had gone wrong. In practice, they didn't, due not a little to Gilly's meticulous hygiene routine with boiled water and insect protection. Every time we stopped a fire was made, water was boiled then cooled, nappies washed and a cool place safe from insects and other predators found for the Moses basket and our infant son. Temperature control was a sizeable issue as our double tent was limited in its ventilation potential and air conditioning remained for us just a bit of modern jargon, a bit like mobile phones - not for us, after our time. We travelled around Kenya, visiting places and contacts that Gilly had, through her family connections there. We stayed a few nights just beneath the escarpment of the Great Rift Valley, on a farm now owned by a black Kenyan political mover and shaker, but managed by a white English settler, whose own farm had foundered partly due to natural circumstances that threatened new farming ventures wherever in the world one is, and partly to the changed political situation triggered by independence in December 1963.

The colonial policy that encouraged British ex-soldiers and others to migrate to Kenya and help build up a vibrant agricultural sector pre-independence changed radically in the early nineteen sixties. Many of the white-owned farms were taken over, either for distribution to the indigenous people for them to set up small farms, or simply to change one elite group based largely on colour for another elite group based largely on political clout. Farming the world over is dependent on so many circumstances beyond the control of the individual, such as weather, political interests, financial costs and the whims of a fickle currency-driven international marketplace. The things within our control such as fertility, pest control, timing of operations and storage dominate our lives; the rest by and large is a gamble. To survive such a world needs a particular personality, more like the Chinese willow than the English oak, more like a fleet-footed scrum half than a sturdy prop forward. In the managed agricultural climate of Europe, with its subsidy-led farming, there is little room for experimentation with new ideas and new crops, but in a short time in Kenya we were to see sheepskin processing, flower production for export, aromatic oils, safari park initiatives and fishing lakes as well as more traditional tea and coffee growing, maize production and cattle grazing.

We slept gratefully in proper beds and were generously pampered with various tropical fruits and some very civilised evenings sat on a veranda whilst listening to the incomparable sounds of the African bush as the sun dropped like a stone and it was suddenly night time.

Whilst travelling, we saw flamingos by the thousand on the mineral-rich salt flats of Lake Naivasha and elephants systematically leaning on fence posts to allow their young to move across manmade fence lines. We assisted with the dipping of longhorn Zebu African cows to protect against the myriad of external parasites intent on a blood fest from their bovine hosts. We swam in the gently massaging waves of the Indian Ocean at Diani Beach. Everywhere, people of all colours and combinations were generous with their hospitality and assistance. We visited the village of Dol Dol, where Gilly's father had last worked to establish a church in the dioceses of Mount Kenya, bending low to enter the mud and wattle manyattas (houses) of the Dorobo tribe (a sub-group within the Maasai tribe). We sat in virtual darkness until our eyes became accustomed to the sudden respite from the midday tropical sun. There we were greeted traditionally by a head bowed, double handshake from the bead-adorned matriarch mother of Peter Sem Olé Matunge, a childhood friend of Gilly's who was at that moment in time studying in Nairobi (my own culture change from suburban England was dramatic enough but Peter Sem's surely was as if on another planet). We left with jars of wild honey and sacks full of humility.

Chapter 23
Back to Britain

Throughout the four fascinating weeks in Kenya, we were aware of a looming problem. Where did we go to from here? The Ugandan border was closed and, in any case, too dangerous; similarly, the roads north to Ethiopia and Sudan via Marsabit were regarded as bandit (shifta) country and though it was tempting to try, baby considerations soon dissuaded us. The best route did seem to be to sail from Mombasa across the Indian Ocean to Karachi in Pakistan. We had heard rumours and rumours of rumours that this service had been discontinued, due to all the Ugandan Asian population having moved or been moved as an initiative of the so-called self-proclaimed King of Scotland - Idi Amin, who was at that stage president of Uganda and a tyrant. This proved to be the case. So, we had a problem and could ill-afford to prevaricate much longer as our fairly meagre financial resources were rattling around at the bottom of the money tin. The temptation to stay and try to carve out a living in Kenya was strong but we were the wrong colour at the wrong time and wider family pressures were tugging.

Whilst in Nairobi, I made a cold call on an Indian businessman who exported strawberries to the UK by plane. Yes, he said. He could carry us, Land Rover and all, but it would cost some four times what we had available! "Ah," he said. "Well, in that case I could carry you on a standby for a quarter of the price." I asked what "standby" meant and he told me that if we turned up at ten to five that afternoon, we and the Land Rover would be on the plane by five! I was learning some vital lessons which were to stand us in good stead for our farming years ahead. Never pay the first price! And ask, they can always say no!

As it happens, we had to return to Mombasa, so we kept the strawberry plane option up our metaphorical sleeves. The following Sunday I took a boat taxi around Kilindini Harbour, having despaired of getting any definitive answers from the shipping offices in the town, who didn't seem to have much idea which ships were in dock and what their onward details were. I was hoping to locate a ship bound for Karachi by the direct route of knocking on the hull and asking the crew where they were going. This proved to be so simple I don't know why I hadn't thought of it before or why so many people had said that that such an approach was not practical. Perhaps they confused the word practical for conventional? Karachi proved to be an unlikely possibility, but the first mate on a Chinese cattle boat said that he was bound for Oman early in the week and if I was able to masquerade as a veterinary trained presence on the ship, we would be most welcome. He would have to check with the captain who was at present in church in Mombasa but yes, he was sure it would be OK. I returned to base and to Gilly, quite sure that our problem was solved, to be met with the news that a missionary from Zaire had just arrived at the house in which we were staying, and his particular job was to purchase a vehicle for his mission station. This also sounded interesting, and as a downer on the Chinese cattle boat option, the only map we could find of Oman showed no roads at all going north!

The missionary was in a hurry; he had a fixed amount of money which would be enough for a new two-wheel drive pickup or our Land Rover with all its spares etc. I explained the necessity of our exporting the vehicle, the carnet and my parents having stood surety etc. and we hatched up a plan.

I was to drive the Land Rover to Embakasi Airport in Nairobi and take the vehicle plus myself through customs. He would meet me in no man's land on the other side of the customs desk and swap the cash for the car. He was quite sure that getting the vehicle into Zaire and off the plane at the other end would not present a problem; God, after all, he assured me, would be on his side. I didn't share his experience of either the Zairean customs routine or God, so I just concentrated on my part in the arrangement.

Within three days, we had executed the plan; I had driven through customs with the Land Rover and walked back through the same office some twenty minutes later with a bundle of dollars and a banker's draft from the purchasing mission via a Dutch charity in my back pocket. No eyebrows were raised, no questions were asked. By the end of the week, we were on a plane to London Heathrow, dropping thirty-three thousand feet through solid cloud onto an England drenched by September rain, with headlights needed in the hammering mid-afternoon downpour.

Danny, in his wasp-like crawling suit, slept not a wink but neither did he cry. He had become content with all the activity and sitting between the two of us. He was to miss the journeying, the sunset camping and the debatable thrill of not knowing what the next hour held, never mind the next day. Throughout my adult life I have always wondered at the promise made by pension companies and shiny suited, silver-tongued insurance salesmen wanting to trade their wares by appealing to an assumed desire for a secure tomorrow. If that what's wanted, then we would all be best off buying a comfortable bed and walking on the pavement!

We blinked our way through a busy Heathrow and introduced the next generation to his grandparents and then we slept. I woke up at Bristol and it was still raining. I slept again and dreamt I was drowning.

Chapter 24
A Different Sort of Journey

For the next year, we worked on a farm near Cirencester which belonged to the father-in-law of a friend of mine who was managing the unit but wanted to move to Devon and sail his own boat. We were not clear whether we were to work as shepherd, shepherding the sheep, or to manage the farm, but we ended up with the sheep. This was just as well, as the farm managing would have required me to enjoy the dubious delights of a weekly pheasant shoot for as long as massacring these beautiful but rather stupid birds was in season! Why this sport (if it can be called such – I have always thought that sport required one to sweat!) was, and is, so popular I have no idea, but I am guessing Freud would have had an opinion based more on the size of the gun than the taste of the bird.

This was to be my first full year on any one farm, and it wasn't a bad one to start on. Having bought our plane tickets from Kenya to London we were again reduced to rock bottom finances so were in an excellent position to put into practice what I had been encouraging my Basuto students to do, that is whatever you earn, spend less. It really was that simple. Gilly was the world's best at making do and mending. We had blackberry and apple crumble for the cost of the flour, home produced eggs, and milk from our British Alpine goat; it always tasted of whatever she had been eating so if you like wild garlic flavoured milk, you know what to do! We did our best to keep her away from aromatic plants, but with little success. Emily, for that was her name, was the most ambitious goat we have ever had and would rock on her heels and land on a sixpence four feet above where she started. It was to be her downfall. One day she was happily hopskippitying over barbed wire fences – not a good idea with an udder full of milk! She tore one of her teats so badly that the tear punctured the teat canal. The flesh wound healed but thereafter she effectively had two milk supply points on the affected quarter (shouldn't it be called a half?). It was an inconvenience we lived with as long as we milked her twice a day and were generous with the Elastoplast. Commercially she would have become dog meat, but you can't talk to or laugh at a can of dog meat, so she stayed with us.

We were surrounded by kindly generous people who shared the produce of their gardens, pointed us towards the best mushroom patches and turned a blind eye to my butchering of a very fat young ewe who had met death before her time in the sun on her back after rain and kicked her last as I ran across the field to up right her again. I like to think that she enjoyed the sun on her tum as I do, but I fancy breathing had become a tad difficult. A sixty-kilo ewe provides about twenty-five kilos of good meat, and that fed a small family like ours for a couple of months or more! Beer was made in buckets from yeast, sugar, hops and barley bought cheaply as a concentrate and wine from whatever we could find that contained natural sugars and a bit of colour. Most of the hedgerow fruits were OK but potato wine was a taste we never quite warmed to.

We went through the shepherding year with the help of the sturdy brilliance of an old farm Collie dog called Tim, despite the addition of our own newly acquired, tri-coloured maniac who occasionally responded to hearing his name, "Sweep". To his credit, Sweep wanted only one thing from life and that was to chase sheep. 'Get away', 'Come by', 'Get on back', 'Steady', 'Down' and 'Walk on' all meant the same thing to him; in his ears he heard 'Chase.' The Welshman who supplied him to us said that he was part trained and so he was; he knew the difference between chase and kill.

I inherited a Honda two-wheel XL, four-stroke motorbike from my friend and predecessor, David, and used it to get quickly around the farm, which was close to one thousand acres so walking would have presented problems. I still use the same sort of two-wheel bike now; it saves time and visiting children think it's the best thing since Disney World. On a dull December day, a burn up around the farm usually does the trick for me, although I still don't admit to it not being work.

Over the years I guess we have changed motorbikes every four and dogs every eight. Most of the dogs we have had liked travelling around on the petrol tank, which has in the past led to some worried looks from passing motorists, as the Collie dogs seem to like to try to sit as upright as possible in order to see over the hedges, and therefore in front of me. I must lean forwards and sideways to look over their shoulders. One day in a hurry to get out to the stock, Sweep tearing along by the front wheel like the lunatic that he was and Tim padding along gently fifty metres behind, the crazy hound suddenly leapt across in front of the bike, straight under the front wheel and then the back. I kept upright for just about for fifteen yards then crashed off the track and into the hedge. I was hurt but not seriously; the bike no longer had brake or clutch levers (someone could have made a good business selling those to me over the years) and the handlebar was bent. My main concern though was for the dog; I thought I might have killed him. I needn't have bothered; he was off on his way to the sheep without a backwards glance. On another day, he could not be found at the end of the day - eventually I phoned the police and Gilly checked with all the neighbours. Darkness arrived and still no dog. I reluctantly had to accept that he had probably been run over on the busy Swindon to Cirencester road, trying his swerve in front trick with an eight-wheeled truck. I was saddened because despite his lunatic disposition, he was loyal and comical in a canine sort of way, wry smile rather than laugh out loud.

On my rounds the next morning, I checked by a group of young ewes in an eighty-acre field of clover - no sheep. Unusual, in clover, sheep usually just eat what's immediately around them and fall into a satisfied sleep, like many farmers I have known after their Sunday lunch. Then in the far corner up against the hedge, I saw them; no casualties but sheep all neatly packed like fish fingers in a frying pan with an exhausted dog holding them up. If the dog could have spoken, it would have asked me where the hell I had been all night. Whether it was the conversation that we had as we returned to the farm or the training trick, I was taught by the local policeman I am not sure, but from then on, Sweep became nearly useful.

The training trick was this. Tie the dog to sixty metres of baler twine. Send him off around the sheep. At twenty metres ask him politely to lie down. Repeat this at forty metres with a little more urgency. At fifty metres scream at him with short consonant rich expletives and at sixty metres pull on the string sharply. I did it twice and after the second time, he always lay down with the gentlest of requests, but I still needed the expletives. That, like the sherry, became a habit.

On large farms like the one I was on, it was normal for all jobs to be specific. I shepherded the sheep, the cowman looked after the cows and the tractor driver operated the field machinery etc. This farm was slightly less regimented than others, but nevertheless roles were jealously guarded, so eyebrows were raised when I was asked to do some post-harvest cultivations following on from a straw burn. This was a minimal cultivation farm which operated on a minimum ploughing policy, to protect the shallow Cotswold brash soil and reduce soil disturbance. Stubbles and straw, which at that time had a low cash value, were removed by fire. We all queued up for that job; in our defence, global warming was not a hot topic and the thrill of a well-controlled fire ripping across a hundred-acre field of wheat stubbles leaving behind a black scorched earth was primal.

Back to my post-burning cultivations – the contractor's direct drill was due in on Monday and it was Friday. Robert Henley, the owner of the farm, had asked me if I could, in his words, "Skip across the field and give it a go" and as was my habit, I said yes and then worked out how to accommodate our proposed London trip to attend the wedding of my hitch-hiking Zambian days buddy, Barbara Lou.

No problem, my tractor driver neighbour Cyril reluctantly allocated me the oldest, worst machine, one that he judged I could do the least damage to, hung on the cultivator and lectured me on possible mishaps. This was Friday evening. I had reckoned that with an early start at three o'clock on the Saturday morning, I could do the field, have breakfast and still make the wedding. So, at three sharp, I was in the yard; it was black as pitch. Tractor and cultivator were parked ready. Unfortunately, Cyril had omitted to tell me to remove the support stand from the cultivator, which protruded some six feet up from the back of the machine. When you are in an unfamiliar machine with levers at every level and the tractor driver's request not to 'bugger up his machine' is ringing in your ears, something is bound to go wrong. As I gently eased the cultivator off the ground with the tractor hydraulics, I didn't see the approaching steel support. The explosive noise as the back window shattered into thousands of tiny glass fragments was enough to have woken Cyril up but to my relief it didn't. I turned the tractor off and free-wheeled past his window out into the field and completed the job before eight o'clock. The tractor, inside and out, and the driver, were a uniform burnt charcoal black in colour. I parked discreetly, showered and ate breakfast and headed off to London in the hope that time would lend proportion to my predicament. We were late for the wedding, the direct drilling did get done on Monday and the window hardly got a mention, though thankfully I was not asked to do any more tractor driving!

Gilly's background in Kenya as the child of missionary parents was certainly different from the norm, so she had had to make some pretty large adjustments in our relatively short time together – I guess we both had. One day that stands out was a rare sunny Saturday afternoon in April when lambing was nearly at an end. Robert and Mary Henley had invited several people up to the farmhouse to watch the Grand National horse race. The assembled company included neighbours Colin and Lindsey Okwell. Colin was a very suave opera singer and Lindsey a talented painter predominantly of race horses. We were all allocated horses and sat in front of the TV whilst the sun was blocked out by pulled curtains and the horses laboured around the four miles of Aintree's sodden turf. Poor Gilly's reaction was similar to twenty years later whilst we sat through a bull fight in Granada, Spain – pained incredulity! Her exposure to such things hitherto amounted to watching the Oxford versus Cambridge boat race once a year to satisfy her father who had rowed in it nearly half a century before. This was a new world.

Had we been able to find a way into farming on our own account at that time, we would have done so but without wealthy, benevolent relatives it seemed unlikely. There was little hope of tenanting, even on the old County Council's smallholding scheme, which was heavily oversubscribed and remarkably demanding in terms of working capital requirements. We, however, were expecting child number two after one year at Cirencester and needed a bigger house than the tiny thatched cottage with its "mattress on the floor" bed. The spiral staircase was not conducive to furniture passage and Gilly had got wind of the fact that other people were washing clothes in something other than old copper boilers which we used. We had, in any event, only committed ourselves for one year.

Chapter 25
Stowford Farm

Our next move was to Devon, for romantic rather than practical reasons, it was the county where Gilly and I had first met. I was lucky to be offered a teaching job at the Devon County College at Bicton and a farm management job on a small farm on the edge of Dartmoor owned by the Royal Agricultural Society of England. This had been given to them by a wealthy, benevolent, oddball lady, daughter of a Boston tea-importing family. This job had to combine practical farming, establishment of a sheep flock and beef cattle herd, financial viability and a strong educational commitment to satisfy the requirements of the benefactress. We opted for the second farm management rather than the teaching although I remained on good terms with the people I had met at the college. I was in any case reluctant to return to teaching lest I choked on the humble pie that I might have been asked to eat at Wolverhampton Technical Teachers college should I have been required to visit. The fact that we were offered the farming job in the first place had a lot to do with the agricultural director of the Royal Agricultural Society, George Jackson. George was a dynamo of a man who had a clear idea of what he wanted and knew better than most how to get things done. I warmed to him immediately and took him on trust when he said that he could persuade his committee to offer us the job. He did and we enjoyed five years with him as our mentor, guide and later, friend.

George was not everybody's cup of tea; he had a direct Yorkshire manner and a steely determination to have his own way, thinly disguised behind a beguiling broad smile and affected bonhomie. He had committees made up largely of the landed, kindly and soft-skinned gentry either eating out of his outstretched hand or whimpering ineffectually in their inability to oppose him. George was the only person I have ever seen dominate a meeting from the floor and end up with the chairman, secretary, treasurer and ninety per cent of the cushion warmers all with opposing views going away each feeling that they had won their corner, but in fact he might as well have written up the minutes before the agenda had been typed! George insisted upon and therefore taught me the essential art of forward budgeting.

We moved to Stowford Farm the same week as our second son was born at the Querns Maternity Unit in Cirencester. Lindsey Okwell took Gilly under her wing and gave her caring support while I chugged up and down the A38 via Exeter with accumulated chattels, mostly gained from auction house sales. Ben arrived safely and all four of us moved into a wing of the rambling Stowford house. The benefactress and previous owner moved out to live elsewhere, leaving behind her long-time companion, Mona Smeaton, who was to become an adopted and very kind great aunt to our two infants.

Mrs Ryan and we overlapped for only three weeks. She was not slow to offer advice and one day called me into her sitting room, woolly stocking-clad feet placed firmly on the ground, sitting in the middle of an ample settee (she was built to match the furniture), a glass of whisky in one hand and a narrow cigar held in the other with pince-nez glasses perched on the end of her nose. 'Now, young Venables,' she started, 'you aren't to become beholden to any of these local farmers and you are to occupy the Stowford pew in Harford Church.' Since this was the front pew beneath the lectern, I thought it unlikely that I would be able to accommodate the second wish and I simply held fire on the first. I fear she would not have approved, as within a couple of years I was, to use her words, totally beholden.

Mrs Ryan had first bought this pretty little edge of the moor farm during the war, intending to revolutionise the local farming practices with the help of her surgeon lieutenant husband. Sadly, he died during the war leaving her to soldier on alone. The act of buying the land had displaced the pre-war tenant who is believed to have taken his own life after losing his farm and livelihood. Louise Ryan was locally held responsible, perhaps a little unfairly. The poor lady should have read the writing on the wall and headed back to the "US of A". Without her stubborn resilience in the face of sabotaged water and electricity supplies, and the devastation of brucellosis (contagious abortion), we would not have had the opportunities that Stowford supplied us with, so I will chink a glass in her honour but in truth I feel a sadness that with all her good intentions and kindness to various children (and those children are now quite elderly), she did not see the need or the joy of working with her neighbouring farmers rather than against them.

George Jackson had joined the RASE as agriculture director in the year before my appointment. Together we had inherited a rather inappropriate beef-fattening system, which depended on purchasing unwanted Friesian bull calves cheaply, rearing them on bucket milk and then feeding them as much rolled barley as possible to fatten them at around five hundred kilos and eighteen months old. Apart from showing it could be done, this had little to commend it above my broiler chicken project in Lesotho. The weaknesses were that it depended on bought in calves and barley – the price of which we could not control and at the end of the day, the beef price was fickle, and currency led. In addition to that, one hundred and twenty calves coming in from different farms meant that we had the potential of the same number of different combinations of infection. Digestive infections due to E. coli and worse still, salmonella were the biggest killers at baby stage. We used to treat all suspect calves with a sulphanilamide bolus (that is a tablet about the size of two Murray Mint sweets stuck together). These we put at the back of the calves' tongues with a specially designed rubber-ended chrome pipe. It was possible to manage without but not if you valued your fingers. On one crisp autumn morning, I had gone along one row of calves, treating the possibly infected ones and was returning up the other side when

I noticed an earlier treated calf on its side, gasping for breath. My fear was that I had somehow pushed the bolus down the trachea (windpipe) rather than the oesophagus but I couldn't feel anything. We had a very bright and helpful student, Helen, working with us at the time, from the Devon College of Agriculture and I sent her chasing off to phone the vet who was engaged on a caesarean but would be with us "directly", meaning within the hour. I guessed this would be to help me bury the calf which was seriously close to giving up the ghost. With nothing to lose, we cut into the contiguous rings of the windpipe with a razor blade and inserted a rubber gas pipe that we normally used for dehorning, into the trachea. The effect was immediate and within minutes the calf was up on its feet, breathing huskily through the dehorning pipe. George, the vet, arrived in time to tell me to cut downwards next time and not across, stitched the wound up and assured me that it wasn't the bolus going down the wrong way but a reflex reaction of the epiglottis, before rushing off to his next crisis. Very good friend as he was and is, George had a bit missing on the encouraging bedside manner bit. The sense of elation when just occasionally things went right was heightened by the fact that it didn't often happen!

The other natural hazard we saddled ourselves with was virus pneumonia. Put a class full of kids into a poorly ventilated classroom and the chances are that little Shawn who had a cough on Monday will have half the class hacking away by Thursday. The same for calves - it doesn't usually kill them, but I am surprised that "Weightwatchers" or "Slimmers Incorporated" hasn't cottoned on and used this as a sure-fire way to shed twenty kilos in as many days. Weight loss was not exactly what we were after. We tried everything: letting the calves out into a yard by day, blowing clean air into the barn with a perforated plastic sausage pipe, taking sections out of the corrugated asbestos roof, but still the coughing continued with the resultant weight loss. We thought of buying them all TVs and feeding them beer and chips as that seemed to work wonders for some of my friends; they put on weight in no time at all. We never conquered the problem completely, although blanket use of antibiotics helped when the policy wasn't so frowned upon. We stuck with the system for two years before abandoning it in favour of a more traditional blue grey suckler herd. There was a lesson here for me; look over the fence; it's likely that the guy who's been doing it for the last fifty years might just have stumbled onto the right idea, since he was still in business.

We eventually secured some blue grey (that is Galloway crossed Shorthorn) cows and made the numbers up with home-reared Hereford cross Friesian heifers. These were all put to a Welsh black bull with the aim of producing small, easily born black calves that would grow well. All fairly straightforward farming logic - it helped that the calves looked a bit like Limousins in the store ring and the auctioneers didn't let honesty get in the way of a good story (no change here). When we came to run these cattle on the moorland adjacent to the farm, the blue greys, having thicker skins, seemed not too bothered by ticks, which the Hereford Friesians at times were seen as easy meat by - the fat little blighters. In this area, ticks and red water fever go hand in hand. We would collect the cattle up on the moor, feed them some very palatable minerals flavoured I guess with the bovine equivalent of sherbet, and whilst they were gorging themselves with their rear ends' outermost, we sprayed them with some wonder chemical to kill the ticks. We had red water fever in some of the cattle but with the ticks removed they recovered and developed immunity to this particular strain of the disease. As the name suggests, the first symptom of the disease is red bloodstained urine; the second is lethargy and the third is death due to kidney failure.

Without the payment of the hill livestock subsidy, it is unlikely that this beef production system would have been economical, but cattle were and are considered to be a conservation-friendly enterprise and successive governments have encouraged the grazing on moorland by beef and sheep. For a long while, there were few limits on numbers or timing and so, quite reasonably, it was seen as an income potential to all farmers who had grazing rights on the moorland as well as some who didn't! This was entirely reasonable as without it, what would the various local commoners' committees have to talk about? Some years later I was to get up close and uncomfortable with this issue.

The Welsh bull we first bought was pedigree and had more barrels to his name than your average aristocrat. Being Welsh, most were consonants, but we called him Heffyn. Not only was he well-endowed where it mattered, he also had a magnificent pair of horns. He was of a much kinder disposition than some other Welsh migrants whom I was later to have dealings with down the years and I don't doubt that he was much better endowed! Heffyn, bless him, used his horns to remove gates. Since he found unlatching them difficult, he simply used his horns as levers as he smashed or removed the gate. Anyone who doubts the driving power of testosterone needs only to meet a Heffyn. One day we received a telephone call from the housekeeper of our neighbours, saying that a bull had just walked past her kitchen window with a gate on his head. She moved on elsewhere soon after that.

We still had Emily the British Alpine goat but by now we had more or less controlled her mountaineering by tethering her to a garden fork. It wasn't testosterone but oestrogen that drove her to pull out the fork one night in November and trot off down into Ivybridge looking for a mate. All we heard was the sound of the chain and garden fork being dragged past our wing of this ancient house and for a moment the house lived up to its ghostly reputation.

Emily never found her mate and was in time replaced with a delightful white British Saanen goat whose milk was closer in taste to that which most of us are used to and whose nature was kind, sweet and gentle. All you young men looking for wives take note – character first, looks second, both if you're lucky and don't worry about the occasional bleat! Daisy was being sold off at Taunton market one Saturday whilst I was up there selling cull ewes. She didn't cost a fortune and as it turns out, pound for pound, she was one of the best value animals we have ever had. The livestock haulier, John Coker, had already left the market, leaving me with no alternative but to carry the goat home in the back of our small hatchback car. She hopped in the boot happily enough and held her head down, gazing out of the front window over my shoulder as we returned home along the A38. She seemed to know that my buying her had saved her from the knacker's yard and she gave me a reassuring little nibble on the ear as we drove back to Ivybridge and the family. No trouble all the way home until I stopped off to collect Gilly from the local school. If Gilly was surprised, she didn't make a thing of it. Daisy however disgraced herself by pressing the panic button when I left the car. Both tanks had been emptied on the front seats and the contents were trodden in. Daisy was to be a family friend for some eight years, just about as long as the car lasted. The odiferous evidence also!

We had another caprine loyal, Smudge the Suffolk cross grey-faced ewe that was a gift to me from the shepherd on Neddy Ayres's farm some five years before. Smudge had taken lodgings with some good friends whilst we were in Lesotho and had produced twin lambs every year since. Now any business that could triple its numbers every year without incurring much cost was worth a closer look at. She was to be the first of a significant sheep flock some years later.

Each year we were at Stowford, we had a different student, each of whom enriched our lives. Helen, who helped with the tracheotomy, soon learnt that a Mars bar in her top pocket was a good idea to keep my energy levels up, although what the politically correct would make now of me feeling around in

Helen's top pocket for a Mars bar whilst she held a ewe for hoof trimming, I don't dare to think.

One fine morning, she walked into our kitchen, Mars bar at the ready and displayed her newly-pierced ears and shiny studs. She was very pleased with herself until Danny, at four years old, trying to be chivalrous, said that he liked her ear tags. I don't think it was quite the compliment she was looking for.

Ben displayed the same candid honesty a year or two later when George Jackson, who smoked as if he owned all the shares in Players tobacco, was visiting. Before he arrived, Gilly would position ashtrays wherever he was likely to go. Neither of us smoked and Ben was aware that the smoke had an irritating effect, particularly on his mum, so as George stomped around, fag in hand, Ben appeared silently from the sitting room with an anti-smoking poster from the Sunday paper (he was three years old at this stage) and laid it out in front of our chain-smoking boss. It was very amusing to us all and hardly surprising that Ben should become a teacher in the fullness of time!

Richard was one of the six students we had and was to succeed us as Farm Manager some years on. As a thank you to mark his time with us, he gave us one of his bitch's puppies. He seemed an intelligent broad-headed dog, so we called him Ruskin after the poet. Byron, Shakespeare and Wordsworth all seemed a bit of a mouthful. Ruskin learnt his trade from Sweep and at six months had more common sense than his teacher had ever had. We entered him for a sheepdog trial in the novice class and had to give up on time faults at the Maltese cross. However, it was enough to take first prize and as that is the only sheepdog trial we have ever done, the average is looking pretty impressive.

The students we had on the farm were all attached to the Bicton College of Agriculture; the Principal was Roger Ferguson, who had offered me the teaching job at the same time as the Stowford farm management job came up. I was to get heavily involved with the college a few years later and indebted to Roger. Altogether we had six students. Helen, Richard, and Paul Hendy who was super competent and conscientiously took notes of every word and action, until he sussed that mostly it was hit and miss at best! Also, Kevin, Andrew and lastly Peter.

Peter was new to machinery, and to farming for that matter. One day I set him up rolling a five-acre field pre-silage making. I warned him to watch the marshy corner and not to take out the fencing; I guessed the job would take a couple of hours. Fifteen minutes later he was in the yard. In this five-acre field there was one drain cover protruding about one foot above the field. Peter was so busy reciting to himself what he must not do when he came to the marshy corner that he had driven straight onto the concrete cover and somehow ended up tractor on one side and roller on the other! I had clearly forgotten this two months later at silage making. I was hauling the cut grass back from the field, the contractor was cutting, and Peter was using the old tractor and buck rake at the clamp. His job was to push and carry the grass up to the clamp and roll it, using the tractor wheels to remove all the air and encourage lactic acid fermentation rather than a butyric one (that is rotting). Filling in time between loads, he turned the tractor around and drove up forwards. The clamp was constructed using large "H" shaped upright steel supports with wooden railway sleepers fitted in between. These steel uprights were about fifteen feet out of the ground and protruded above the last sleeper. If you accelerated hard on the clamp, going forwards with the back wheels digging into the grass and a loaded buck rake, then the compaction effect was exaggerated. There was also a ten thousand to one chance of hanging the front weight-carrying frame of the tractor on one of the steel supports. I returned to find the tractor neatly suspended and at a forty-degree angle to the horizontal, with the back wheels sinking as I watched, into the soft fluffy grass. Peter realised his perilous situation and went off to make me a sweet coffee. Using a jack, chains, the other tractor and another of my nine lives, I coaxed the tractor off the vertical steel support and took comfort in the fact that it could have been worse;

he could have driven the tractor right off the clamp in which case the roll bar wouldn't have done much good!

Being close to Ivybridge, we were an obvious magnet for all the boys from the estate on the other side of the railway line. On holidays and Saturdays there was usually a group of five lads between ten and fifteen years old, hanging around ready for jobs, fun or mischief. Jobs were the best option as far as I was concerned and I had a system that they could stay up at the farm as long as they didn't put a foot wrong but as soon as they did, they were off home for that day but could come back again the next week. This they had no problem with, and I later found that they had a league table of their own making with the top one having been sent home the least times. They were great lads and I looked forward to their company. Two brothers, Jason and Darren, stand out as the most regular. Darren was the youngest and had a photographic memory for detail, but this was not apparently useful at school.

Chapter 26
Arrival of Number Three

The Christmas after we had arrived was memorable for the last really heavy snowfall in the area. Anticipating its arrival, I had put all three hundred Devon and Cornish Longwool sheep and their Finn Dorset crossed daughters (a shearer's nightmare, with wool covering every part of their body except their teeth) in one field with high hedges for maximum wind protection. It began to snow at dusk, so we walked out just to check the sheep were where we had left them. The wind was so strong and the snow so icy that we could not walk straight into it and in any case when we got to the gate the snow had already drifted over it; time to head back inside and keep the stove company. At this stage the house was only a few degrees warmer than it was outside, with its high ceilings and ill-fitting windows. Ben, as a new baby, slept in the handmade wicker Moses basket on top of the freezer to make use of the heat from the cooling unit. Why we needed a freezer at this time isn't clear! The next morning dawned crystal clear with snow drifts of up to twelve feet deep and sculpted extravagantly into elaborate curls around the edges of the fields. The middle areas were blown clear, revealing some very sparse grazing. In the supposedly safe sheep field, the drifts were at their deepest to match the size of the hedges. All the sheep had headed uphill into the north-easterly wind to shelter in the lea of the top hedge. That must have been quite cosy in a sheep sort of way, until the snow began to blow over from the other side and then drop like a wintry white duvet onto their heads.

When we got to the field in the morning, a few children were already there with sledges, and about a third of the flock were picking around at the odd blade of grass showing in the middle of the field. The white humps soon showed us where the other two hundred sheep were, so we organised shovels and bean poles to rescue the flock. There is a very strong reassuring "bounce" to a bean pole as it hits the soft body of a sheep. Soon all the sledgers and several of the parents were engaged in a "save the sheep" operation. It took us three days to locate and free all the sheep and they were all alive, although one had to be shot as its leg had become irreparably dislocated because of an over-zealous rescue. Devon and Cornish Longwool sheep look something like Dougal from the Magic Roundabout and when they have ice balls attached to the ends of their curly locks, it is hard to take them seriously.

Having been somewhat focused on the sheep problems, we had neglected other possible areas of disaster. The fine snow driven by wind had found its way into the roof space of the main house. The first we knew about it was when the damp patches appeared on the wall a week later as the snow melted. It turned out that the building system favoured by the sixteenth century constructors of this old house was a diagonal timber frame filled with rubble stone. If you wanted to design a building style better suited to being destroyed by dry rot, you would be hard pushed. Soon we were growing dry rot fungi from the walls like there was no tomorrow as the latent spores awoke like the Sleeping Beauty after being kissed by the prince's moist lips. This listed house became a building site and we moved around it with hastily erected plastic sheet walls as the builders chased along the wooden substructure to find the extent of the rot.

Whilst using the large, front south-facing rooms to sleep in, we woke one spring morning to see the sheep flock pushing through a gap in the railway fence and walking in a single column along the Plymouth to London line, suicidally towards the

Paddington-bound train due on the hour in ten minutes' time. I ran down the field in my pyjamas and wellingtons trying hard to look and sound like a sheepdog. I doubt the pyjamas and wellies were very convincing, but the bark seemed to do the trick as the sheep uncharacteristically did the sensible thing, turned on their heels and walked back along the track, through the hole in the fence and into the field.

The same track but another field saw a similar thing happen with a three-month-old calf about two years later. This time we didn't see it, but a guy living in the new houses below the railway line did and climbed through the fence onto the track, caught the calf and lay on it whilst a train thundered past then shouted for help until help came.

The weather was often grey at this sea-facing side of Dartmoor, but the days rarely were. Steve Wilcox, who lived in one of the cottages attached to the farm, usually sported shoulder-length, dark, curly hair, a black, over-sized trench coat and large, unlaced, leather boots. He and Peter, his rather pukka bagpipe-playing neighbour and Spanish Vince Alonzo, married to the dramatic and enveloping Isabel, along with Mona Smeaton (our adopted aunt), our student helper and ourselves made up the Stowford community for most of the five years that we were there. We were an eclectic bunch and apart from the odd blip such as sheep poo on Peter's new fitted carpets, we all got along fairly well. Vince was super capable, and Madrid was the poorer without him. One day he was really excited to have secured the contract to remove all the lighting towers in the old Plymouth railway sidings. This he achieved by hiring a steel angle grinder and chopping them down like trees! Isabel, his wife, might have stepped off a flamenco dancing stage and was a serious suffocation risk to anybody about four feet high with her enveloping cuddles.

We had a very amicable advisory committee at Stowford who met every six months, and Gilly spoilt them with a meal and generous hospitality. They thought it might be a good idea if I had a horse to check the cattle on the moor and one of them had "just the thing". "Just the thing" turned out to be a heavy-boned, one-speed ageing cob who took me more time to catch and saddle than I could spare, so we sent him back and bought a three-quarter thoroughbred from Exeter Market named Delmonico. Delmonico was a fine-looking horse, with a crumpled ear, that needed riding two hours a day and then feeding a generous dose of sedative. He was the opposite of his predecessor and seemed intent on punishing me for daring to imagine that he could have been used for cowpunching. I stuck with him for six months but decided then that our ways should part. Until the arrival of this horse, I had always imagined that I could decide and control, if I needed to fall off, how and when I would fall. The final straw for Delmonico came when we were visited by some Anglican sisters from a Malvern convent whom we had first met in Lesotho. The dynamo that was Delmonico took exception to their grey "Florence Nightingale" headgear and took off around a small paddock with me, totally out of control like an unwired cork on the top of a bottle of well-shaken champagne. He eventually got rid of me five feet from a concrete drain cover, head to the grass. I pretended it was part of the act, but by this time, with two children and a third on the way, there was too much at stake. I rode him once more to restore some honour, put him back through Exeter market and have stuck with motorbikes ever since. I realised that I was perhaps a little past my best when I caught myself telling the bike, later, to stand still!

Our third son, Matt, was born three years into our time at Stowford. There was a pattern emerging here which we were empowered to take control of, and we did so! Fifty years previously and in much of the third world today the birth control option was and is absent. The consequences socially in a few years' time, when the developed world has effectively curbed its population growth and the third world has not, will be political dynamite and will dwarf the present crisis of the world's population shifting away from the inhospitable equatorial areas.

Matt just fitted into the routine; we were already busy so another child would not cause too much of a rumpus. Various older people living in the village took an interest in the family and at that time, if you had a problem, it was everybody's problem and as such, was soon solved. Things were to change with the increased suburbanisation of the village.

On a damp and dull winter's day halfway through his second year, Matt contracted meningitis. Gilly was the first to recognise that his symptoms were more than simply a childhood chill. She phoned our GP, Rodger Dadge, and he was up to the house in five minutes. We were lucky to have Rodger as a GP. He didn't hesitate and sent us straight to the Derriford Hospital in Plymouth and phoned through to arrange for us to be met at the door. An associate of his, Ruth Harker, was waiting at the casualty entrance and led us at a run past all the possible snags and delays to the appropriate ward. Our minds were in a spin. Part of me is reliving the moment as I write it. Part of me is unclear of the order of events, but I suspect the explanation is that I was unclear even at the time. Thirty minutes previously at home, I had been holding my baby son, unaware of any significant problems and now we were in an unfamiliar hospital ward with our son undergoing dangerous tests involving his spine and brain. Gilly and I reassured each other that we were lucky to have such superb facilities and doctors on hand, but my brain was careering around the regions of my childhood - my brother's life and illness, again involving the spinal region - and the "what ifs", what if Matt had been taken ill late in the night before, what if it had happened with Danny on route in Africa etc. Had we been offered a secure tomorrow at that time by a silver-tongued insurance salesman, he would have had a taker I have to admit. I think the meningitis was first confirmed by analysis of spinal fluid, which was extracted by lumbar puncture and then, whilst the sensitivity test was being carried out to determine which antibiotics to use, Matt was given a cocktail of all the possible ones intravenously before the results of the test streamlined affairs. Parents at this time are reduced to by standing impotent spectators, desperate to help but incompetent to contribute. We stood by counting the hours as they passed – how long before his temperature would drop, should he really be asleep now, is he in need of more bedding, less bedding, does he need a drink, why is he so pale?

The neighbours in our village rallied around and we could focus just on Matt. After a haze of three days, when we had little idea of what the outcome would be, I remember Matt's brothers, who were six and four years old, being in the hospital ward and playing at being animals crawling under the bed and over the chairs to try to engage Matt's interest. Did we see a flicker of a smile? We looked again, both of us; Matt moved his head to follow Ben as he disappeared beneath the bed and then smiled, this time there was no doubt, as Danny followed him out of sight. It was to be a little while before he was out of the woods and even longer to clear his system of the toxic effects of so much antibiotic, but from that smile on we both knew he would be OK. We would choose to keep close to our children for the next twenty years on the premise that though we might not be able to cure problems, we could at least identify their presence.

Gilly had spent all her school years from when she was six at boarding school to allow her father to carry on his work with the Church (not unusual at that time) so this was a big change for her. We were beginning to look forward to our next move and had started to consider possibilities. We reckoned that we would stay at Stowford for five or so years and that was how it worked out.

One of the jobs that we did whilst we were at Stowford was to host school and other groups that came to the farm for a hands-on experience or more, depending on their age and stage. We offered this free to whomever wished to use it. The visits ranged from second year degree students at Seale Hayne University, who never said a word to avoid looking and sounding silly, to groups of five-year-olds who couldn't stop speaking and sent very telling letters and pictures back to us as a thank you. One I particularly liked was, "Mr Venables never has a sick sheep." I puzzled over this for a time until their teacher reminded me that I had in fact said that we never had a sick sheep; they were either alive or dead! If you must make jokes, check out your target audience!

The whole student visit venture nearly foundered when we instigated a farm open day in late August of one year. Someone foolishly suggested that we invited along the Health and Safety Executive. We did, against what proved to be my better judgement. The local officer paid us a preliminary visit as, in his words, if they were to be part of the event, then the farm, and more problematically the farmer, would have to be like "Caesar's wife"... Being like Caesar's wife cost just over two thousand pounds in yesterday's money, mostly in raising safety bars to make them more difficult to fall over but a whole lot easier to fall under! A new visitor washing facility had to be built as it was apparently unacceptable for visiting children to wee behind a bush and the more refined or needy to visit our house which was just fifty yards away. I have never got on with petty bureaucracy and this was doing nothing to change things. I asked him which wife we were supposed to model ourselves on. Was it the young Cornelia who I believe died in childbirth? Because if it was her, we knew a bit about those problems, since some of our undergrown heifers had got rogered by our neighbour's Charolais bull (not known for easy calving) and their birthing had been a tad problematic. Or was it Pompeia? She, it seemed, got into the history books by playing catch-me-if-you-can with a young transvestite with the unlikely name of Publius Clodius Pulcher at the festival to the goddess Bora Dea whilst Caesar considered affairs of state. We opted for the second, as she sounded more fun, but our new, shiny brown-shoed friend was not amused; in fact, he was positively unimpressed and continued to niggle on about sharp edges on the holly bush and the need to muzzle the hens.

In our last month of paid employment before stepping out into the competitive battlefield of the self-employed, we took a tractor and transport box up onto Dartmoor, constructed a rope slide across the river and camped for a week with our three children and, by this time, three sheepdogs. In the days we walked, played cricket, swam and dried in the sun, thanking whoever or whichever for Matt's recovery, and all that was past; tomorrow was another day. In the evening, we watched the brown trout somersaulting out of the river, obviously also feeling flush; all that energy couldn't be just to catch a fly, or could it?

Chapter 27
The Beating Heart of a Village

Moving to a new farm some seventy miles north, although still in Devon, was always going to be a challenge but it was made worse by all the things that we left behind. In the village of Harford we had been treated to some extraordinary characters who had become friends.

Anita and Tony Knox lived just above the farm and enjoyed a bird's eye view of all that went on. Anita was the local optometrist and Tony was newly retired from history teaching. Tony had a shed in his garden where he housed twenty-five years of back copies of The Guardian. Anita and Tony had a house built on the site of a former piggery. Within the field, just below their house was a sizeable three-foot-deep, shallow reservoir built in Mrs Ryan's time in order to control the flow of water to the waterwheel and in turn to provide power on the farm and electricity for milking of the cows. This had long since been out of use, but I had restored the flow of water through the neighbouring woods, to keep the reservoir topped up and we stocked the reservoir with rainbow trout. We fed them every day and, as such, had a constant and ready supply of fresh trout. One day, whilst walking across the field on a hot summer's afternoon carrying my shirt, the goat caught sight of me and became agitated. This fourth-dimension vibe was immediately picked up by a young Galloway bull we had on loan to work with some heifers. He became excited and then looked around like a switched-on teenager to see how he could best express his excitement. I became his target and by this time, the goat had pulled out her tether and was galloping up towards me with the garden fork tether dancing crazily behind her. Ruskin the dog did a quick mental calculation and bolted for the gate, leaving me to quickly reach the conclusion that a galloping goat and a snorting bull had more than an odds-on chance of seeking revenge for the Spanish cousins of the said bull before I reached any safety. Waving my shirt at him and shouting 'Go away!' didn't seem a good plan, so I legged it to the reservoir and jumped into the middle just as goat and bull arrived, slithering up to the edge but no further. Anita was in her bathroom, watching all this as I stood, shivering, waiting for the bull to lose interest.

Rosemary and Brian Howell lived a little further up the hill at Lukesland House and Gardens, which included a fine collection of rhododendrons and other more exotic species and was regularly opened to the public. It was this paradisiacal garden that I chased an escaping group of cattle into about a month after I had arrived at Stowford. Being well-behaved cattle belonging to the Royal Agricultural Society, they miraculously kept to the gravel paths and eventually turned tail and trotted all the way home – perhaps they had heard Rosemary's very classy shrieks as she saw what was happening and just felt intimidated… I certainly did.

Miss June, Rosemary's sister-in-law, helped by Julie Cole and Linnie Davis, sent, and still does, flowers and greenery to London each week from her shrub garden. She was to comment some years later to us that the noise that came across the valley from one of our son's parties reminded her of the blitz when Plymouth was flattened in the last war.

Johnny Cole stepped up to offer his dip, and then helped us dip when we had only been two weeks at Stowford and needed to re-dip the flock due to an earlier dipping having been rather low on the measured chemical. At that time, sheep had to be dipped usually under supervision of the local bobby (police officer). My mum was helping us at the time and was bowled over by John's old-fashioned generosity in wading through mud and wet sheep to bring coffee out mid-morning. Then there was Commander and Mrs Edwards, with their neighbours, Pat Honnor and his vibrant and petite wife Nell, who had a hat full of white hair and piercing blue eyes that missed nothing. Pat had sold their big house to Commander Edwards in order to bail out his boatbuilding business in Plymouth which would otherwise have been declared bankrupt with all the knock-on distress such declarations bring. Pat was an honourable man. Michael and Kerry were our artist and potter friends; Michael was the third of four children to Pat and Nell. Together we transported an old lithographic printing press, by tractor and trailer across open moorland, fields and through woodland to their remote home by the river Erme.

Peter and Elizabeth Riley lived at a beautifully kept, small and remote haven nestled amongst Dartmoor boulders, with a stream tumbling along the edge of the garden. Peter had been in the Kenya police and Elizabeth had grown up in the same country. Uncannily, she had also been head girl at the same school in Kenya where Gilly had held the same position some forty years later, that being Limuru Girls' School. Eric and Muriel Pearce were mother and father to our later friend and neighbour Vic Pearce, who lives then and now five fields away with Peggy, his wife. Sybil Greenwood, who had been matron to a local school for severely handicapped children and was only just over four feet tall but made up for it in width, kept our boys in order by telling them that she had a revolver in her Mini's glove compartment! Betty Hawker, an elderly spinster, rode with the hounds well into her seventies and as she was losing her sight later, still used to walk her terrier dog along the moorland lanes and stop whatever traffic came along with an upraised stick, until she and her dog had walked safely past. Betty used to wear a woollen hat with side tassels but for her they were only on the side by accident, not design. Eric used to like to tell the story of his quietly watching Betty in her late seventies and clad only in her nightdress, crossing the icy road on her hands and knees with a steaming bucket of bran mash for her horse on a particularly frosty morning.

There was also Ken Watkins, who was deaf, and his wife Mary Watkins. Ken had raced motorcars at Silverstone and Brands Hatch and established a very successful agricultural machinery import and export business with his brother Leon. This business started with Ken driving tractors from Cambridge tractor sales to Devon in the nineteen fifties. Ken was later to find some fame as a wildlife film maker and he set up the Woodland Trust. In due course, he was to have a very significant effect on our lives. After his death, he remains the only person I have ever seen as a ghost, or least I thought I did - who knows, perhaps I did?(Three months after his funeral I was so sure that I had seen him, head on one side walking his little Collie dog on a short lead, that I walked several paces to greet him before looking again!! Alas no Ken and no dog.)

Patty and Leon Watkins lived close to the church. Patty first moved to Harford with her friend Mary (now Watkins) as a land girl in the war and they lived in a stable and milked five cows. For years, Patty used to be chairlady of the parish meeting, which although largely a bureaucratic irrelevance, was well worth going to just to hear the banter from Leon as he rocked on his chair in the middle of the room, referring to Madam Chairman. 'Could Madam Chairman possibly enlighten us as to the state of the land drain to the south of Homewood Bridge?' etc. etc. The meetings were often held at Stowford House in the cold Tudor kitchen and we provided coffee and biscuits.

John Pearce sported heavy round glasses and his bright little collie dog used to hide under his coat as John squeezed backwards into the hedge, with his not inconsiderable frame, to allow traffic past. John's brother-in-law, Fred Wilcox, was the opposite in stature but a master craftsman, who with the Hosgood family in

Ivybridge have contributed so much to the survival of many of the old local buildings. Down in the valley, by the humpback bridge over the Erme lived Lee Pym, who had been in business with Pat Honnor until things fell apart. Lee was later to lose one of his legs as a result of illness, but still managed his isolated cottage lifestyle with its intermittent spring-fed water supply – intermittent due to it getting clogged up with frogs and small rodents. Lee's tea always had that little something extra in terms of flavour!

There were others of course who added to the colour of this delightful village which we had been privileged to become part of. Moving away was always going to be difficult; we knew not what the future held.

In Ivybridge, similarly, there were many outstanding characters who had come into our lives and many of whom are still in our lives. Bill Blackett used to work for the gas supply company and from his retirement in his mid-fifties up to the present day, he still works a day a week with us whenever he can and is full of good humour and wise advice. My good and loyal friend David Moulder has been part of our lives for more than thirty years, adding to his cv. tractor driving, fencing, worming and endless log splitting. His former day job was as a marine librarian.

Chapter 28
Stepping into the Unfamiliar

Our journey into farming on our own account was about to begin – failure was not an option – we had no Plan B. I would do whatever was necessary to succeed and succeed we would. At times it felt that we, like the trout, were snatching at gnats, then a great big juicy dragonfly would come our way. All my predecessors at Stowford had gone on to manage large farms, but I didn't fancy being somebody else's mouthpiece or dogsbody. We applied for and got a tenancy on a one-hundred-acre farm (part of a large estate) in North Devon, managed by a local firm of land agents and owned by a very wealthy, elderly, over-landed, over-privileged Knight of the Realm, Sir Robert Throckmorton. Actually, I need to subjugate my republican sympathies and judge him as I found him, and I found him OK; a bit slow to put his hand to the wheel when there was a job to be done but in that he had plenty of company.

Tenancies at that time were like gold dust. It seemed that a large group of the existing tenants on the estate had grouped together to take the land agent and owner to a rent tribunal some few years before we were involved. The tenants won and so the agent, either under instructions or independently, decided to break with the tradition and offer the next vacant farm on the open market, to try to establish a commercial value. At the time, we knew nothing of this and did what we have always done – that is we bid what we could afford. This happened to be slightly more than double the average of the rest of the estate! Unsurprisingly, we got it although the circumstances were such that the chalice was sour if not quite poison. I had no problem with it – we knew what we wanted, and if needs be, I could work away from the farm doing whatever was possible in order to subsidise the new business. Our established neighbours were doing similar things. One of them ran the bookmakers in South Molton, another man ran a haulage business of sorts, collecting "fallen stock" in order to convert it to saleable meat on whatever market he could hit; our close neighbour Fred used to collect fox skins and others similar, to lay in salt and send to London by mail train for the fur trade, yet another traded in straw and hay and others contracted with whatever machines they had available. Our plan was not so very different. However, ideally, we intended to rear surplus calves from the dairy herds and move them on at three months, weaned and ready for some more established farmer to fatten them to beef.

In effect, we were taking the risk of young calf rearing, doing a lot of the work and getting paid twenty pounds per head for our efforts. At the same time, we intended to establish a flock of mule cross Suffolk ewes by buying in some broken mouth old mule ewes and squeezing one more crop of lambs out of them to give us a young flock (their offspring) to carry on with. Well that was the plan that we had; it's the one that we presented to the interviewing agent and it's the one, with a five year forward budget attached, that we presented to our sympathetic bank manager and then we were able to persuade him to support us with an overdraft. Though in fact, since the bank had the security of my parents' house set against the overdraft, I guess he wasn't taking too much of a risk! We borrowed a lump of cash from friends but taking a leaf out of Mrs Ryan's book, "Don't become beholden to etc. etc." we insisted that we paid a competitive interest rate. Since I was sure that one way or another, we would make things work, barring an early death, I also took out a term life insurance to cover our borrowings. Our plan at the bank showed that we had significant capital of our own in the form of a sheep flock, tractor and sheep-handling unit, a bucket of rusty nails and nine spare left-footed wellingtons kept for the day when I wore out a left foot ahead of the right one! Now it is true that we had those items, but we were generously optimistic in our valuations! This enabled the bank manager to tick his box and we hurried onto other things.

It has been pointed out to me that this was not strictly honest, but since most of the establishment individuals and organisations that might have split hairs over the issues were perfectly comfortable to have their pensions met by someone else gambling on the stock market with jobs and businesses at stake, I was not unduly concerned. Morality is not an absolute. The one hundred rand that I had lost in Lesotho – did it do more for the family that ended up with it than if it had stayed in my pocket? Was the fault not more mine for not giving it away in the first place, when the need was obvious, than the opportunist who redirected the asset to where it could do better? At heart I am a benevolent socialist in a capitalist world. It concerns me sometimes that the competitive edge which is part of my make-up fits me up better for the capitalist economy than the other. Capitalism in its simplest expression and the meritocratic system that supports it is the route by which my journey from suburbia was made possible, so as an agent for change, I can't knock it.

We knew that we had to hit the ground running at this farm on the edge of Exmoor, so had arranged for the purchase of three hundred broken-mouthed mule ewes from a dealer in Cornwall. He had advertised them in the farming section of the regional paper – I went to see them, and a deal was done. He agreed to look after them for ten weeks at a price per head per week whilst we finished at Stowford and before we moved onto the new farm. Big mistake! A lot can happen to three hundred old broken-mouthed ewes in a hot, dry summer over a ten-week period when they are grazed on two ten-acre paddocks. They arrived, or at least half of them did, on our haulier and friend John Coker's transport lorry. John was well experienced in the ways of farming. He had done our haulage at Stowford for five years and knew what we were moving into. He wasn't too impressed by the stock he was delivering - big-boned sheep probably in their second year of losing teeth and some of them would be lucky to see the end of the month. He was right and I knew it; I had made a most simple and stupid mistake. I had rushed into a deal and been let down badly. These sheep hadn't been kept well; in fact, they had been pretty well starved. John told me that he had only brought up the best of them but even they were pretty bad. The one saving grace was that I had paid only for half of the sheep. Together we agreed that the best plan was for John to return to the farm with a handful of sheep to make it exactly half and I would come down by car and meet the seller and confront him on their condition.

This was my first stock purchase and it wasn't going to be my last. This wasn't the way I had thought I would start, but as John counselled, 'You've got to let them know you're not a soft touch, let them know who's boss'. I drove down behind John's lorry, in trepidation at the anticipated showdown. We met up on the scorched paddock they had been kept in. John was right about their condition; some of these sheep could barely walk and collapsed under any pressure from the dogs. They were not the only ones who hadn't got a leg to stand on. To his credit, the dealer owner did not try to defend his position and accepted that the sheep were in a dreadful state. He had taken, as he said, a bit of grass to graze them on and had been let down. I think he was expecting to be left with all three hundred, so I guess he was relieved to have moved at least half of them. We parted not exactly the best of friends, but a least we had not hit each other! I would never in the future lose control of stock of any sort whilst I owned them. John had helped me through a tough deal, as he has since when the occasion has demanded. He has not had an easy life, but like others we have met through farming, he was bred and reared on, and in part made of, Dartmoor granite and I am indebted and delighted to have had him on my side. He is well into his eighties now and still drives the occasional lorry load of sheep to Exeter for us; I think he likes to come up just for Gilly's flapjack and a cup of tea. He came up to a farm party last year and sang Uncle Tom Cobley and other songs to sixty or so guests whilst sitting on a rickety stool in the field by the pond. Life has its diamond moments and that was one of them.

Chapter 29
Family Dynamics

I guess in every family there are various difficult-to-solve problems - children struggling to establish their own identities separate from their parents, parents desperately wanting what's best for their children and not surprisingly thinking that what was best for them will also be best for their offspring. Our family was no exception. We struggled to accommodate both of our sets of parents' hopes and expectations whilst we trod the tricky path to become parents ourselves. Eggs were broken as the deference expected by the retiring generation was replaced by our focus on the coming one. Our social shift from being a patriarchal society where the oldest male was regarded as head of the family to the new meritocracy where respect needed to be earned was not to everyone's liking!

We were both fortunate to have had parents whose hearts were in the right place and they brought very different gifts and colour into our lives and those of our children.

My own parents had had a tempestuous and troubled journey but had largely risen above their problems and helped us in whatever way they could; even so we had moments when conflicting loyalties caused tensions. Gilly's parents had returned from Kenya the same year that we had met. They had been working as missionaries in the declining post-war years of what must go down as one of the world's most unlikely empires, the British Empire. They were present in Kenya as the violent struggle for independence ground its bloody progress. From six years old, Gilly went to a Kenyan boarding school. They returned to England and its unfamiliar, consumer-orientated society in the dying days of the sex, drugs and rock 'n' roll revolution, having spent most of their lives cocooned in private schooling and church society of one sort or another. A change in employment in advanced middle age, no golden nest egg and a family of three teenagers all at vulnerable stages must have added up to a challenging period. Gilly's mother Margaret needed a home to call her own, whilst her father Mike needed a job, a roof and a new space in which to assert his identity. Both remained loyal to their religious traditions and beliefs.

My common ground with Mike centred on Gilly, his eldest daughter! Rowing, public schooling, the church, Cambridge and crosswords were not really a big part of my history and football, sheep, farming and funny "ha, ha" were not noticeably part of Mike's! We could no doubt have found some other common ground, but I don't think either of us tried very hard. Mike took a series of church-related jobs in which he was more or less comfortable before both he and Margaret settled in West Devon, where Margaret could at last close the door and breathe a sigh of relief and Mike could fill every moment with some sort of activity. Alas, not farming! If Mike was cognisant of the financial, social and physical pressure points that we experienced in our early farming years he was very quiet about it. An encouraging word, some light-hearted banter or a shared anecdote over a beer or two would have been appreciated but it wasn't his way, sadly. He was perhaps stronger on the Old Testament prophet bit than the comforting New Testament foot washing idea!

Gilly's mother, Margaret, came down to stay with us for the time that Gilly was in hospital when Matt arrived. Gilly had prepared some dishes and put them in the freezer to make things easier to manage. That presented no problems for the first course, but for afters the "yoghurt pots" filled with a cream-based pudding looked suspiciously to me like cow's colostrum, frozen for use in the next lambing should we be short of this vital first feed for lambs. This was indeed what they were, and it was entirely my fault for not labelling them clearly; we did without pudding that night as one of the qualities of the colostrum is that it is a strong laxative, to encourage the newly-born animal to vacate its bowels of all the debris accumulated whilst in the uterus.

Every year we were visited by Gilly's Uncle Peter and Aunty Jo with their immaculately kept Sprite aluminium caravan. At first the visits were for two or three weeks, but over about twenty years they gradually stretched their stay out for most of the summer and well into the autumn. They were slow to call it a day lest it was their last. Peter and Jo would, like my parents, get involved in anything that happened on the farm and would christen the worst of jobs with some jingle. Dagging (which is removing the soiled wool from the back end of sheep) became daggling which somehow made the job lighter. His 'Goodness gracious me,' as I accidentally removed the window plus frame from the side of the house with the tractor and loader, turned a foolish mistake on my part into an amusing memory. The resetting of a young cow's broken front leg using plaster of Paris - couldn't be done you say - well yes it can, but you need an Uncle Peter and Aunty Jo to hold the animal still for long enough! Their visits were eagerly anticipated and are fondly remembered, along with the bowls full of hedgerow blackberries collected and the second breakfasts enjoyed by anyone passing the caravan at mid-morning when the flag (tea towel) was flying.

Michael did once offer to help and so I got him set up harrowing a field, which didn't really need it, but I was so surprised and pleased at his offer that I didn't want to say, 'No thank you.' After a couple of hours, I took the motorbike out to see how he was and take him a drink; he climbed down from the tractor, stopped long enough to say how boring it was and went off on one of his endless walks, leaving me stuck with two machines, one pair of legs, half the morning gone and a cup of cold tea… During the early years and largely to make things easier for Gilly, I deferred to her father as did almost everyone else. I tried to overlook the times when a word or gesture of parental encouragement, which would have done much to lift Gilly at difficult moments, didn't come. He was, as we all are, a child of his time. He believed he had a direct line to the Almighty and as such any communication was a tad one-directional. Single minded or stubborn? Cathedrals, both real and metaphorical have been built based on such belief but it can't have been much fun for the stone mason! We have some long term and very loyal friends who want to know every detail of what we are doing and what the family are up to, which can on occasions feel a bit heavy and intrusive. I guess if we put them and Gilly's father in the same bag and mixed them up thoroughly, the average would be perfect! The problem may of course be with my expectations, but after a long period of trying to get alongside and failing, I guess it's not unreasonable to concentrate on where one can make a difference.

Our contacts in the village and in Ivybridge seemed to be coming to an end with the move from Stowford up to Luckworthy. If Gilly was cognisant of this, as she must have been, she didn't register it, and without her saying with a smile, 'Yep,' when I said let's go, we would not have got past Old Kent Road. My squash and tennis were to go on hold as well.

Chapter 30
Government in Farming

Our journey into the unfamiliar territory of the self-employed did not begin well. Firstly, the episode with the starved sheep and then politics came to play its part.

Government support to farming had become part of the farming scene which I didn't like (along with many others) but as long as your competitors, both local and international, were getting it then the market place was skewed, and it became a vital part of one's income. For those near the edge, without a good few years under their belt or money stacked in the bank, this was particularly the case. Peter Walker, the Conservative Minister of Agriculture (when agriculture was considered important enough to have its own ministry), tried to change the situation. At the time, there were grain mountains and milk lakes in the form of butter, cheese and dried milk surpluses across Europe. Some of this went to the third world, where it provided valuable short-term relief, but also destroyed the market for local African and other third world farmers. "Set-aside" (i.e. the forced removal of land from production) was introduced to curb the cereal production – sadly the bureaucrats responsible for this idea hadn't allowed for the fact that your average farmer would take out his poorest land and up the fertiliser on the rest, so maintaining his saleable asset, and therefore his income. 'Dairy cows,' said the same school of bureaucrats. 'Ah, we have a cunning plan; if you sold one thousand gallons last year then you can only sell eight hundred gallons the next year,' hence the eight hundred gallons would become your "quota". Within six months, quota was being sold amongst the dairy farmers and within two years it was worth more than the cows producing the milk. Why these bureaucratic numpties didn't put a prohibitive tax on the one input which increased everybody's production, i.e. nitrogen fertiliser, is difficult to fathom. The cynics among us wondered aloud if perhaps the powers that be had self-interest in the companies producing the fertiliser. The fact that ground water supplies were becoming contaminated with nitrogen runoff, thought to be cancerous, might have even proved to be a vote-earner had the politicians embraced the idea.

The milk lake response of dairy quotas affected us dramatically, in that the dairy farmers had an immediate problem with what to do with their surplus milk. 'Ah, good idea, feed it to the surplus calves,' they said. These were the surplus calves that we were relying on as our bread and butter income. Too bad, it's a tough world! To make matters worse, the calves that we already had in the system had a much-reduced market value. However well one bucket rears a calf, it never looks like a naturally suckled one at three months old. (There is a lesson here for all young mums keen to maintain the "I am just eighteen" look, but it is probably not an area I should blunder into!) Consequently, our second sale of calves never happened, which rather changed our forward budget profiles.

This was the winter of 1984, memorable to most for being the title of George Orwell's prediction of social collapse, though for us it was more akin to a nightmare version of "Animal Farm". The old ewes, some of which we had nursed back from starvation the previous autumn, started to lamb. About a quarter of the way through our first lambing season the lambs began to develop sore lips, which soon became inflamed gums. Ears down, drooling copious amounts of infectious saliva, they stopped drinking and then died in their dozens. I had seen orf (contagious pustular dermatitis) before, but never at this age and never affecting the tongue and inside of the mouth. We had not vaccinated, as a cost cutting exercise; this was always a dilemma and as we have gone on through farming, one of the luxuries that I have most enjoyed is being able to vaccinate as a "just in case" strategy, without having to worry too much about the cost. That way at least, whatever happens, one can take refuge in the "Well I did all I could" shelter. On this occasion, there was no shelter or refuge to hide in.

Our local vet, proved to be unhelpful, – no, they didn't think it was orf and in any case if it was, vaccination would have no effect at that stage. Crucial days passed and we buried more and more lambs as well as having to milk off the embarrassed mothers. In desperation I phoned my friend and vet George Austin back in Ivybridge. 'Don't mess about boy, or you will lose the bloody lot. Vaccinate everything in sight and antibiotics if it blinks at you.'

Within ten days, the orf outbreak was over and the sun peeked through the clouds. Spring was on her way and so, unfortunately was Pasteurella. This is a bacterial infection, which causes septicaemia usually in the fastest growing lambs and the first symptom is a dead bloated lamb with a bluish tinge to its skin. Easily vaccinated against but not if you can't afford the vaccine! Of course, in retrospect one can always afford the vaccine but at that time the overdraft, borrowed money and a hundred other considerations meant that we felt that we couldn't. I spent all my time checking stock, working out how many lambs had to die before the cost of the vaccine would have been justified! If you've been there, you'll know what I mean. Eventually we were forced to bite the bullet and vaccinate. They stopped dying, although one never knows, perhaps they would have stopped in any case?

Our first year was agriculturally disastrous. Fortunately, Roger Ferguson, the Principal of the Devon College of Agriculture, came to our aid and I was able to work two days a week teaching day-release classes all over east, north and central Devon. The income was enough to persuade the bank manager that we were not yet worthy of a red letter; we lived on market-reject fruit and vegetables, eggs, goat's milk and overcooked Ambrosia puddings, normally sold on from the factory for dog food. We soon learnt that the dented cans were the best, having been rejected on grounds of shape rather than taste.

Otherwise, we spent nothing that wasn't essential. The small Ford 3,000 tractor with its roll bar and link box doubled up to transport the boys to the school bus, and Gilly doubled up as farmer as well as mother whilst I was away teaching. At that time, Gilly was also doing an Open University course to qualify with a degree, partly to keep her sane, partly to make her employable and I think partly to satisfy her parents' requirements that she complete her degree. Whatever, she used to get up at five thirty a.m., work for a couple of hours before the boys woke and then carry on with a normal day. My parents, thinking we needed a break, gave us a caravan which we, with their reluctant approval, sold to buy a tractor to continue to protect ourselves from the bank manager's red letter. Birthday or Christmas presents were all tools for the farm and going out meant a walk around the fields together looking for the next problem. For a while we had no television.

Our immediate neighbours, Fred and Marge Pook, were supportive and generous in ways that they were able to be, but they were farming on their own with only eighty acres so theirs was also a deep and steep furrow. Marge had been a wartime evacuee child from London and was always laughing, with her dentures just that bit out of step with her jaw; she had a three-wheel Robin Reliant car which probably accounted for the fact that we saw very few hedgehogs in the area!

The two elder boys settled in the local primary school at East Anstey and we soldiered on, but it was hard going. Our second year saw fewer catastrophes and with the teaching we had hit a very low but sustainable plateau. The farmhouse was in a dell but with an open south-facing aspect. It was a traditional Devon cob longhouse, where in the past, livestock were kept at one end and the farmer and family lived at the other. We still had livestock in the form of rats that we could hear running around in the inside of the cob and in the attic... The whole house was leaning downhill to the south such that if you parked the hoover in the hallway, it would freewheel happily onto the small flower-bordered garden. We had a regulation one electric socket in every room; any more would have been excessive in the eyes of our land agent, although I did notice that in his house, he had a TV, record player and lamps all in one room - perhaps he had one of those new-fangled multiple socket extension leads?

During our first year at Luckworthy, with Gilly struggling to cope with the isolation, we had a phone call telling us that our dog had gone walkabout, and would we like to collect it? I suggested that Gilly go to establish a contact and meet someone new. She changed out of her wellies and drove the mile or so to collect the dog. When approaching the farmhouse and about to knock on the front door, she heard the kitchen window open and a woman's voice say, 'Dog's in outhouse,' then the window banged shut! Luckworthy on the Molland Estate wasn't all like that, but it did sometimes feel that way.

The village hall found use for several events during the year, mostly church related. One of the more secular uses was for the annual estate meal, which to be fair, might not have happened at all. Recognising that, we were a bit surprised to attend and find the head table was occupied by the land agent, the owner, the hunt master and a couple of regular guns on the shoot. They drank wine. The three tables stretching away from the top table were for the tenant farmers, with beer provided for the men and orange squash for the women, and if my memory serves me correctly, the outside of the room was for the cottage tenants, whom I presume had water! We sat through a ridiculous address from a drunken member of the shoot, which had absolutely nothing to remember it by other than that he laughed occasionally, so I guess it was supposed to be funny. I had to fix Gilly with an unblinking stare, which said, 'No, we can't get up and walk out.' We didn't, and the mealtime conversation started and stopped with sheep and cattle. We might survive at Luckworthy, but it wasn't going to be easy; at that time, I couldn't think of beef or sheep without visions of carcasses awaiting collection by the kennel wagon.

Year two was easier, but it was a case of getting by rather than anything else. My teaching got me away from the farm and provided me with some social interaction, but Gilly was suffering with none or very little of the above. Neither of us could comfortably embrace the idea of killing anything other than for food or self-preservation so the interests of the hunt and shoot didn't really attract or entertain us. Our children, however, had no problem at all with getting pleasure from murdering wildlife. They would spend hours on end sitting inside an old caravan, in which we used to store stuff, killing flies with rubber band catapults and piling them up on the table surface...

We were pretty naive on the subject of country sports and although I had been hunting, I certainly could not pretend to know much about it, nor shooting. I would have to concede that galloping across the country with a group of other horses and riders, not knowing where you were going or what you might have to do is a thrill all its own. (Not, however, up to skiing on deep, fresh powder snow). In defence of hunting though, if I were a fox living in a democracy, I would vote for it on the grounds that mostly I would get away and, in any case, if I didn't, death would come mercifully swiftly. I can think of many worse ends; old age and longevity have, I think, always been overrated. One day, Gilly was at home when one of the joint hunt masters, a lady, was polite enough to call in the day before the hunt to announce that they were going to "draw the copse" the following day. (Drawing the copse being a hunting term for running the hounds through to flush out any foxes). I was glad for Gilly that she didn't ask to see the results to assess its artistic merit. The final straw for Gilly I think was when she got into the awkward position of holding the gate open for a lone horse and rider to pass through and then found herself holding the same gate for the rest of the hunt as they trotted through, touching their whips to their peaked, velveteen-covered hats. However, you say 'Thank you' from the back of a horse, it is always going to seem condescending.

The days I spent away teaching not only earned our bread and butter but also provided me with a welcome glimpse of other people's lives. Whilst taking a class at the Cullompton church hall, one lad was showing off his new motorbike during a coffee break. For some reason, he took the cap off his petrol tank and at the same time one of his mates flicked the stub end of his fag towards the bike. Chance would suggest that the fag would drop harmlessly down to the ground and no one would know about it. No such luck. Not only was I watching, as I munched my way through a break time sandwich, but also several of the elderly people in the adjoining old peoples' home witnessed events from their picture window just fifteen feet away. The fag end winged its way contrarily through the air, straight into the petrol tank, where thankfully it was extinguished by being submerged in the petrol oil mix, but not before lighting the fumes rising invisibly from the tank. Elderly schoolboys behind the windows jumped out of their enforced lethargy and phoned the fire brigade, who eventually arrived. In the meantime, I grabbed somebody's jacket and smothered the tank, so putting out the flame. Suspecting what had happened behind the picture window in the care home, I got all the students into the room after tidying up the area by the bike. Without wasting time, we pushed on with the lesson and were about thirty seconds into it when we heard the bells ringing. Within five minutes we had a good few yellow-hatted, blue-coated firemen at the door. 'No,' I said, "there is not a problem,' and 'Oh really, did they say that? Well, I think they must have imagined it.' The firemen went away seemingly not too worried and I saw their chief talking to the late arriving police car and that was the end of it. However, the story must have got around the City and Guilds Agricultural Student Community, because after that, with all the groups I could have walked on water, much to the puzzlement of my fellow teachers.

Meanwhile, back at the farm, our youngest son Matt, who was too young for school or playgroup for the first year, necessarily had to spend long periods amusing himself with the goats, numerous cats, bantam chickens and dogs for company. Inevitably, he would get into a fix from time to time that ended in tears. On these occasions, Daisy, our white Saanen goat, would charge from wherever she was browsing and up to Matt to see what the trouble was. She would assume that it was the dog, on the grounds of genetic instinct, and then headbutt Ruskin our collie. Poor Ruskin quickly learnt that a crying child meant he had to head for the kennel for the next twenty minutes until the goat had lost interest!

Daisy needed the company of a billy goat occasionally and since we didn't have one, I had made enquiries as to where I might find one. Mervyn was apparently the man to speak to, so I was told at the market. I got him on the phone – yes, he said, he would be along directly, no problem. Good to his word, he arrived at the end of the day in an ancient Volkswagen Dormobile van, the sort that you normally associate with surfboards. Out slid Mervyn along with beard and shoulder-length hair, black, heavy rimmed glasses and a duffle coat; soon after followed Bovril, his incredibly odoriferous pet Billy. Bovril was the size of a small horse, with a superb set of swept back horns and ridges of coarse hair stretching from the back of his head to the tip of his tail, giving him a sort of "just got up" look. He took one look at Daisy and if goats can smile, he smiled. Getting to know each other and consummating their relationship took about ninety seconds, after which Bovril jumped back into the Dormobile and settled down on the folded-down back seat to recover from his exertions. He was soon followed by Mervyn, who would only accept a cup of tea for his trouble on the grounds that Bovril enjoyed his outings and they were friends. Somewhere in all this there was a lesson for society, the church and its attitude towards sex, but I am in danger of digging too deep a hole for this book! All the same in this little farmyard tryst it's difficult to find a loser.

Other than Fred and Marge, we had two other fairly close neighbours. Derrick was just a very good farmer who had the advantage over the rest of us mortals in that he had come from a family line of very good farmers, probably going back five hundred years. There are many farming families that could boast the same. One day in mid-May I met him on the road. He was driving a group of young ewes up to his top field to make the most of some newly planted pasture. For every ewe, there must have been at least two and a half lambs, and every lamb had that fluffy, round, contented, filled-out look which said, "If I have another suck, I'll simply pop." These were in stark contrast to our scrawny specimens, whose starry-coated, head down, hollow-sided message was, "I just want to lie down and die." Trying to be cheerful, I greeted Derrick and complimented him on his lambs, his grass and the sunshine for which he was also probably responsible. His response was, 'Whrr, yeh alright I s'pose, mind now, thar be two moons in May, so no corn 'n' no hay!' Sometimes you just can't win.

The other close neighbour was Sam. Sam was the brother of our predecessor tenant farmer and maybe he had hoped to take on the farm when his brother moved on. Whatever, Sam used to do a bit of contract work and it seemed the neighbourly thing to do for us to use him as our contractor where we could. I did, and dreaded every contact I had with him, partly because his dog seemed to share his animosity and would nip in and bite my or Gilly's ankles or calves at any opportunity, which led to us backing off in a crouched bowing position to avoid attack. (It is possible that the queen's corgis behave similarly, since I've noticed that people sometimes back off in a similar way from the queen.) Also, partly it was because whatever I had done, in Sam's eyes, it was always wrong. I had cut the grass in the wrong direction, rolled the silage fields too late, sheared the ewes too soon, opened the gate the wrong way or painted the door the wrong colour. Underneath Sam's flat hat, which I think he slept in, was an angry man whose mouth had taken on a permanent downwards curl – I was not equipped to change it. Sadly, the glass half empty rather than half full syndrome seems a common characteristic among farmers. I have a favourite cartoon which depicts a farmer at the end of a very successful year surrounded by shiny healthy-looking stock, all his hay barns full to bursting and golden harvested grain piled high in the newly built barns. His response to the question "Have you had a good year?" is "If this lot catches fire, it'll be the worst year yet". I had to accept that whilst I could be some of the answer, some of the time to some of the people, there are others whom no amount of effort or help was going to change. For Sam, I was never going to be able to fill his glass, so we changed contractors and drove into the village on the other road!

Chapter 31
New Horizons

We were kept afloat by little acts of neighbourly kindness during our time in North Devon (they were like tiny glimpses of blue sky on a wet November day), and by visits from family and friends largely dating back to our time at Stowford. Well into our second year there, we had one such visit from one of our Stowford farm students, Richard Pine, it was he who had given us the puppy who became Ruskin the dog. Richard had arrived with wicker basket, tablecloth and girlfriend of the day and we picnicked in the top field, looking west down towards the valley. We were trying hard at this stage to remain buoyant on our nearly level, albeit very low, plateau. Relative to the first year, things were better, so when Richard told us that a two-hundred-and-fifty-acre farm on the edge of Dartmoor, some two and a half miles up the road from Stowford was to be let by the new charity owners, we were only slightly interested. Then I remembered Uncle Jim's offer of a ride in his car when I was four and I said, 'No thanks,' and we got a bit more interested. We were both of us aware of the limited options for the children's schooling in North Devon and the chance to expand, possibly to diversify, and therefore increase income seemed worth looking at. It was really too early to consider moving but if we didn't have a go it might never have been offered again.

Once we had got to that stage, it was inevitable that we were going to apply for the tenancy of Hall Farm. Opportunity for diversification, a bigger house, wider schooling possibilities, more acres, better layout of the farm and most importantly social considerations for all the family - they all pointed us towards having a go. If we were to get it, all the people and things we had reluctantly said goodbye to at Stowford we would be saying hello to again. Those autumn evenings sat on the Erme estuary as the sun dropped in the west over the sea would no longer be just memories. On the very few occasions we had left Luckworthy to revisit friends in South Devon, it was always difficult not to feel low as we drove back up the A38, up Haldon Hill and then north into the depths of Exmoor. But it was early to be moving on; we could not allow ourselves the luxury of a dream; the waking might be too painful.

At around this time and whilst we were in the throes of applying for Hall Farm, Gilly unsure about another change, this time with three children, and both of us stretched close to breaking point, I thought it might be nice to go out in Exeter to the small Northcott Theatre. We had in the past enjoyed most of our visits to live productions, so phoned up to see what was on offer. We booked tickets and found a boy sitter and looked forward to our evening out, the only one that we had in the two years that we were in North Devon. What was on offer was a stage presentation of Raymond Briggs's graphic novel about a nuclear attack on England. It was labelled as a black comedy; it was certainly black. Hilda and Jim were an elderly couple living in the countryside at the time of a nuclear attack. It ends with death, gore and destruction five days after the attack. I must have blinked at the comedy section. There was no interval so the bottle of cider and two glasses that we had discreetly carried in didn't get drunk. Apart from the usher who offered to sell us a programme, we met no one and talked to no one. It was nearly dark and raining when we went in and properly dark and raining when we left. Determined to make the most of our one night in two years at the theatre, we pulled off the road near Tiverton and in the light of a streetlamp, solemnly drank the cider as the rain pummelled the roof of the car and coursed erratically down the windows. As we pulled off, there was a dull, unmistakeable bump, thud, bump coming from the front left wheel - we had run over glass and had a two-inch gash in the tyre. Not a lot was said as we drove the next thirty miles, wet and cold, having changed the wheel, but both of us had arrived at the same point when we got home. We burnt some midnight and early morning oil drawing up a forward budget and farm plan for Hall Farm.

First the bank manager and then the agent - we were well rehearsed in what was required. The farm walk revealed a beautiful tree- dominated edge of the moor farm with lots of small fields, good perimeter fencing, natural leat water to about half the fields and an old farmhouse and buildings with a small asbestos-roofed modern shed. The house had not been lived in for six months and many of the windows were either stuck shut due to rusty hinges or had glass so loosely fitted it rattled in its frames. It was south facing though, with a rampant and neglected walled garden, and like an abandoned kitten seemed to cry out for attention. Not for the first or last time, we were smitten and pulled out all the stops. No doubt it helped that we were locally known and that we had been at Stowford for five years just some two miles away, and that we were naturally very sympathetic to the aims and interests of the newly-formed conservation charity owners. I guess it helped that we had proved our commitment to farming in our own right in that we had made the move to North Devon. Whatever, we were, after really quite a short time, interviewed by the local agent and chairman of the Woodland Trust, Ken Watkins. They promised to decide quickly and Roger German the agent phoned us at teatime the next day to offer us the farm. There was one issue though. Roger paused on the phone for dramatic effect; Ken Watkins thought that we had been too generous with our rent offer and so wished to reduce it by a significant amount! There are moments in life when everything has a golden glow and that was one such moment. We were both ecstatic. The fact that we would have to run both farms for twelve months was an irrelevance; we didn't know how but yes, we would do it somehow and we did. Gilly's uncle Peter and his wife Jo were staying with us at the time and conjured up a bottle of wine, perfect!

We took on Hall Farm from Michaelmas, the traditional end of summer quarter day when it was most easy to assess what crops had grown and how to calculate the "ingoings". This was a word that had meant little to us until we made the move from employed to self-employed two years previously. "Ingoings" are what the incoming tenant pays to the outgoing tenant via the landlord, or more likely his agent, as compensation for the value of any improvements that the outgoing tenant has done. The same applied to the "unused manurial value" or any crop not yet harvested. It was a well-conceived idea in that it gave the sitting tenant some incentive and protection to improve the holding, confident in the knowledge that if they were to quit the farm after having carried out improvements, they would be compensated for what they had done. Buildings were usually depreciated over ten years. Not knowing a lot about these things cost us heavily as we moved into Luckworthy. We were faced with a cost of eleven thousand pounds to buy a barn lean-to that we didn't want or need that our predecessor had erected. At Hall, no outgoings had been paid to the previous tenant and so no ingoings were due from us. Since our ingoings at the previous North Devon farm had been depreciated, we were effectively paid by our successors seven thousand pounds for the white elephant which was effectively a covered feed passageway access to a concrete-based, hole in the ground, unlined silage pit. I hope but doubt that our successors valued it more than we did!

September the thirtieth 1986 saw Gilly at Hall Farm with our only car, a newly acquired Renault Pear that we bought through the North Devon Motor Auction Company, three children under seven and a very cold, old house in desperate need of heating. We spent the generous rent reduction on making the house a little more comfortable and were physically helped by many family and old friends. I was to be for much of the next year based at Luckworthy with our Ford 3000, hand-painted and cabless tractor. Coming back to Harford was a relief and in every respect a homecoming. The village of Harford and its resident population had hardly changed, with the exception that the prestigious brick-built house on the hill, Harford Lodge, had new owners, Graham and Jan Adam. They were to become firm and valued friends, among many others. Together, with Michael and Kerry Honour, our artist and potter friends and their two sons, we made up what was the younger generation in a rapidly ageing community. Change was inevitable, but for fifteen or so halcyon years, things bumped on gently and the speed of change was mercifully at a snail's pace. Patty Watkins would trot by on her pony with positive encouragement on how good it was having the old house coming to life again and frequently dropped off some bantam eggs. Australian Nell, on her long rambles, frequently stopped by with a basket of goodies, mostly hand-picked, home grown or home cooked. Peter and Elizabeth Riley rarely drove past on the way to Plymouth or the supermarket without checking Gilly was not in need of some errand or shopping. Jan Adam would slither to a halt on the road, run up the lane and bubble over with some salacious tale and old John Pearce and Gilly swapped gifts of cakes and vegetables.

From Ivybridge and particularly the Methodist Church, we had and continue to have great and valued friends, such as Bill and Ilsa Blackett. Ilsa was a Jewish war refugee from Austria, and in continuing gratitude to the church that was instrumental in her escape from the ravages of the war, worked a clothes recycling business to raise money for Christian Aid. By giving Gilly first pick on some of her acquisitions, she saved us the need for a clothing budget. Bill began his thirty years of weekly days at the farm. David Moulder retired from his work as a librarian in Plymouth at the Marine Laboratory and announced that he was going to spend a good part of his retirement helping us farm and so he did and still does. Jeremy White and his artist wife Lynn and their two children camped on the farm each May, as did our West Indian cousin Kurt and Joanna Lapage Brown and whenever there was a job that could be shared, they did so, and we had numerous expanded family meals in the kitchen or camping barbecues in the fields. One year, eager to help, Jeremy with his boundless enthusiasm took over from me worming the ewes and administering the "Pour on" insecticide for the sheep. I went in for coffee and came back to find that the wormer that was destined for within was going without and vice versa. We watched the sheep carefully for several days but saw no difference which does make me wonder what the value of the job was in the first place!

Scottish Linnie with her printer husband Roy Davis, loyal friends for nearly forty years, helped in all sorts of ways including farm sitting to allow us to go on holiday at odd times, as did American Shawn and English Rosie. Anita and Tony, our neighbours at Stowford who converted a concrete pig emporium to a tranquil Dartmoor garden shared their Christmas Eve party with our family for many years. John and Gill Cole farmed between us and Ivybridge so in effect we drove through their farm every day several times, especially when the children were at school. One year they had a suicidal calf which dropped down off the field, down the bank and into the road every morning. There it stood and bellowed for its mother. John sensibly erected a new post and wire fence. He must have learnt his farming from the same source as me, in that having bought new stakes and new wire he couldn't quite justify staples as well, so he tied the wire up to the stakes with baler twine. It worked – only for a few months, but he did save the cost of the staples. Rosemary and Brian Howell provided us with the occasional Christmas tree and pocket money for the boys in return for wheel-barrowing mulch to their specimen garden trees. Danny in particular remembers sitting under a tree with a cup of tea whilst Brian waxed lyrical about the value and satisfaction of manual endeavour. Mmm! I think my son was hoping for a demonstration. George and Lynn Austin, our veterinary friends, were always there if we were in a fix. They provided a trailer for us to move furniture, sheep and food etc. when we were so tight for funds, we couldn't really justify buying a wheelbarrow, let alone a trailer. John and Pam Hall provided us with their pedigree Dorset rams to work out of season with our own ewes, which lifted the genetic quality of the next generation by several hundred percent and Derek and Jennifer Dennis, David and Vicky Craig, Cliff and Anne Rogers, Geoff and Zoe Sayers and many others provided us with winter grass for our rapidly expanding sheep flock.

All these people and many more have been integral to our lives. Without their contributions, life would have been the lesser and more pointedly, the changeover year would have probably foundered.

Gilly pretty well managed the family and house on her own with me moving between the two farms using the little Ford tractor as personal transport. We had christened the Ford 3000 "Tembo", in part to recognise the elephantine contribution it made to our lives. The seventy-four miles between farms would be covered by this little tractor in a remarkably consistent four and a quarter hours, down the country lanes of Exmoor via Tiverton to Exeter, along the ring road around Countisbury Weir and then onto the A38, known now as the Devon Expressway. One day I drove down to Harford before lunch, worked at Hall in the afternoon and went back to Luckworthy after tea because the people that we had let the house to had a problem with the heating!

I had had to give up the teaching line at Bicton but did continue to help with an input into the examination of students at the end of their course, similarly with the Seale Hayne degree students who used our farm as a case management study. We tried all sorts of things to ease the pressure of running two farms, including letting the house for holiday use, sub-letting grass keep and selling hay. They all added up to more work and little income and could have been avoided if the agent for Luckworthy had been imaginative enough to allow us to quit after two years rather than insisting on us serving a full year's notice, which although written into our tenancy agreement, was practically unnecessary as our eventual successor was known to the agent and keen to get going as soon as possible. This would have been to everybody's advantage.

With all the pressures of setting up our farm business and coping with new challenges, we clung pretty well to four "must do" imperatives – one had been to do ourselves anything that was remotely possible rather than to get into a dependent and expensive arrangement, two was Dickensian in its simplicity – spend less than we earned, three was wherever possible go against the tide – never swim with the shoal, and lastly, as hard up as we might have been, settle bills immediately. I have been truly astonished at the tardiness of many farmers who seem to take some perverse pride in not settling bills or obligations promptly. A contractor friend cites this as his number one business problem and yet most of his customers boast shiny four-wheel drive pickups and the latest model flash machinery and tractors. We sold hay to one such before we eventually shook the North Devon dust from our shoes, eventually getting paid some eight months later. In the meantime, we paid interest at the bank on the equivalent amount. Drive hard bargains, yes, walk away if you don't like the price, yes, but once you have agreed then settle the deal and move on.

Whatever problems and demands our farming business was to make of us, we would not lose sight of the fact that its function was to serve the needs of our family and not the other way around. Necessarily this was often achieved by stretching the day and streamlining the work. Rarely was one job finished before another two were started.

What we were doing was not, for me, the fulfilment of a life's ambition as it may have appeared. It was a pragmatic attempt to provide a home and a base for us from which we could rear and launch our own children. My own preference would have been to be growing food where the result of my efforts would have been filing hungry bellies rather than faffing around filling in some movement form or applying for this or that subsidy. In the real world, most of us must make these compromises just in order to put food on the table and keep the slates on the roof. We have had lots of people through our various farms and homes as guests, friends, students, holiday visitors, school groups, playgroups, children's friends and friends of friends. Like farmhouse kitchens all over the country the kettle is rarely cold, and the therapist is usually redundant. Those social occasions probably tip the grand scale when weighed against the total agricultural contribution we have made!

Due, I suppose, to farm and livestock commitments, Christmases were always spent at the farm. Work always had to be done although we would reduce things to a minimum on such occasions, bedding up the day before and leaving food conveniently placed to just pour out. One particular Christmas was the same as every other day for a sheep farm; prolapses, abortions, head stuck in feeder, twin lamb disease, sore feet, sudden deaths etc. Having coped with whatever that morning brought, done all my chores, lit the fires, joined in the stocking opening activities with the children and been around the fields to check the stock, it was time for a coffee as Gilly's parents arrived mid-morning. After normal family greetings, I slipped out of the kitchen into the sitting room to relax and recuperate – as a cover I turned on the TV, which had a smiley, snow falling and crass American film on, the sort of "Sound of Music" Christmas day film that gave the newsreaders a day off. Complete rubbish as it happens, but it was a cover. Within five minutes, my father in law was at the door with a loud clearing of the throat. 'Do we have to have the telly on? I thought we'd like to go for a walk.' (If only he could have said 'Great job, take a break, Gilly likewise, we'll go and check the stock.')

By this time, my feet were up on the arm of the settee and my eyes were nearly closed. Caught off guard, I snapped 'Yes I do,' and stubbornly insisted that I was engrossed in the film, which I then watched to the bitter end just to make a point.

I had obviously just got my timing wrong; TV on Christmas day apparently started and finished for Mike at three o'clock to three fifteen p.m. for the Queen's Speech with the predictable opening, 'My husband and I,' etc. as the Duke of Edinburgh stood by awkwardly looking for all the world like he wished he was somewhere else.

Chapter 32
Hall Farm

In the July of 1987, having helped us make Hall Farmhouse habitable and seen the farm which was to be our home for the next thirty years and more, my mother was to suffer a massive stroke, which in its severity and suddenness might as well have been a lightning strike. She had always had a fear of being incapacitated by illness and since the death of my brother Neil she had carried a sort of tragic resignation alongside her courageous vibrancy. She wrote poems and prose which I was later to see when my sister Anne sorted through my mum's personal possessions. They were an eloquent testament to her underlying despondency triggered by Neil's illness and her inability, along with all of us, to make a difference in the face of his aggressive cancer. These poems were for my mum and the Almighty, with whom she had some unfinished business.

In her wish to not suffer long in incapacity, she was satisfied. She died some four days after the stroke and the morning after I had seen her at her hospital bed on route between farms during haymaking. I would love to be able to say that I had spent the night at her bedside holding her hand, but cruel circumstances don't live well with poetic niceties. In the car in the hospital car park, I had a student helper whom I was ferrying back to Hall; he had been helping me with the haymaking in North Devon. I took him home and my mother's hand was not held for the last night of her life.

The summer was dull, damp and dreary as was my mood in the days following my mother's funeral. She was laid to rest in a grave at Chilwell which she shared with my brother Neil – the grave having been intentionally dug deeper in anticipation of such an event. In the fullness of time, my father's ashes would be buried in the same location but that is jumping forward in time. Soon after my mother's funeral, my father lamented to me the things he hadn't got around to saying to mum during her life. The milk of this kindness regrettably was poured too late and only left a stain on the rug that is my memory.

But we had crops to gather, sheep to sell and children to muster so life went on and autumn eventually arrived with its crispy blue skies and russet curtain pulled over the dreary summer of 1987. Luckworthy was a stage past and in many ways endured rather than enjoyed. Today was indeed the day that, well lived, would define the colour of our tomorrows and the memories of our yesterdays. This Sanskrit sentiment was to become my mantra and largely replaced the contradictory complications of the religion that I had grown up with and grown out of.

Hall Farm had been bought by the two Watkins brothers, Leon and Ken, on the back of their successful agricultural machinery importing and distributing business known as Watveare Engineering, later to become Western Machinery. Land at that time in this sort of area was very cheap and land on the edge of the moor, not known for its productivity, was particularly affordable, so not only was Hall Farm bought but also much of the adjoining land around the village of Harford. Commercially, it was an inspired move; rarely in a fifty-year period can any commodity increase in value by five thousand per cent. Almost matching this inspirational purchase was Ken's initiative to set up the conservation charity which is now the Woodland Trust. At a time when most of the population was remembering the austerity of the war years and the early 1950s and celebrating the socially liberating age of rock 'n' roll, Ken was recognising the need to preserve deciduous woodlands both for their own sake and for their habitat value. He began the process of replanting and re-establishment of field boundaries as linear woodland and wildlife corridors. At least that is what we call them today. As a result of his early work, which we have, together with the Woodland Trust, continued for the past thirty years, the two hundred and forty-seven acres that make up Hall Farm includes some four thousand trees and bushes, mostly growing in enhanced hedgerows and providing valuable mammalian habitat and home for forty-four species of birds (British Trust for Ornithology Survey 2002).The thirty-five fields are necessarily mostly less than seven acres in size but well able to generate enough farming income for a family, including a rent payment to the Woodland Trust. It is, I think and hope, exactly what Ken had envisaged back in 1986 when the initiative was begun - an effective, self-sustaining collaboration of commercial farming with conservation principles paramount.

For twelve years up to his death in 1998, Ken used to be a regular sight and occasional counsellor to me as he walked with his dog for his statutory minimum two miles per day, either along the road when it was wet or across the fields when dry. Some three months after his death I had the previously referred to ghostly experience, there he was walking his dog down the bridle track opposite the farm. Never again, though I often think of him; he was a good man to have known. He was quite deaf but seemed to be able to catch my tone or read my lips (not so with Gilly or the children). When he had had enough of conversation, his usual phrase was, 'Well, I expect you've got work to do, Clive,' and then he would toddle off back home. I'd know then that he was tiring of the effort needed to listen. Ken had a desire and vision to rebuild the barns, widen the hedges to create wildlife corridors, establish ponds and generally to increase the habitat diversity whilst at the same time providing a commercial return as a family farm. Now thirty years on I hope his ghostly walks give him pleasure. We can boast egrets, herons, ducks, a healthy population of brown trout and even an escaped stork on the farm visitor list along with a vibrant community of all the usual British mammals one would expect to find in this area. Fallow and roe deer, foxes, badgers and rabbits are common sights, with stoats, weasels, polecats, otter and sea trout making occasional appearances.

Perhaps the best part of spring for me was and is the arrival of the swallows and house martins from their winters in Africa, usually in about the third week of April. Watching them line up like spitfires to dive low over the length of the pond and drink whilst in flight with a bob of the head at thirty miles per hour is a delight I don't tire of. Similarly, the brown trout leaping right clear of the water. If these trout could play the violin and kick their heels up in a Yiddish dance before they jump, then I think they would. Who knows what happens below the surface - perhaps they do?

Harford has its own small eleventh century Anglican church dedicated to St. Petroc. It is the only public building in the village and as such the weekly services were useful social events if little else. Over the years, a succession of ministers has conspired to make the mystic side of religion so mysterious as to be, for me at least, either above or below my ken. In the early days we soldiered on largely for social reasons and for several years hosted an annual inter-church barbecue with the Methodist Church of Ivybridge, which was largely supported by emigrants from the drab Anglican service conducted in Ivybridge's main church. Our efforts at integration were limited in their success and it was notable how the Anglicans tended always to want to identify their own sausage after ten minutes cooking and our best efforts to mix everything up! The Methodists were pretty happy with whatever came their way!

Though our own good friends Jan and Graham Adam, who lived at Harford Lodge (a 1930s brick-built house a half mile to the east and over the river next to the church) were not regular church goers, the church goers for their part were regular visitors to Jan and Graham's house, where by tradition we all met after the carol service on Christmas Eve. Mostly, these evenings would start with mince pies and then as numbers thinned out, the whisky would make an appearance. Patty, the land army wife of Ken's brother Leon and soon to be the matriarch of Harford, was central to these occasions and hosted a similar event after the harvest festival.

Our contribution to village life started as a Boxing Day hockey match and pond swim, which quickly outgrew its Harford origins and still happens today, although now the sport is touch-rugby with mulled wine, and it has expanded to a second Christmas meal buffet in the farmhouse. Our summer contribution to the village social life was a village summer party by the pond, which was eventually taken over as an around the village idea and now, with the rapid suburbanisation of the community, is in danger of death by discussion as the inevitable committee takes control.

Jan and Graham, who were significantly better heeled than their sheep farming peasant neighbours, did us the great service of pointing out that with the progress of years comes the passing of opportunity, by which they meant that your kids are only this age once. Although many weekends were dominated by the need to move, check, bury or sell large numbers of sheep, we did find time every year to go skiing in the first weeks of January (cheaper by half than the New Year or Christmas week since we took the first few days of the school year when it was not considered a crime worse than bigamy to do so), and to go camping and surfing at Polzeath in North Cornwall in the summer. We financed these jaunts by raiding the budget box labelled, "Funds for new machinery". Consequently, all our machinery was bought from the nearly scrap ends of local farm sales and I honed my skills at repairing and patching up. For interest's sake, one new green and yellow tractor is equivalent to about forty years of family skiing, and at the end of the day, I would challenge anyone to look at a cultivated field and tell me the age of the machine that did the work!

Chapter 33
The Numbers Game

In the very early days at Hall Farm, we were assisted at lambing by an Australian vet called Mandy - we were probably the only farm in all of England to have a resident, fully qualified vet to assist with lambing, but she needed a bed and an excuse to be in the UK and seemed content to work all week for a bed, banter and the occasional Mars bar thrown in. Mandy may have forgiven me for my enforced penury, but she never quite forgave me for not waking her up to do a caesarean section on a ewe. Preferring instead to manage myself, I pulled off two extremely large and eventually dead lambs, with the mother soon to follow them to the local hunt kennels. (The hunt kennels perform a useful rural service by collecting dead carcasses and serving them up as hound dinner.) At breakfast, she dismissed the whole saga with a very Australian, 'Bloody farmers.' In my defence I will say that a fair few lambs have been saved by this particular "bloody farmer" by carefully manipulating and separating tangled legs, heads, tails and whatever and that the economics of veterinary intervention rarely satisfied the demands of profitable farming.

Along with Mandy came her friend and buddy Louise. Louie, as she became known, came from a family of at least a hundred and arrived without a plan at nineteen years old and stayed with us on and off for five years, helping with children, sheep, buildings, machinery repairs etc. She eventually returned to Australia but never fails to ring us up on holidays and birthdays - even now some twenty-four years on. She would save up a few pounds and spread them thinly like Vegemite over as much time and travel as she could before limping back to the farm to start the process all over again. To us, she was a solid gold Girl Friday.

Along with and succeeding Louise, came tenacious Sue who joined our lambing squad at eighteen as she retook her A Levels, re-applied for veterinary college and returned again and again until she qualified some eight years later. Sue was the only person to actually fall through the rotting floorboards in the long barn into the shippon below, although we all had near escapes. Due to shortages of covered space, we had built lambing pens for our rapidly expanding sheep flock in the long loft. The floor was a sort of composite block board that stood up to a certain amount of wear and wetting but would then spontaneously disintegrate and as well as losing our vet student Sue into the lower level, a succession of lambs would end up "down below", having wandered off from their penned-up mothers. This ad hoc maternity unit had other drawbacks as well as the porous flooring. We arranged a double row of pens down the middle, leaving a passageway each side to allow access for feeding and sheep. This would provide a useful aid when driving wild, reluctant new mothers out into the yard and into a waiting trailer. Occasionally we would move four to five ewes at a time to speed things up. At such a time, judicious placement of hurdles became a necessity to prevent an orderly sorting out becoming a very disorderly chaos. An ill-timed blockage of a passageway or doorway could easily cause the latter. So, it was one day with the unexpected arrival of Gilly's parents. I became aware of the young two-tooth ewes hurtling majestically over the temporarily arranged hurdles, followed by the splintering sound of destructing lambing pens as they landed in the "TLC" area, rather than going into the trailer. They had turned right rather than left and I realised that something or someone was in the way. My verbal response was less than eloquent! In my defence, I didn't know from my position that it was Gilly's parents' presence that had deflected these sheep, and as is well known in shepherding circles, sheep don't understand much English if it is spoken quietly, and none at all without the help of preceding qualifying adjectives so fondly appearing in every day farmyard discussions!

My colourful monologue was perhaps a bit pointless, as the damage had already been done and I must concede that such an outburst was perhaps over the top and self-indulgent. But then again it was me who was sleep deprived, me who would have to mend the "TLC" pens, me who would nurse the trodden-on lamb until it gave up on life and me who would have to mother up the traumatised ewes and their clueless lambs. At these times, I have since learnt to bite my lip and swear later at the dogs in the security of the open fields. Dogs are such good listeners and rarely judgemental!

Our life was enriched by annual visits of veterinary students to help with lambing. Michelle, with her explosion of red hair and wire-rimmed glasses perched on the end of her upturned nose, kept fantastically detailed records of lambing numbers, birthing problems and a column for explanations. After the first page the explanation was just "It's a sheep". Freya lived locally and after three years assumed managerial status, while I happily skulked in the kitchen for a second cup of coffee. Kat was also local and suffered in that she was weight challenged - that is she didn't have enough of it so was often to be seen being dragged around the barn by a rampaging Dorset cross ewe intent on lambing unaided. Kat had a boyfriend, Dan, now her husband, who together with his brother Luke on the keyboard, Tim on lead guitar and Harry on the drums, formed a beat group known as "The Days". Never to make it into the big time, it did look hopeful at one stage as they were signed up and generously supported by a large record label company. For a couple of years, they were a regular feature in our lives as they practised in what was the old shippon, built to house milking cows but now reinvented as a snooker and table tennis room. Above them was my woodwork shop known as the piano loft due to it housing an old honky-tonk piano when we first took over the farm. The music wouldn't have been everybody's choice, and as if to register the fact, the paint tins and screw filled jars stacked neatly on their shelves would steadily creep forward in inanimate response to Harry's drumming, eventually to fall on the floor. Screws could be put back in the jars; paint proved to be more of a problem. We had a good commercial arrangement with the boys - they got the space, the heating, the light, endless cups of tea and Gilly's flapjack and we got lots of smiling help with rebuilding the cottage adjacent to the farmhouse that we would eventually use for holiday guests. Perhaps I exaggerate the smiling help bit, but I do definitely remember them holding plasterboard in place while I screwed it up to the framing. We were glad of their cheerful company and happy to be included in their plans and enthusiasm.

One summer's afternoon, we filmed a sketch for their website. It consisted of them driving my father's old Volkswagen Passat car along the seven-foot wide sunken road approaching the farm. I was to approach from the other direction with a tractor loader and a bale of silage. The boys would refuse to go back and generally barrack me whilst hanging out of the open window and its skylight. Assuming the guise (with little difficultly) of a truculent Devon farmer, I would approach the car at speed and proceed to beat up the car with the tractor loader and half-ton bale of silage whilst conducting a dialogue with the boys on the subject of their hair length, proper jobs and the general depravity of today's generation! Apart from stifling the urge to cry with laughter, all went well and to plan, and in retrospect I can perfectly well understand the family of holidaymakers that witnessed the event and beat a hasty retreat along the narrow road to the safety of the neighbouring village. Whether or not they did actually report it to the police I don't know. Sadly, all the preparations and practice did not end up in the glitzy life of London clubland or international jetting - I rather fancied being their travelling songwriter or guitar gofer - a good change I thought from sheep's feet and tail end daggling. This was not to be, unfortunately; the group disbanded and went their separate ways in the fickle forest of what is the music scene – I can't quite bring myself to call it an industry.

Nick Patrick first joined our orbit as we moved six hundred sheep to grass keep, on a dairy farm in Ermington about five miles south of Hall Farm, still on the banks of Britain's fastest falling river, the Erme. We thought that since we had got used to trekking sheep across the nearby Blatchford Estate and Hanger Down to get to Derrick and Jennifer Dennis's farm, just geographically over the hill and down the valley, then it wouldn't be very different to walk them down the Harford Road to Ivybridge, past Stowford Farm and then on over the railway bridge and through the new housing estate to one of several farms in the Erme Valley. We would start as dawn broke on a Sunday morning and aim to be back before the sound of the church bells at ten o'clock. It was, of course, a whole family job plus anyone who was available. We had an excellent dog at the time, a red and white collie called Kelpie whose strain we still have today. Good though Kelpie was (she would stand on her hind legs behind the sheep just to be able to check what was happening ahead and look for confirmation that she was doing the right thing), even she was powerless to affect the sheep a quarter of a mile ahead of her, around corners and up and down the hills so it was constantly necessary for one or other of us to be moving from the back of the flock to the front to fill in gateways etc. Six hundred ewes fill an awfully long stretch of road as they move along, four abreast down the sunken Devon lanes. As we crossed the railway bridge and cut left along the suburban feeder road, it was possible for the flock to concertina on the wider road and associated grass verge, and for those of us at the back to see the lead sheep once again. This was three miles into the trip. By this time, we were pushing one hour on the road, so hopefully these early pregnant ewes had

settled down to a plod rather than a skit. That was until the seven o'clock Penzance to Paddington train went past with its noise and its cant on the gently curving route over Brunel's extravagant viaducts and on through the southern edge of Dartmoor. The sheep moved at speed en masse like a flock of acrobatic starlings away from the train and across the grass towards the gardens. It was at this moment that Nick and several of his buddies joined us on their bikes. Nick lived on the new housing estate and this was too much like Rawhide and the Ponderosa for this ten-year-old to ignore. Together they saved the day and the gardens, and we trekked on for another three miles to winter keep and endless days of electric fencing dairy paddocks. From then on, Nick and occasionally one or more of his friends would be a regular presence on the farm at weekends and for Nick at least, any day he could get away from school. Nick's life and interest became the farm and his loyalty and enthusiasm was then and still is something I value deeply. At the other end of the age spectrum was Bill Blackett. Nick, as an early teenager, and Bill in his early seventies made an unlikely team. We have had a lot of Nicks, Bills and Louise's join in our journey through farming and at the end of the day, I am of the opinion that they altogether, too many to name, have not been just a means to an end, they have been the end in itself.

The farming and all that it is and has been was a slowly moving train on which we were joined by many working passengers; it is the passengers themselves that made up the point of it all. Without the passengers, there would be no train, without the train no journey and as with all life it's the journey that matters; arrival is just a target, sometimes an irrelevance.

I recognised that the secret of success or otherwise, financially at least, lay in numbers of sheep as units of profit. At that time at least, not only did every breeding ewe have lambs which made up our crop, they also attracted a subsidy payment roughly equal to one extra lamb per ewe. This was at a time when the wool income matched the cost of shearing, so making wool a net nuisance rather than a net gain. It was of course wool that had sparked the keeping of sheep in the Middle Ages (and provides the physical and historical background to the Lord Speaker's Chair in our Parliament's upper chamber today). Now here we are some six hundred years on with a massively expanded world population and therefore a high demand for clothing and fibres, scratching around trying to find a use for wool and reduced to chopping it up and spreading it on the sea to flocculate oil spillage from the world's leaky fuel tankers!

Back to numbers. In obedience to both our African-inspired instinct and more modern economic incentives, we built up our sheep flock and started a herd of suckler cows to graze the summer months on the open common land on Dartmoor. This was at a time when Gilly, encouraged by her parents, had decided that she needed to escape the confines of the farm and take a job teaching English at a large suburban secondary school on the edge of Plymouth. Having gone through the lonely and largely unsupported period on Exmoor and then the physically demanding first few years at Hall Farm, I suppose I should not have been surprised or troubled by this move and yet I was. I had in my own mind put my preferences to work in the third world to one side, partly out of the necessity to provide my wife and family with a comfortable, stable home. Now, at a time when I was pushing all the boundaries to cement our position and in the knowledge that most others in our situation coming into farming with little more than a pocketful of pennies and a bagful of energy and enthusiasm had foundered on the shoreline rocks of cold reality, I was to be coming back to an empty house with no one to share the news of that day's disasters and death, and there were many!

The old farming adage that where one has livestock one also has deadstock could well have been extended to include the words "large numbers" twice over. The problem for many in livestock farming is that the stockman is always looking for the problems whereas the poet sees the bigger picture. At that stage, life allowed little time for poetry and I was constantly looking for problems before they occurred and beating myself up for missing the symptoms before the event. A stitch in time needed a needle and good eyesight at the same time; one of them was usually missing.

For the second time in our lives together the elastic was tightly stretched. I had already done all that I could to make Gilly's study possible by stepping in to fill the gap left by a preoccupied mother! I had thought it was on a "just in case we needed it" basis. However, I did know that Gilly had gone through a lonely time and had said yes when most would have said not likely, so we both stuck to our tasks and Gilly's teaching would go on for eight years or so, stopping dramatically in 1999. Mealtime conversations widened from the problematic lambing and the post-mortems to the difficulty of dealing with aggravated teenage pupils and the prescriptive demands of that year's favoured teaching fashion.

The income was useful, and I learnt to keep the disasters under wraps although I still wake up in a panic even today as my unconscious mind tries to cope with past catastrophes. With fourteen hundred ewes stretched between the open moorland, the home farm and the winter grass keep, the beginnings of a fifty cow suckler herd (we bought in Hereford cross Friesian calves to rear on as heifers eventually, to bull them and graze them on the open moor), I also took on the chairmanship of the local National Farmers Union group and became a parent governor of the local state secondary comprehensive school that all three of our sons attended. The accounts and record keeping were done late at night and we had a steady stream of guests through the house. We were well busy.

Something was bound to give, and it did. One spring I omitted to fill in a form before the deadline date in March, which led to our not receiving the support payment on all the ewes for that year and since that year was to be taken as a base year for all subsequent years, it would have a knock-on effect for as long as the subsidy lasted. This was not sustainable; if I could not resolve it, we would go under.

Chapter 34
Giants and Dwarfs

The fact that I had not received the form in the first place was not excuse enough (it turned out that those with names beginning with the letters close to the end of the alphabet had been cut off the mailing list). I had to agree and didn't push that as an argument; pressure of work, personal injury (I had damaged my back wrestling with six-month-old stirks (young cattle) needing dehorning) and my undisguised abhorrence for form-filling did not add up to "force majeure". I appealed for a sympathetic ear from the bureaucrats at Exeter, then Bristol and then Whitehall and got just that but nothing else, a sympathetic ear! Eventually, Bill Hosking who was the union's livestock convener of the NFU put me in contact with my local MP, Anthony Steen, and through him I met Sir Leon Brittan, one of Britain's two European Commissioners. Anthony's wife provided lunch and Sir Leon took notes on a ten-minute conversation with me after coffee. Within four weeks I was in Brussels after a long train journey, sitting on the edge of a conference table with the Flemish man who was responsible for all European sheep support payments. Francois Broeders, along with three assistants and a couple of solicitors, listened to my story intently, and promised to investigate the matter urgently. He gave me his personal telephone number with instructions to use it only if I must and assured me that if I did, I would get him or no one. If he didn't answer it, it would be because he couldn't, he was in a meeting. He was good to his word and a couple of months later the whole issue, which could have easily been settled by sensible discretion at an early stage, was sorted out and settled in our favour. Francois Broeders, Bill Hosking, Anthony Steen and Sir Leon Brittan all had one thing in common – they were "can do" people in a "can't do" world. As such they stand out as beacons in my memory, high above the stagnant, lethargy-poisoned marshland of mediocrity in which so many of our paper-shuffling bureaucrats presently reside. History may well chronicle ours as the "age of the bureaucrat" in that we made rules to cover every eventuality, buried common sense and lost the guide book and the plot in a plethora of multilingual jargon.

We were to be sucked down into this small-minded, energy-sapping quagmire again several years on with the planners of the Dartmoor National Park and their largely inept managing committee. But as I said, this is several years on – I am jumping the gun again.

As time passed, we settled into a routine which started early and finished when all that absolutely had to be done that day was done. I cut cuttable corners and learnt from my mistakes. I had spent too many NFU meetings, hearing too many farmers bemoaning their lot and pontificating about how this or that support payment coming out of the public purse was their right, and how they were facing imminent collapse, before retiring to the bar and a comfortable ride home in Land Rover's latest offering. There are farmers on bikes, but they are few and far between! I took my leave of the active NFU commitment and concentrated more on our own business. No more missed deadlines.

Similarly, with the parent governors; the principal of the school was well competent, and the governors were largely occupied folding envelopes and wielding the official stamp for the management team. I don't easily fit into the role of sycophant, so after four years I didn't look for re-election. Our suckler herd had started to produce calves and so we pushed up onto Dartmoor with them, since we were already grazing several hundred ewes up there at different stages of their lives. The local common of Stall and Penn Moor, some three and a half thousand acres, became a useful grazing resource for us which our predecessors had not utilised.

Chapter 35
Dartmoor Commons

The system of common land usage which is similar on many of the national parks across Britain is complicated and convoluted. The land is owned by individuals privately, but that ownership does not necessarily confer the rights to graze, cut peat or practice any other activity usually associated with ownership. Those "rights" might be partly held by the owners, but more usually are held by the local farmers, or indeed the not so local farmers. The rights are known as grazing rights, to distinguish them from the rights of turbary (turf cutting, not now widely practised). Sporting rights often do go with the owner as do the mining rights, although the national park and planning administrations have a large say on these issues. The duchy, which really means the royal family in the present guise of Prince Charles, owns a large section of the middle of Dartmoor, although I am yet to see him cutting turf or driving sheep. No doubt he would if he could - if the system allowed him to. But the system is God and he can't; he has compensations not afforded to the rest of us born in different beds.

The grazing rights, which are the ones that affect us, are the most relevant to this story and most others. Originally, they were allocated in an informal way to local farms, providing one unit of grazing (that is one cow and calf or five sheep and their lambs) to one acre of "in-bye" land. The principle was that stock would be wintered on the "home" in-bye land and then turned up to graze to coincide with the moorland spring flush in mid-May. The growing season on this acidic, granite-dominated moorland is short, and the goodness drains out of the grass by mid-September. Traditionally, productive lactating stock were kept on the moor for this period, and outside this period the moor would be used to graze non-lactating stock which only needed to maintain their body mass. Surplus grass was usually burnt off (swaled) in February or March the following year and would green up magically and succulently to provide sweeter grazing later in the season. Generally, stock can be found on the ground that was burnt earlier in the season, so it is a useful tool for learing, (that is to teach animals to graze in a certain specified area). In theory, once on the open moor, there is nothing to stop stock, be they cattle, sheep or ponies, from roaming thirty-five miles right across the moor. In practice this rarely happens, although ponies are more inclined to roam than cattle or sheep unless they are driven. Their natural tendency is to return to the sweeter in-bye land from where they came as soon as the conditions deteriorate.

The learing process is therefore important to hold stock in a given area and to avoid excessive livestock roaming, which is not wildly popular with the neighbouring farmers. (To drive someone else's stock is seen as a sure sign of an intention to steal them, so it is not usually smiled upon.) Stock does go mysteriously missing from time to time but given the relatively low value, I doubt theft is the usual reason. Let's be generous and call it a playful way of protecting one's own lear. Playful or otherwise it is madly frustrating, and I doubt there are many graziers who haven't felt its effects.

Back to the grazing units. Up until the 1960s the so-called grazing rights were recognised as a grazing privilege - an opportunity to de-stock the in-bye land and make hay to feed to the animals during their winter home period. Enter the post-war subsidy on grazing livestock known as the HLCA or the Hill Livestock Compensatory Allowance. Compensating for what, I have no idea, but I guess it was the poor quality of the grazing; it sure changed the economics. Suddenly, farms got paid to keep stock! It wasn't a big jump to realise that if it were possible to keep stock up on the moor all year as well as stock at home, profits would not be hurt much. Welsh Mountain and Scottish Blackface ewes and hardy Galloway cows were seen as the answer, and supplementary feeding on the moor during the winter helped keep them alive and productive. There is no doubting the sweetness and quality of the eventual meat produced, but the real motivation was the government's support payment. What limited the potential was how many grazing rights a farm had. Faced with the perfectly understandable farming response to exploit an income potential, the government panicked at the prospect of over-grazed moorland and tried to regulate moorland usage by registering the rights of a grazing farmer. Astute cookies in the farming world registered as many rights as they could in whatever ways they could. So called "straying rights" were registered as grazing rights; and tenants, landlords and the farm cat registered rights separately on the same land. Ingeniously, other multiple rights were registered under the so-called "Man of Devon" title which I guess was a sop by the then Ministry of Agriculture not to discriminate in favour of only edge-of-the-moor farms. (I believe that some time ago it was possible to claim "Man of Devon" grazing rights just by qualifying as a man of Devon i.e. living in Devon!) Whatever, I can't blame the individual farmers for reacting to incompetent legislation. The result was a dog's breakfast of iniquity, with some farms ending up with no rights at all and others with up to four rights per acre of in-bye land. Yet more were allocated to bits of woodland and odd people related to the original Man of Devon concept, but now living in the Mediterranean sunshine with rights to graze twelve and a half sheep on this, that or more probably, this and that common!

Grazing rights became a very contentious issue and dominated the proceedings of the local commoners' association meetings. Our own particular commoners' association met once a year in the infant school room of the local village. Always aggravated and belligerent, with insupportable accusations and unfathomable legalistic responses, the meetings were entertaining and an educational experience not to be missed. On one occasion, the validity of one of our member's rights on a farm that had been a spoil heap for the local china clay extraction works was challenged. His steely blue-eyed response was to point out that since the arrival of the spoil heaps on his farm, it now took twice as long to try to cross his farm so he thought he might be due twice the grazing rights and furthermore, if for no other reason than to spite his accuser, he would so exercise these rights and would lear his new stock right adjacent to his accusing neighbour's. The whole conversation was recorded in the minutes as were countless others.

The sight of these hardworking, stubbled, heavy-coated men sitting with knees up to their chins on infant school children's seats, whilst grinding out insults and accusations at each other based on nothing more than interpretation of grazing right allocations will live with me forever. Many of the population of our small island would have given their back teeth to have swapped their suburban mediocrity for the chance to live and work in this breathtakingly beautiful part of Dartmoor, so it seemed contrary to allow such a small item of self-interest to so dominate and colour local relationships.

The chairman at the time of our commoners' association was called John. He was a mild mannered, kind man who was keen to do his job well and frustrated by the vitriolic nature of the invective. He introduced a spool to spool tape sound recorder to assist his cousin, who was then acting secretary and struggling to record the nuances of the meeting, if indeed there were any. At first, music was the result of the machine being switched on, but once the record button was located, the meeting proceeded to the repeated "click - whoosh - click" as the tape wound around its empty spool. The whole company of fifteen people was transfixed by the passage of celluloid from one spool to the other. Apologies, minutes, accounts, reports, election of officers and any other business all happened without acrimony and barely an unnecessary word was uttered until just before the slot for the date for the next meeting was reached, when the tape ran out. All hell let loose as the next hour was spent making up for preceding silence. The "Any other business" for that meeting was the largest on record!

John was looking for a way out and eventually I ran out of excuses at a time when everybody else was better prepared with theirs. It was 1998 and we had been grazing stock on the moor for ten years. During those years, the original HLCA had been supplemented and increased by the suckler cow premium and the ewe premium. The cash incentive to keep stock had increased with extremely predictable farmer responses, me included; we had worked too hard and suffered poor prices too long to ignore the generosity of our government and Brussels' benevolence. The moorlands all over the UK were becoming over-grazed and so through the quasi-government institution that was to become Natural England, a new initiative called the ESA or Environmentally Sensitive Area scheme was floated. This was to pay farmers to reduce stock grazing levels on the moor and introduce a level of vegetation management to increase the dwarf shrub and heather population and avoid poaching. They also introduced a stick to assist the carrot; if we didn't take up the scheme, then support payments would be reduced or removed. It was a no-brainer - the only difficulty would be persuading farmers to cut stock numbers - there was something primal in building up stock populations and it was against instinct to cut them however good the economic arguments were. We had only relatively recently built up our stock numbers so to reduce them was not such a primal leap for us; neither had we long established bloodlines to lose.

The discussions went on forever and plans were drawn up, re-drawn, scrapped and resurrected over a two-year period, but eventually agreement was reached, and stock numbers would be reduced. We were the first large common to go into the scheme; many, but not all, followed. There was, is and probably always will be a deep-seated farmers' resistance to anything that has a whiff of outside control being imposed from above. I share it but not to the extent that I blame the bureaucrats for the rain coming on the wrong day. We are, like it or not, in a controlled industry and I prefer the sort of control that comes from reasoned incentive rather than the heavy stick of government-imposed regulation. The ESA scheme was largely an incentive carrot held out to hungry horses short of income and with a half chance of achieving some environmental benefit. It was fuelled by money from the public purse and as such it was perfectly reasonable for the public to expect some benefit. I had been to farmer meetings where the beneficiaries of these payments were arguing the case that the incentive payments, they were receiving were theirs by right! Thin ice and skating come to mind. In due course after ten years the ESA scheme was replaced by the HLS. The higher-level entry scheme recognised some of the weaknesses of the earlier ESA and sought to redress them. Unfortunately, it was difficult to argue with the criticism that some of the new regulations were close to being counter-productive. For example, having persuaded farmers not to graze cattle in the late autumn to avoid poaching damage to areas of moorland areas used by the public for moorland access, it was unhelpful to those of us trying to manage the implementation of the new scheme to effectively pay incentives for reintroducing late autumn grazing. I don't think this was ever the intention, but a lack of communication between the quasi-government providers, the participating farmers and facilitators led to unnecessary problems for all concerned. For my part and that of other individuals caught between the participating farmers and the government providers, it was unhelpful to have not been consulted before policy was fixed. Potential problems could have been avoided.

One of the largest problems on our particular common was how to equally benefit all members of our farming group. Was it fair to compensate non-graziers for not exercising their grazing rights? If they weren't compensated, then all the incentive payments or compensatory payments would go to the minority active graziers. Needless to say, the non-graziers would then wish to exercise their grazing rights in order to benefit from the payments on offer and why shouldn't they? Achieving a balance was Solomonesque but without Solomon's autocratic advantage it proved beyond most of our earthly abilities. Most of our members were eventually satisfied that a reasonable compromise was reached, but alas, not all. Inevitably, the biggest recipients had the most input into facilitating discussions and this was not unreasonable, but when reason became superseded by competitive greed, then the end point was bound to mean disappointment for someone. My eighteen years working with and for this particular common ended last year with, I think, a significant improvement in income for all members and a much-improved level of cooperation and repartee, but not for all the people all the time. I have had many sleepless nights trying to satisfy competing aspirations, but just when I thought I had got there, the goalposts would be moved yet again.

Eventually, an administrative error on the part of the providing agency meant that the original agreement, which had cost me heavily to achieve would have to be renegotiated. At a time of significant pressure from other directions, I could not face the agony of the acrimony that was going to be involved. Fortunately, others were willing to take over, which ended for me an interesting, sometimes entertaining and always challenging job. We had come a long way in our farming journey and had well passed our target of a couple of acres and a caravan and an experience of the "Good life".

Our three sons had arrived, grown up and moved on in their separate ways; we had bought a good part of the farm that was our home; the vision of Ken Watkins as the chairman and instigator of the Woodland Trust was well on the way to being achieved. The buildings had been carefully restored, slate roofs replacing their asbestos predecessors, doors fitted, lofts replaced, stonework repaired and repointed using lime and local clay-based mortars, stone banks and dry-stone walls reinstated, and ponds dug. The farm was in regular use for school groups, individual visits and similar. In time, with active input and enthusiastic Woodland Trust employees, more than two thousand new trees had been planted.

I had been recognised by a national conservation body for what they referred to as my "outstanding contribution to conservation" at a small award ceremony presented by the then Environment Minister, Ben Bradshaw. Much as I appreciated the recognition, it did feel a tad over the top since most of the conservation work, I had done was thanks to generous European funding. Perhaps I should in turn recognise the European Union for their outstanding contribution to me!

Two things happened some twelve years apart which threatened to spoil the party. The first might have been called an "act of God". The second was very definitely an "act of man".

Chapter 36
Dark Days

Gilly was diagnosed with breast cancer in 1999 and as I suppose is the way with these things, at every stage the prognosis seemed to get worse. At first we thought that symptoms could be explained away by the fact that whilst competing in the River Dart raft race (a charity event where competing rafts enter the Dart River at Buckfastleigh in an innocent enough slow water section but within a quarter of a mile are tumbling down significant rapids towards the finish at Totnes, culminating in the weir), Gilly had been hit hard by a branch that had flipped back and hit her in the chest area. However, that proved not to be the reason for the symptom. With successive visits to the Derriford Hospital, the outlook seemed to be becoming increasingly grim until tests were done to see if the lymph nodes were infected. They had been. After that, my and I'm sure Gilly's mind went into a blur.

We were supported by everyone. Our good friend Jan Adam pulled strings, and linked Gilly up to the surgeon and he talked us through the implications, possible treatments and timing of procedures. No time was wasted, and the National Health Service hospital staff and treatment were magnificent. Due to the advanced stage of the cancer, Gilly and I opted for every possible treatment on the belt and braces approach. We didn't want to feel afterwards, oh, I wish we had done this or that. However, any treatment has consequences, mostly unpleasant, and so it was a brave decision by Gilly to opt for this tough option. Radical surgery, radiotherapy and chemotherapy took the lion's share of that year, with treatments having to be taken subject to red blood corpuscle numbers. If anything happened on the farm that year, I don't remember - we switched to autopilot and focused two hundred per cent on Gilly. Our sons, family and numerous friends were superb and catered for Gilly's and my every need. Whilst in hospital, Gilly was surrounded by flowers and when she came home, the village community and others surrounded her with kindness. Patty Watkins provided us with a case of champagne - one bottle for every month of the treatment and George Jackson, our boss from the Stowford days and others sent so many bouquets of flowers that there was hardly room for them in the bedroom. We took care to mark each cycle of chemotherapy with a trip somewhere in the week preceding the next therapy, to avoid the period being just needles and sheets. We were also super careful to monitor visitors and social situations for possibilities of infection. A cold or a sore throat can postpone vital chemotherapy, so anybody with any hint of infection was kept at arm's length.

There is, I believe, frequently no reason for cancer, it just "is". So I had to struggle to control my reactions to the minority viewpoint that there were reasons. Equally it was difficult to cope with the well intentioned comments of religious friends asserting that cures could be affected by the right sort of prayer. Meditation and prayer have their place, but not as a wish list, as if pressing the right button and then asking in the right way for the right things in the right numbers would somehow magically effect a change in circumstance! Flowers, kindness, smiles, medicine, meals, phone calls, visits, sunshine, cool hands on a hot brow, moisture to dry lips, warm cushions on a cold day - all that is vital aid to recovery, but for me the assurance that prayers were on offer cut no slack and was not a comfort, though no doubt that was the intention. As with other things, there was no reason; it was not part of some overall plan, it was a physical illness needing a physical cure; we did everything we could and left no stone unturned.

Ten months of treatment had pretty well left Gilly exhausted - a return to teaching seemed unlikely and proved to be so. We tried to keep stress levels as low as possible and focus on positives. On one occasion, we took a holiday in Finland whilst the boys looked after the farm. Some very good friends looked after Gilly like a princess as she was just recovering her head of hair. One notable night we sat by a lakeside, singing Finnish and English folk songs, keeping warm by a log fire whilst the sun went down and rose again, and the loon croaked its haunting melancholy cry across the glassy black water.

The next day I was treated to a sauna with the same folk. My response to their question of whether I was comfortable, as we three men sat naked in the sweltering fir essence-filled steam, which was a very British, 'Yes thank you, I am comfortable,' was a big mistake. The Finnish idea is that if it doesn't hurt, it won't help, so we had more steam. I dropped my reserve and admitted to being indeed extremely uncomfortable. It worked - no more steam. The other two seemed rather keen that we leave the sauna and go to the lake naked carrying our white towels neatly over one arm at a very exact moment. It neatly corresponded to the moment when the Helsinki-bound train from Rovaniemi went past the old railway cottage where we were staying. There were trees, should we have looked for cover but that of course was not part of the plan! We three, somewhat past our prime, smiling gentlemen stood stark naked, towels on arm, waving to the amused passengers before crossing the line and cooling off in the lake. In England it would no doubt have been an arrestable offence; there it was just a huge joke. I had been "had". I pretended that it was perfectly normal and so did they - for them, it probably was.

Again, as part of Gilly's recuperation, we took a holiday to visit some friends living in Tobago. The radiant heat of the sun and the warm sea was a pick-me-up for both of us. This little episode might be better told than written but I'll give it a go. Two of our friends and Gilly had gone out beyond the not insignificant surf and were comfortably flip-flapping their way around, heads down, snorkels fitted, no doubt engrossed in colourful tropical submarine wonders. I had earlier decided that my natural tendency to sink rather than float was good enough reason to keep me beach side of the surf. However, as the three of them seemed to be having such a fine time, I was tempted to give it a go. Like buying a dress, there are things you must know. One is to fit your flippers on the beach and walk backwards into the surf; secondly, don't pull your mask down and engage with the snorkel until you are in the water and lastly once your head is down, if the snorkel gets full of sea water it's better to blow it out rather than try to breathe through it! These are basics and I got them all wrong. By the time I got beyond the surf I was in deep water metaphorically and literally. Fortunately for me, Gilly tired of the little striped tiger fish and noticed that I hadn't succeeded in extracting oxygen from water. She arrived and was slightly irritatingly calm, but at the time it was what I needed to continue living so I mustn't knock it! Swimming for me was and still is a matter of staying alive whilst I'm in the water.

From then on, Gilly got stronger and stronger and having stood so close to the edge, we gripped closer together and swallowed hard on the cool life-giving air of new horizons. Like the American poet Robert Frost's character, who sucked in the vibrant air of his neighbour's planted woodland by the fading light of a winter's moon, we had "promises to keep, and miles to go before we sleep."

During the nineties and noughties as they were to become known, we took the chance to purchase the Hall Farm house, surrounding buildings and a good bit of the surrounding land. Building maintenance was obviously outside the remit of the Woodland Trust, yet many of the buildings were in a poor state of repair resulting from years of neglect. The Woodland Trust, in particular Ken Watkins, recognised that we had invested a significant amount of cash and a large amount of time into making the house comfortable, improving access to and bringing the old buildings into a usable state. We had got to the stage that large amounts of capital needed to be spent on building work and a new livestock barn. Ken was helpful in persuading the Woodland Trust to allow us to purchase the buildings and land, although at the time the purchase price seemed daunting.

The logic was simplicity itself. We had family labour and given a bit of luck and a gentle breeze, we would get clear of the necessary borrowing in twenty-five years or so. In the event, we bettered that. All unnecessary expenditure was driven to the minimum - stock numbers were pushed up coincidentally with a generous input of headage subsidy from Europe. We squeezed twenty-five hours into every day and kept our fingers crossed. I reckoned that as long as I didn't die in the attempt, we would be OK but just in case I took out another life insurance to cover the mortgage. One way or another, we would have bought our farm against all expectations. Whatever foolishness my mother's father had got involved in to cause them to lose Cleyhill Farm in Wiltshire all those years ago would have been expiated and we would have a secure base from which to launch our family in whatever direction they wanted to go. Family helped where they could in ways that they could. In a particularly difficult time, my sister subbed us with a sizeable, unasked for loan which was massively appreciated. My dad was ever-ready and willing to come over for a day's work, usually arriving with a supply of wine, chocolates and other goodies. Bill, with his Cumbrian flat hat, anorak and intelligent good humour helped focus our sights on the wider world. Our children at different times in our farming journey had been vital and although they were the main reason for the venture, they were also integral in our getting to where we got to.

There was mushroom collecting and selling before school, endless lambings, calf dehorning, reseeding, hay making with our temperamental old square baler, riding behind the bale sledge, moving stock onto the moor and bringing the same stock back again - sometimes the same numbers and sometimes they were fatter, searching out the odd missing ones, moving to grass keep, erecting and moving miles and miles of electric fencing and early morning market jaunts after starting at four thirty a.m. to reach Taunton before seven o'clock after a good sale the preceding day at Exeter. Breakfasts have never tasted better than at Taunton Market where the brilliant yellow eggs floated around in a greasy sea of bacon, sausage, beans, and mushroom, topped off with ketchup. For me, these were diamond days and still glitter in my treasure chest of memories.

Sadly, my father passed away in 2002, after a short illness, just after his eighty-third birthday. We smuggled a bottle of sherry and some birthday cake into his hospital bedroom, along with Scamp his terrier dog, which he had inherited from us after the boys found him wandering around on the moor. No more would he arrive with a bottle of Blue Nun, Liquorice Allsorts and Milk Tray. No more would one of us get dispatched to make yet another cup of tea, whilst the last one stood half-drunk by his chair and no more would the boys have to go scouting around for his car keys which would inevitably be in one of his many pockets.

Eventually, we sold his bungalow with the stained-glass image of my mother with Chipper, her Cavalier King Charles Spaniel built into the porch window, and with some of the money inherited we built a hut over the stream in the field facing west and the setting sun. We have spent countless evenings with supper, a glass of wine and a radio concert sitting in the hut watching the swallows dive past for an inflight drink, the doves glittering brilliant white on route from the pond back to the barn, the heron stalking ponderously around the stream looking for croaking and juicy frogs and of course the playful trout and their acrobatic leaps into the summer gnat- filled sky. Dad always said that it was a shame we hadn't got a west-facing window in the house to sit by. Well, thanks to him, we have now, and it was built by me and his grandsons with love and in his memory – he would like that. He was like us all, a child of the age in which he was born; generous to a fault, politically an enigma, he struggled with some irrational prejudices, but you don't remember the odd patch of tough skin when the apple is sweet, and he was a sweet apple and I miss him a lot.

Margaret, Gilly's mum, died in 1995, just before the birth of her first granddaughter - she had five grandsons. She and Mike had moved to Tavistock on the west of Dartmoor some years earlier, and for Margaret I think it was the first home that she could feel comfortable in, and in her words, where she was not on display or on duty. She had, I think, always been the vicar's wife. Duty and appearances were paramount. It seemed like she was only beginning to emerge from underneath the suffocated weight of other people's expectations when she died. Sadly, I never really knew her, just her shadow; I think we may have got on.

Chapter 37
Building Projects

One of the two biggest building projects that we took on was to make a holiday house out of a dilapidated cottage, which was rat infested, having been used as a feed store previously. One wall was collapsed; it had an asbestos roof, a bramble patch and an old adjoining cart shed.

The other was a new barn to provide covered space to house six hundred ewes at lambing. The barn was actually second-hand or pre-used, to use the vernacular, bought at a farm sale in Launceston and previously used as an indoor riding school. It first had to be dismantled, and then reassembled on site in January when it rained endlessly. Since the roof steel spanning beams were thirty-two feet long, Danny my eldest son and his friend Glyn, who had been a regular helper on the farm, used a borrowed tractor and a load of straw to lift the steels above the hedge height and get around the corners. Four loads at eighty miles per round trip and "hey presto". It's quicker in the writing than in the doing. We dug holes and laid concrete pads for the uprights. A genius contractor friend, Richard, levelled the site for us, cleverly leaving the top surface a sort of crumbled granite which set like concrete and yet drained freely just like he said it would. One by one, we positioned the uprights, welding extra feet on as necessary, propping them up with wooden slats whilst the concrete set, measuring and re-measuring to ensure the sixty-foot roof span and bracing diagonals would fit. One or two uprights had to be leant on by the borrowed telehandler to shift them an inch or two, but otherwise all went well. Danny, Ben, Matt and Glyn were the workforce and although it was our first such attempt, we had a barn up and useable by the beginning of that spring's lambing.

The carefully screwed-on roof now supports photovoltaic cells and we have buried all the previously hanging electric supply wires so unfortunately no more do we have the sight of enough swallows (literally hundreds) collecting on overhead wires to weigh them down as they congregated, waiting for the starting trigger for their perilous journey over the mountains of Europe, the Mediterranean and the Sahara to their winter homes in Central Africa.

The cottage took a little longer; in fact, we dragged the job out over five years, working on it usually between five o'clock and supper time. It became a labour of love and, as such, didn't want to be rushed. From the first guest to the last, many of whom were from outside the UK, they have all left generous and glowing reports. We were booked more than thirty weeks every year and without any doubt, could have repeated the venture three or four times over with other barn conversions, but for the unfathomable preference of the Dartmoor National Park Planning Department to see buildings fall into dereliction rather than be sensitively adapted and used to provide much needed housing, tourist accommodation and local employment as well as supplementing income.

Chapter 38
Chance to Raise My Gaze

The friends that we stayed with in Tobago had a touch of style to them; Rosemary is a vivacious sixty-year-old who met Gilly in the hospital at Derriford, where she worked as a reflexology medic among other things. Patrick is her high-maintenance, high horsepower husband. He spent his working life in the army, taught himself which end of a boat was which, mortgaged their house in Plymouth and built himself a sailing boat to take out to Tobago which was Rosemary's family home. There, he intended to set up a charter business. Sadly, on his way through the Bay of Biscay the weather took up a bit nasty, and running out of ways to steer, he had to abandon ship and abandon a lot of other things too. The thing that I love about Patrick is that he didn't abandon his smile. My father liked to quote Rudyard Kipling's poem "If", "If you can make one heap of your winnings and risk it on one turn of pitch and toss and lose and start again at your beginnings etc. etc.", well that's Patrick. Anyway, they introduced us to Carol Trewan, who at that time was producing the weekly Radio Four programme "On Your Farm" and in due course she thought it might be an idea to slot us in, largely I think because we were first-generation farmers, unusual in that we had not inherited our farm or had any significant outside or family money to aid us.

The normal routine for the radio interview was to focus on some whizz kid who had returned home from college with a headful of gross margins and was now keeping four cows where father milked one and growing gold-encrusted wheat where grandfather grew wild oats. I didn't fit that category and the interviewer was Robert Foster, the beef wizard. He didn't know where to start but he was OK once I had settled him down! The BBC must have thought it not a total disaster as they played it twice.

Carol went on to edit the farming section of the Western Morning News and asked me to write an article on computers in farming. For someone who didn't and still doesn't know the difference between a mouse and a modem and considers a laptop ought to be a baby, a cat or a pretty girl depending on your age, this was quite an ask. However, I did and went on to provide several years' worth of occasional "farmer takes a sideways look at life" articles. I confess that I really enjoyed it in that it lifted my head from the soil and the toil. I am amazed even today to meet people who actually read them. Carol was a great friend who sadly died young with leukaemia. Her slot at the Western Morning News was taken on by someone else and the sideways look idea gave way to more grown-up stuff involving figures and the latest models (tractors that is - you need The Sun or The Star for the other sort).

Chapter 39
Beyond Our Control

In 2001, foot-and-mouth struck Britain and ten million cattle and sheep were slaughtered. There were cases very close to us and so, in common with many other farmers, we closed the gates, discouraged visitors and generally battened down the hatches. The cost to the country was about eight billion pounds. The emotional cost to many farmers and their families was unbearable. It might be difficult to imagine if you haven't been there, but when you work with animals every day and you get to know them as individuals, their little quirks and foibles, and you have little human company to share the everyday care and decisions (and these are frequently matters of life and death) concerning the animals in question, the distress felt when things go wrong is difficult to bear. To watch a whole herd or flock be slaughtered sometimes on a "just in case" basis must have been terrible indeed and was more than some could bear.

This followed the bovine spongiform encephalopathy, BSE or mad cow disease of the early 1990s, which was later linked to the occurrence of new variant CJD (Creutzfeldt-Jakob disease) in human beings. This was a tragic disease, but it was avoidable. It does not take a genius to do the sums. The BSE outbreak is now known to have been caused by feeding the dried and compressed animal carcass waste back to animals as a protein source. I suppose in times of great famine it might have been just about acceptable to risk feeding dubiously sourced protein to livestock in the pursuit of food security to a hungry population. But what might have been acceptable in the post-war years when food, and in particular protein, was in short supply surely could not be justified in the 1970s and '80s when food surpluses were more the problem. The individual farmer or abattoir could do little on their own to influence this. In fact, I suspect many farmers had no idea what was included in the neatly packed and pelleted "fast finisher nuts" or "early weaning supplements". When I heard that a cluster of cases of new variant CJD had occurred in the East Midlands and were traced back to baby food (that is two-ounce little jars of tomato and beef or similar and fed to babies by mothers thinking they were doing the best for their children) being made using mechanically recovered meat, I was, in common with others, flabbergasted. Mechanically recovered meat is meat that has been removed from the butchered carcass by a high-pressure water jet once the standard joints have been removed. OK for the pet food trade perhaps, but baby food? That surely is mercenary greed taken to unacceptable levels. I am not a great fan of bureaucratic intervention, but it was surely the job of government to put a stop to that. Many farmers would have chosen not to support such a penny-pinching approach, but they would have been powerless to stop it themselves.

The cheap food policy so close to the hearts of successive post-war governments has benefitted no one. Government refusal to release land for building over the years has forced up house prices to double that in much of Europe and food prices as a proportion of income have shrunk proportionately with the result that farming still needs to be subsidised for farm businesses to survive. I didn't choose to go into farming to fill in subsidy application forms, but if I hadn't done it, then the farm would have been just a dream. The system sadly is king.

By the mid '90s I had slowed down a bit; I guessed age, workload and our sons having all moved on in their own lives, (so our family labour force had gone) were the main reasons. Gilly and I hung on to a reduced cow herd, but the economy was in numbers and we didn't have enough. The worry and aggravation caused first by BSE and then foot-and-mouth had also taken its toll. One day whilst blood testing to see if TB (another disease) had got into our cattle, one of the heifers rocked back on her heels and vaulted the galvanised gate that Gilly was holding up to push the cattle towards the crush and George Austin the vet. Fortunately, Gilly saw what was happening and let the gate go; she jumped out of the way and it crashed to the floor, but the heifer had I suppose just not worked out that where front legs go, back legs normally follow. Either that or she had caught sight of the size of the needles in George's bag! We regrouped and finished the job and the three of us sat down for some soup, bread and cheese. As we recapped the morning's events and counted our blessings, we heard on the news the sad inquest conclusions concerning a lady who had died having been accidentally trodden on by her own bull. It was to be the final straw for our cattle herd. We sold all the remaining cattle, including our sons' one cow each that weekend. I missed seeing them, scratching their ears, and the odd conversations we had but if I'm honest, not the work.

I was soon to find out that the reason for my energy drop was more than Anno Domini. I was playing squash with a doctor friend one day and my shoulder hurt - then it didn't - I restarted and then it did again. My squash partner realised the pain was related to increased heart rate. Lucky me, I could just as easily have been playing a librarian! Within a couple of weeks, I had three stents (these look like expanded biro pen springs) slid into my main heart arteries and watched on a TV monitor screen whilst the blood flow expanded like the tributaries in the Nile Delta to reach places it had not been for a long time. I substituted my occasional games of squash for even more occasional games of tennis and I ran a half marathon six months later partly as a thank you to the heart medics and partly to prove to myself that if I was strong enough to do this then I was also strong enough to continue farming I ran with my new daughter-in-law and she kindly let me just beat her to the line though I think she was staying behind to pick up the pieces if I collapsed.

For five years all was fine, until the symptoms reappeared. I thought I would be pulled in for another bit of plumbing and a few more biro springs but no such luck; this time it was considered to be a job for the hacksaw. I had a triple heart bypass in 2004 when the genius surgeon removed a vein from my left arm and chopped it into three, turned it around and tacked it into my heart. Within two days I was walking up and down the stairs and within five days I was back home. Gilly was strong and supportive and she and I, over a period of about two months, walked steadily around the farm, getting a little faster every day. Somehow, with family help, we kept the farm going.

I had had two visits to the hospital which the system deemed serious enough to ask me during them what my religion was. The first time I had said I was a "creationist", intending to mean that I acknowledged a creative force behind existence but that I was not convinced about the rest of it. Son number three pointed out that a "creationist" was actually a name chosen by the "and God created the world in seven days (literally) starting with a serpent, an apple tree and Eve etc." brigade, prevalent in the bible belt of mid-America. Next time I did some homework. I was a "theist", I told the nurse. 'How do you spell that,' she said, 'with an "f" or a "th"?' Since it might have been my last form, I was at pains to get it right so was in full flow explaining what I thought a theist was, and how it was spelt, and how I thought that if there was indeed a God, then I didn't recognise the need to identify him, her or it, and that if I had got it wrong then it probably wouldn't matter in any case. She stopped me before I had finished to inform me that she had actually found it on her list after all and I was wrong, it didn't start with an "f" or "t" but an "a". I was top of the list, ticked and accounted for as an "atheist!" I wouldn't want to be part of any heaven if the Big Cheese didn't have a sense of humour – it would probably be full of planners and barristers and I would just hate that (more later). If I get there, I will explain the atheist bit to the angel on the gate and if I arrive at an inconvenient moment and it's St. Peter, I will probably hang around until he goes off duty. I prefer the idea of a heaven full of laughing butterfly angels than long faced, bearded old men in long white robes! First impressions have always mattered a lot to me!

About two months into my recuperation, we looked southwards out of the upstairs window of the house to see that what looked like one of the far fields had been partially ploughed. We hadn't been there since my operation, it being winter, and all the stock were either in the barn or north of the road closer to the buildings. Closer examination revealed a small drift of wild boar had taken up residence. There were seven in total, ranging from the heavily-tusked father who would have tipped the scales around sixty kilos, through to his daintier (hardly the word for any wild boar specimens) wife and five following family of different ages. In France, these are called sanglier and taste wonderful in a stew. Gilly stayed to keep watch from about twenty yards and I took myself off as fast as I was able back to the farm for a means to convert these destructive porkers to sanglier stew. The only gun I had was an air gun, which might have just about been powerful enough to make a mouse jump at close range, so I settled on a pickaxe handle and some African spears that we had mounted on our hall wall. My ever-sharp penknife was always in my pocket. So armed, I drove our ancient Toyota into the field ready to join battle. Thinking I was cleverer than they, I hedged them towards the corner of the field, excitement and taste buds rising to the event. Gilly walked on steadily behind. I reckoned at least two of the smaller ones were a near certainty when the vehicle snapped over a fallen branch. I might as well have fired a starting gun; the whole group dispersed in seven different directions, with the big tusked old boy crashing directly through the sheep fencing and into the woods; he didn't even slow down! For several weeks after that, we would see the group trotting around the farm with the unperturbed authority of the invincible, heads down, tails up like their African warthog cousins. A little later in the spring, I heard they were over at the neighbouring village of Cornwood, where they were making friends with the groundsman of the pristine cricket pitch!

With the gradual inflow of suburban conformist attitudes to our village, came a change to the cooperative and slightly cavalier spirit that had contributed so much to village character in the past. At the time of Barack Obama's elevation to the White House, the dreary black railway bridge at the southern margin of the village was unimaginatively sporting the hastily dubbed letters KUFC, but not in that order. Its lack of creative genius had irritated me every time I crossed it, so having left it for a year to see if there was any subtle nuance I hadn't appreciated, Barack Obama's inauguration provided the excuse I needed. I got up on one moonless morning at two a.m., armed myself with head torch, a brush and rainbow paints and tentatively set up my stool on the offending bridge. It took me an hour and I only had to clamber over the wrong side of the bridge once when a slow-moving police car cruised by some thirty yards away. After that hour, KFUC had been over painted by a smiling Thomas the Tank Engine with an even wider smiling Barack Obama at the wheel and the words "Well done America" on the following carriages. It wasn't an artistic masterpiece, but it was passable and clearly had a positive upbeat message to our friends over the pond with whom we are supposed to have this special relationship. It made at least two other people in Harford smile but only lasted three months until the bridge was overpainted again in an unimaginative shade of British Rail black. It is interesting to me that "KFUC" was considered acceptable, but my goodwill gesture to our gullible cousins wasn't.

WELL DONE

Chapter 40
Planning Pantomime

If Gilly's illness had been the higher-level challenge to our party, then the pantomime that was orchestrated by the planning department of the Dartmoor National Park (DNP) was the lower one. At about the time of Gilly's hospitalisation, I replaced the windows of our farmhouse with hardwood, double-glazed and purpose-built replacements. In truth, these were not an exact copy of the ones they replaced and in one way in particular they were clumsily built with a heavy horizontal drip bar between the vertical frames. Also, the new ones had an integral sill to deliver water away from the stonework. Other than that the windows matched their predecessors in numbers and size and panes. In overall size they were exactly the same, having been purpose-made and the pane sizes were so similar as to be almost impossible to discern any difference on an A4 sized photo of the house taken from some fifteen metres and with the house filling the page!

The windows they replaced were poor quality (all that was available at the time) softwood, post-war, simply-made insertions themselves, some of which had been altered to fit the spaces and were so dilapidated that it was necessary to support the glass with one hand when closing the frame to stop the panes from falling out! By replacing the windows, I had, the planners asserted, "caused criminal damage to an historic building!" It is true to say that I had made the change without their consent, but I was genuinely under the impression that like for like didn't require consent and deeply offended to be accused of having caused criminal damage. I was in any case happy to both modify the new windows and apply for retrospective consent. Like Shakespeare's Shylock in the Merchant of Venice, they wanted flesh, by the bucketful.

Since we had been personally visited by the chairman of the Dartmoor National Park Authority to see what all the fuss was about and been assured by him that it was "a storm in a teacup" and that he would, in his words "show them", that is the planners, "who's boss", I really thought that retrospective permission, which we applied for, on recommendation from the planning officer, would be granted and that would be an end to it.

I should have heard the alarm bells ringing when the chairman referred to the "who's boss" bit. I was obviously to be a pawn in some petty bureaucratic struggle for authority.

This whole saga started when we were entertaining the historic building officer with coffee after she had visited us on entirely different business to do with one of the outbuildings. I had known this particular lady for many years and although she was thoroughly pernickety and pedantic, I respected her as a person and doubt that on her own volition she would have abused our hospitality by returning to her office to check the files and see if the double glazing she had noticed while drinking coffee in the kitchen was authorised. She had a rather transparent tendency to blush when she was on dodgy ground and she blushed a lot when I next met her, and she was taken off the case by the new director of planning. She was replaced by a reluctant second historic building officer. I know from a mutual friend who worked in the planning department that the new historic building specialist was not at all keen to get involved for whatever reason, internal politics I suspect.

The penny was beginning to drop. Soon after this garrulous Welshman had taken over his job as director of planning at the Dartmoor National Park, I had invited him as a courtesy to walk the farm with me and in so doing had also looked at the house and the buildings. He had made polite noises about the barns being the best maintained that he had seen for a long time on Dartmoor (fine examples of original design and twentieth century craftsmanship, preservation and maintenance etc.). He too would have enjoyed Gilly's ever-present hospitality in the form of a cup of tea and some flapjack. He probably walked through our handmade, home-grown, spalted beech front door with which his chairman had been so taken and was to so excite his imagination in the months to come. No mention of "double glazing" here or of "inauthentic front doors" or "different reflectivity" of single glazed and double-glazed windows. (In all the inspections and nonsense that was to follow, no one noticed the "different reflectivity" of one of the forty-nine windows on the front of the house that was not double glazed!). This "man from Del Monte" lookalike had a penchant for sweeping importantly across the meeting room in a white-waisted suit topped off with a gushing tooth-filled smile and a bundle of supposedly incriminating papers crooked into his high bent arm.

Our retrospective appeal some eleven years after the windows were fitted was allocated a site meeting at which I had little doubt that good sense would prevail, especially as we had significant and professional supporting evidence and testimony. However, I was surprised to see the new head of planning take control of the meeting in the way that he did. I remembered then the words of the chairman of the park authority (that we would show them who was boss), and alarm bells were tinkling.

"Del Monte" assumed total control of the meeting, side-lined his inadequate chairlady and young planning officer, informed me that I was only to speak to answer questions when asked (I wasn't), and informed the four (two of whom were professionally and relevantly qualified) supporting "witnesses" that they could not contribute in any way to the meeting. In writing up the minutes of the meeting after the event, he actually reported some of his own comments as if they had been made by the historic building officer.

The "witnesses" that were not allowed to speak included Glynn Hosgood, the original window maker for the post-war windows and now well into his eighties, Kerry Honour, a resident of Harford Village going back some fifty years who knew the house well, Ted Pinsent, one of the previous tenants of the house in its previously dilapidated state some thirty five years ago and Roger German, the professional land agent who had made a very thorough record of the condition of the farmhouse, acting for the landlord when we first moved in twenty-five years earlier. Eventually the land agent Roger German did speak, over the objecting squeaks of the chairlady, to point out the unfair and undemocratic way the site meeting was being held. With obsequious arrogance, "Del Monte" turned to the attendant members of the committee and metaphorically licked the mud from their boots.

This was a crucial meeting for me as it was the site meeting and the consequential report that the members of the full planning committee formed their opinion on and made their decisions. It was therefore important that they received a balance representation of evidence, especially as the issue was more subjective than objective. There was one practical committee member, a carpenter who was clearly horrified at the way the meeting was being held and the pointless nature of the impasse, one devious peacock, keen to inform anyone who would listen that two of his uncles six times removed were farmers, as if that conferred for him some sort of credibility and another joker, who was I think there for the day out and to claim expenses.

Up until that morning, I had been prepared to compromise and accommodate in a reasonable way, but the manipulation of the minutes and the undemocratic and unreasonable conduct of the site meeting were a step too far; they had chosen the wrong person to be a pawn in their power struggle.

Over the following two years, the local government ombudsman was to be involved, my local MP Gary Streeter, the then Minister for the Environment, a recently retired director of the National Heritage Council, the Council for the Preservation of Rural England, the Dartmoor Preservation Association, the BBC, a professional solicitor and the overwhelming majority of our local village. This village support was somewhat undermined by a small self-appointed group grandly titled the "executive committee", who took it upon themselves to instruct the new chairman by email not to attend a subsequent appeal meeting to represent the views of most of our village. What prompted that over-step of their imagined authority is open to conjecture, but it may be that several of them had planning applications of their own in the pipeline.

Given the astonishing levels that the director of planning had stooped to in order to win his battle for authority with the chairman of the national park, I doubt any clear decisive intervention from my village committee would have made a difference, but we will never know. As it transpired, the whole sorry saga dragged on some two and a half years and cost us heavily in cash, emotion and time.

After some thirty-five years of village life, during which time we had as a family pitched in willingly whenever anyone had a problem, it was a hard thing indeed to take such a blow from a group I had thought of as friends. The winds of change that had swept out the old stalwarts had sadly left us with some much-reduced shoe sizes, the imprint of which I doubt will trouble history overmuch.

After the pantomime of the site meeting, a few of the Dartmoor National Park committee forced the dispute to be referred to a national appeal. We employed a solicitor on the advice of our Member of Parliament. I regret that we did so; she was incompetent and expensive and way out of her depth in the job that she was asked to do and failed us completely at the first planning appeal hearing. She failed to point out to the appeal judge that if he dismissed, as he did, the fault-riven enforcement notice served by the DNP on me to remove the windows without saying that they had to be replaced by something else, then the DNP planners would simply go away and serve another notice and we would have to fight the case all over again. That little error cost us twelve thousand pounds, her fees! I fought the second appeal against a re-served enforcement notice myself, with much patient support from Gilly.

It was not all doom and gloom though; late one dreary afternoon, a man from the Dartmoor National Park phoned up to say that he was coming to visit the farm and would need to see the inside of the house. He gave his name as Christopher Porridge which, pronounced with a lisp as he had, led me to think it was a joke. Perhaps I had misheard him? It wasn't. He went on to say that he was the legal advisor for the Dartmoor National Park and was qualified as a barrister and would arrive at two p.m. the following day. I enquired about the reason for his visit. I had seen this character before, fond of the sound of his own voice and fancying himself as a bit of a wordsmith. 'Words are my forte,' I remember him saying at one meeting, thumbs in the waistcoat, monocle falling from his eye socket (well, at least that's the image I have). He declared that he was 'not bound' and these were his exact words, 'to give me a reason for his visit.'

I responded, 'In that case, Mr Porridge, I would not be bound to open the front door to you.' He countered that I would have to do so since he would arrive with a legal right of entry document. This clown and I were never going to get on! No solicitor was going to enter our house uninvited, I told him.

He seemed perturbed, mostly because I had confused his legal status. 'Barrister,' he said and repeated, 'Barrister, spelt with a "B", followed by an "A" Mr Venables.'

I guessed he was trying to intimidate me with his professional status. His lisp, however, sounded the letters more like p, a, – it was too much of an invitation. 'Oh p, a,' I nearly cried in gratitude, 'would that be a p, a, as in "pompous ass"?' I told him that if he did arrive, he would be met by the BBC Spotlight news team.

The BBC was news-short when I phoned up and they jumped at the chance. At two p.m. the next day, the shiny black shoes of the green-anoraked Mr Porridge passed through the gate to our walled garden and slithered across the wet granite cobbles as he, head down, and careless of any courtesy, made uncertainly for the front door, past my wife and the waiting and primed BBC cameraman. He feebly waved his little bit of legal paper like a creepy schoolboy handing his homework in. The whole interview was recorded and shown on the news that evening and generated a good response. If the Dartmoor National Park had had any credibility before, it was certainly running on half empty after that. It was repeated again at the end due to the public response that came in through social media and again the following night.

At the second appeal meeting, the enforcement case presented by the Dartmoor National Park was QUASHED. The enforcement notice served on me by the Dartmoor National Park was lifted and I was given a reluctant written apology by the director of planning for having misled the planning committee about the doors. (The main focus of the DNP was on the Windows but as the case dragged on the director of planning did not hesitate to expand the argument. He chose to include the front door on the grounds that it was "inauthentic" and " temporarily fitted". Since the door was built and fitted to recorded professional standards by the resident occupier who had been farming on Dartmoor for nearly forty years using wood from a beech tree that used to grow adjacent to the house it was a tad difficult to see how it could have been either inauthentic or temporary.)

To have applied for costs would have dragged the fight on. I was ground down by the pointlessness of the dispute, which had lasted nearly three years and I didn't want to inflict further pressure on Gilly, my family or indeed most members of my village community.

In 2008 the Dartmoor National Park published a useful booklet on "Standards of Excellence" concerning building repairs. It refers to and even has pictures of a local development by a neighbouring estate. I applaud it; I agree the development is excellent and it has made something useful out of an otherwise wasting asset. Jobs have been created, buildings saved, and tourism encouraged. However, on further inspection, many of the things that the director of planning found specifically so unacceptable in our windows (the very same ones that I was accused of having wilfully caused great harm to an historic building by fitting) are celebrated as beacons of excellence just down the road!

The planning laws and regulations in the UK are well intended but need intelligent interpretation and sensitive discretion. If we can't trust public servants to act reasonably and responsibly in the interest of the public whom they are supposed to serve, then they should not be allowed the privilege to exercise discretion. The inconsistencies apparent in this small area of Dartmoor and the contradictions between government policy (i.e. the provision of housing, energy preservation, employment and provision of tourism facilities) and local government's interpretation do nothing to inspire confidence in the public to trust the system.

Chapter 41
Crossing the Rubicon

The financial struggle to get started in farming and then service the mortgage, the intransigence of the layers of ineffective bureaucracy in the Department of the Environment on our ewe premium saga and the soul-destroying frustration of trying to equably share the conservation goodies coming into our group of commoners in the face of irrational argument and stubborn greed had taken their toll. The physically debilitating battles with illness for both Gilly and me and the totally unjustifiable and unreasonable stance of the national park planners, as they kicked us around in their childish power struggle in pursuit of the pointless, topped off by my disappointment in the weak-kneed support of my fair-weather friends and neighbours had left me drained at a time I could ill afford it. In the wake of all the above, I hit a barrier from which getting up again was difficult.

With the sheep I carried on thanks to Gilly's help, but I was now going through the motions. What I had seen before as a challenge I now saw as just work and I woke up in the mornings dog-tired. We had many positives in our lives but the responsibility and the pressures of running a business in the mind-numbingly over-bureaucratised world we now occupied was beginning to weigh me down. My mornings were a trudge through sticky mud in heavy boots. None of our family was able to take over the farm (perhaps we had been too successful in encouraging them to follow their own paths!) but Gilly and I needed a different horizon. I had no intention of dying in my wellies, which is a life-threatening tendency among farmers.

In the summer of 2015, my youngest son Matt bought a ten-pound bike from a recycling centre, pumped up the tyres and cycled across Europe to Slovakia and then down to Croatia and back through Italy. I joined him for two weeks, cycling from Frankfurt where I bought a bike, after a long bus journey from Plymouth on the hottest day of the year, and we cycled together along the rivers of central Germany to the Alps and then to Munich. We slept by the river banks, cooked a lot of porridge and put everything into the saucepan for suppers of seafood stews, washed down with locally sourced white wine at the end of the day. We swam to cool down and to wash and drank ice cool Weizen beer and milk for energy and because it tasted good. Gilly looked after the farm and I had my own Damascus road revelation. Whilst cycling, I remembered the times on Sunday mornings, rushing off to fence in yet more sheep and passing people walking their dogs and going to fetch the newspapers. I remembered thinking what a luxury it would be to wake up one day with just a dog to walk or a newspaper to fetch. Here I was and for a while the only thing that mattered was keeping cool, eating and finding a place to sleep. Gilly didn't know it at the time and perhaps neither did I, but we had crossed the Rubicon - "Alea iacta est", the die was cast.

In the autumn of 2015, we both fell in love with a place, a house, a community and a lifestyle in the high French Pyrenees. It was to be a new stage for us. My sheep knife is now not always in my pocket and I can look over the Pyrenean mountain pastures in a detached way. The snowy peaks, lush green gullies, the profusion of flowers, the lop-eared sheep, the long-horned cattle and the majestic Comtois horses make a picture now beyond the pixels. The stockman and the poet may well wear the same hat and walk the same path, but not usually at the same time. Perhaps I was always a poet, playing at farming. In which case it has been one heck of a game!

No longer am I looking for the problems and after forty-five years of doing so, I am well glad of it. I shall take care not to enquire of my farming friends if everything is all right. With livestock farming everything is never all right, it's enough that some days are better than others!

Our train is still rolling along steadily; the destination is unclear and unimportant. It is sufficient for me that we are travelling at a pace that allows others to mount and dismount.

SO FAR SO GOOD…

Postscript

My own grandparents lived through massive social change bought about by colonisation, revolution and international conflict yet what I know about their lives can be written on two sides of paper. This book has primarily been an attempt to ensure that my own grandchildren will be able write down a few more pages.

Some of the anecdotes in my book are amusing, some are not, all are true. Life is a journey made worthwhile by the people we share it with. Some are giants to me, some are dwarfs. My hope is that to others the latter may appear as the former.

The last time I can remember saying "no thank you" because I thought it was the correct thing to say I was four years old. Since then I have by and large run for the mountain when rain threatened. Where most would say no, I have said yes, where they have said can't I have said can. I have not recognised false barriers set up by bureaucrats who so easily contain aspirations and dampen dreams and I have valued loyalty and unconditional friendship, both the giving and the receiving.

I have struggled to find some existential meaning (some would call it religion), under the smothering shrouds of suffering throughout our world and have paused for the moment in a glade in the woods where the dawn sunlight is warming my back as it penetrates the impossible spring greens of promise for a new day.

Beneath my feet are the crisp and fragile leaves of past years. Those leaves have been the pages of this book. Tread lightly and look to this day, all our tomorrows and yesterdays depend upon it.